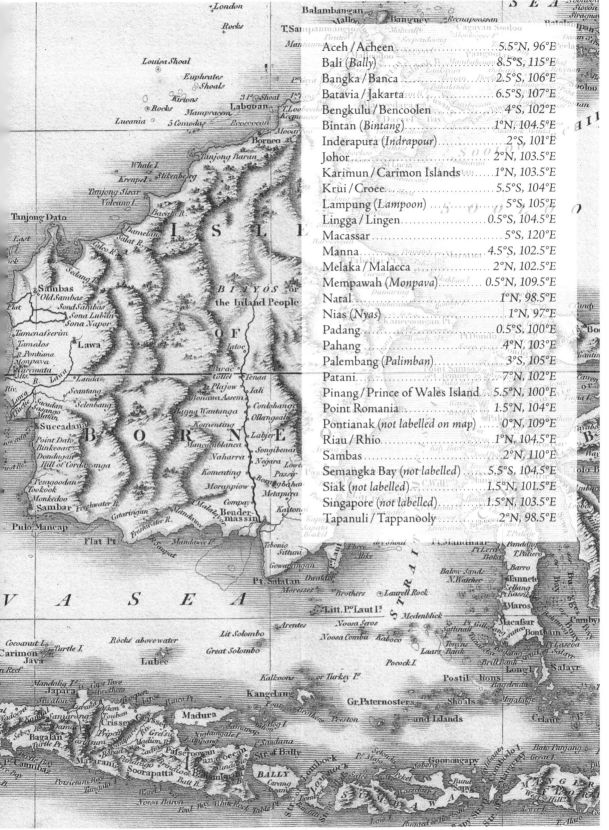

Aceh / Acheen	5.5°N, 96°E
Bali (*Bally*)	8.5°S, 115°E
Bangka / Banca	2.5°S, 106°E
Batavia / Jakarta	6.5°S, 107°E
Bengkulu / Bencoolen	4°S, 102°E
Bintan (*Bintang*)	1°N, 104.5°E
Inderapura (*Indrapour*)	2°S, 101°E
Johor	2°N, 103.5°E
Karimun / Carimon Islands	1°N, 103.5°E
Krui / Croee	5.5°S, 104°E
Lampung (*Lampoon*)	5°S, 105°E
Lingga / Lingen	0.5°S, 104.5°E
Macassar	5°S, 120°E
Manna	4.5°S, 102.5°E
Melaka / Malacca	2°N, 102.5°E
Mempawah (*Monpava*)	0.5°N, 109.5°E
Natal	1°N, 98.5°E
Nias (*Nyas*)	1°N, 97°E
Padang	0.5°S, 100°E
Pahang	4°N, 103°E
Palembang (*Palimban*)	3°S, 105°E
Patani	7°N, 102°E
Pinang / Prince of Wales Island	5.5°N, 100°E
Point Romania	1.5°N, 104°E
Pontianak (*not labelled on map*)	0°N, 109°E
Riau / Rhio	1°N, 104.5°E
Sambas	2°N, 110°E
Semangka Bay (*not labelled*)	5.5°S, 104.5°E
Siak (*not labelled*)	1.5°N, 101.5°E
Singapore (*not labelled*)	1.5°N, 103.5°E
Tapanuli / Tappanooly	2°N, 98.5°E

110° 115° 120°

CHAPTER I

Beginnings of the Relationship

The crucial role played by the Governor-General and Commander-in-Chief in India, the Marquess of Hastings, in the founding of Singapore, and especially in its retention during the early critical years of its existence, has never been fully recognised. He made the fateful decision to establish a British settlement at the southern entrance of the Straits of Melaka and it was his determination that led to its retention despite strong opposition from the Netherlands colonial government at Batavia, the British and Dutch authorities in Europe, and the government of Prince of Wales Island (Pinang). This opposition led him to waver briefly in his support of Raffles, inviting the comment by D.C. Boulger in his *Life of Sir Stamford Raffles* (London, 1897) that his "vacillation" deprives him of much of the share in the establishment of Singapore.[1] This is a partisan view designed to give credit to Raffles's single-mindedness in pursuing his objective and does less than justice to Hastings's resolution in maintaining the British settlement. When Raffles sailed from Calcutta on 7 December 1818 as Agent of the Governor-General with instructions to establish a British trading post, Hastings's last words to him were, "Sir Stamford, you may depend upon me".

During the ensuing months, despite some initial concern about Raffles's actions following the Dutch return to Pulau Bintan in the Riau Archipelago, Hastings remained steadfast in his support, writing to the Chairman of Directors of the East India Company in May 1819 strongly advocating the retention of Singapore, and in the same month to the Secret Committee describing it as "a valuable post, which it is desirable to retain".[2] Hastings's support was fully recognised by Raffles when he stated in a Farewell Address to him from Singapore in 1823 that the British settlement had been "planned under your Lordship's auspices, and maintained against jealous rivalry by the vigour and firmness of your counsels".[3]

Francis Rawdon-Hastings, 1st Marquess of Hastings and 2nd Earl of Moira, was a prominent member of the Anglo-Irish aristocracy. He was born on 9 December 1754, the eldest of six children of John, Baron Rawdon, in the Irish peerage, who was later created Earl of Moira, the title passing to his son on his death in 1793. Francis Rawdon's mother, Elizabeth Hastings, was the eldest daughter of the 9th Earl of Huntingdon, and in 1789 she succeeded to the ancient baronies of Botreaux, Hastings, Hungerford, Neumarch, Moels, Peverel, De Homet and De Moleyns, following the death of her brother, Francis Hastings, 10th Earl of Huntingdon. Her son inherited these ancient baronies when she died on 11 April 1808 and, as heir to the 10th Earl, he became Rawdon-Hastings. He was educated at Harrow and matriculated at University College, Oxford, but left without taking a degree. He was gazetted Ensign in the 15th Regiment of Foot at the age of seventeen, and in 1773, with the financial support of his uncle, he purchased a commission as Lieutenant in the 5th Regiment of Foot. In his nearly eight years' service in America during the War of Independence, he distinguished himself at Bunker's Hill and in the battles of Brooklyn and White Plains, and in 1778 he was promoted Lieutenant-Colonel and Adjutant-General to the British forces. On his return to England he was promoted Colonel and appointed aide-de-camp to the King, who elevated him in 1783 to the peerage of the United Kingdom as Baron Rawdon, of Rawdon, in his own right. In 1793–94, with the rank of Major-General, he commanded a division of 10,000 troops supporting the Duke of York's army on the Continent during the French Revolutionary War, his services there and in America being adjudged so highly by the historian of the British Army, J.W. Fortescue, that he placed him after Wellesley and Moore as "probably the ablest soldier in the army".[4]

In his political career, he initially sided with Pitt, but subsequently acted in loose association with the Whigs. As spokesman, agent, and financial backer of the Prince of Wales he attained considerable political influence,

Fig. 3
Francis Rawdon-Hastings (1754–1826),
1st Marquess of Hastings, Governor-General
and Commander-in-Chief of India, 1813–23.
Contemporary engraving.

and on the formation of the Fox-Grenville ministry in 1806 he was appointed
Master-General of Ordnance and a Privy Councillor. He resigned in the following year and in 1809 he declined the post of Lord Lieutenant of Ireland
in Perceval's ministry. At the beginning of the Regency it was widely considered that he might become Prime Minister,[5] but disagreements with the
Prince persuaded him to abandon politics and to accept on 11 November

1812 the post of Governor-General and Commander-in-Chief in India. He was created Marquess of Hastings, Earl of Rawdon and Viscount Loudoun on 7 December 1816, from which time he was known by his foremost title.[6]

On 14 April 1813 he sailed for India with his wife, Flora, Countess of Loudoun, and his three eldest children on HMS *Stirling Castle* (under the command of Sir Home Popham), and after a brief sojourn at Madras between 11 and 18 September, he assumed the duties of Governor-General on his arrival at Calcutta on 4 October 1813.

The details of his ceremonial reception by his predecessor, Sir Gilbert Elliot, 1st Earl of Minto, at Government House are described in his Private Journal, which he commenced on his arrival in India. Because of "excessive pressure of business", however, he found no time to make further additions to it until February 1814, when, curiously, in the very first entry we find him writing critically of Raffles.

Hastings wrote of Raffles not by name, but as Lieutenant-Governor of Java responsible for causing a heavy financial drain on the Bengal treasury. Various factors are attributed by Hastings to the "great pecuniary embarrassment" of the Indian Government at this time, including the remittance to London of £300,000 in gold pagodas on the orders of the Directors of the East India Company, and bills drawn on the government by the Governors

Fig. 4
Sir Gilbert Elliot (1751–1814), 1st Earl of Minto, Hastings's predecessor as Governor-General of India, 1807–13. *Portrait by James Atkinson.*

of Isle de France and Ceylon; but he considered that "a still worse drain" than these was the island of Java, whose Lieutenant-Governor, instead of providing the surplus revenue he had promised, now stated that "he cannot pay his provincial corps unless we allow him 50,000 Spanish dollars monthly in addition to the prodigious sums which we already contribute to his establishment".[7]

This criticism hardly presaged a good working relationship between the two men, but Hastings had every right to be critical of Raffles, who had addressed a number of despatches to Bengal containing exaggerated accounts of the economic benefits that would accrue to the East India Company from the capture of Java from the Dutch in 1811. He had referred to the large surpluses of rice, coffee and spices available for sale as well as supplies of Bangka tin, and had calculated that with the addition of revenues from customs and farms, especially the opium farm, Java would yield an annual revenue of more than 5 million Spanish dollars against disbursements of less than one-eighth of that sum.[8]

As it happened, large quantities of colonial produce were seized as prize property by the British military and naval forces, and in the absence of neutral shipping during the American War of 1812, and the closure of European markets by the Napoleonic decrees, the loss of export opportunities led to a glut on the local market, with coffee prices falling by four-fifths. Having no other sources of revenue to meet the cost of the large military contingent on the island, Raffles was forced in 1812 to issue one-quarter of a million Spanish dollars in treasury notes covered by bills of credit drawn on the Bengal government. Further large sums were expended in withdrawing from circulation the Dutch depreciated paper currency, and without sufficient silver to meet the government's expenditure, especially the payment of troops, Raffles had no recourse but to appeal to the Supreme Government for permission to draw bills on the Bengal treasury to the extent of 50,000 Spanish dollars a month.[9] This request was directed to his patron, Lord Minto, who, as the one responsible for retaining Java under British control, might have given it sympathetic consideration. Instead, Raffles's request was received in Calcutta by Lord Hastings, who saw no reason to bestow favours on one of his predecessor's placemen, even though Lord Minto had solicited his support for Raffles's administration in Java and for his succession to the reserved post at Bengkulu in west Sumatra.

Fig. 5
Major-General Robert
Rollo Gillespie (1766–1814),
Commander of the Forces in Java.
*Contemporary print after a
painting by George Chinnery.*

Hastings's view of Raffles at this time was also strongly influenced by
the charges of maladministration made against the latter by the former
Commander of the Forces in Java, Major-General Robert Rollo Gillespie,
who had arrived at Calcutta from Batavia (Jakarta) in December 1813, two
months after Hastings. Harbouring bitter feelings against Raffles's initial
appointment as Lieutenant-Governor of Java, he now levelled serious charges
against his conduct in government, including his personal involvement in
the purchase of colonial lands.[10] These charges he discussed with Hastings,
whose sympathies naturally went to a fellow soldier, whose military exploits
and "heroic valour" he admired.[11] Hastings's antagonism towards Raffles
increased after Raffles counter-charged Gillespie with immorality, alleg-
ing that "a virgin was forcibly demanded by his orders from the Orphan
School at Samarang", and that a "similar outrage" had been perpetrated
by his alleged agent. Hastings's evident distaste for the subject, involving
the examination of a witness before the Supreme Council, led to Raffles
being condemned for making an unwarranted and unproven charge against
a British officer, and a communication to this effect was sent to the Court
of Directors of the East India Company in London.[12]

The examination by the Supreme Government of the Gillespie charges
against Raffles was unnecessarily protracted, but the matter was eventually

resolved in Raffles's favour, except in the matter of his personal involvement in the purchase of lands, which was characterised by the Governor-General in Council as "an act of the highest indiscretion, evincing a perfect ignorance of the principles of Government, as applicable to the State of affairs in our Eastern possessions".[13] This was written in December 1815, after the Supreme Government had received instructions from the Court of Directors of the previous May ordering Raffles's removal from the government of Java.[14]

In October 1815 Raffles had addressed a personal appeal to Hastings for a resolution of the case, the first of his extant letters to Hastings in the Bute Collection at Mount Stuart.[15] The Governor-General's reply, however, simply conveyed the order of the Court that he was to be removed from his office as Lieutenant-Governor of Java and its Dependencies:[16]

Letter 1
Hastings to Raffles
4 December 1815

Calcutta, Decr 4th 1815

Sir,

I have the Honor to acknowledge your Letter by the Nautilus. It gives me much concern that you have been kept so long in suspense regarding the opinion of the Supreme Government on the matters of which testimony had been required from Sir: G: Gillespie and Mr Blagrave.[17] The delay occurred from a correspondence which by distance rendered slow, between the V: President & me as to how far we might be justified in abstaining from the execution of an order from the Court of Directors for a further investigation of the transactions. That question has since been set at rest by the subsequent Commands of the Honble Court that you should cease to conduct the Government of Java. The resolutions of the Supreme Government on the charges & defence, as far as the loose nature of the enquiry warranted an opinion, are now transmitted to you; & they of course supersede the necessity of entering into any detail. You will perceive that the Council decides in favour of your occupying the Residency of Bencoolen which has been remained open to you.

I have &c

The Honble T: S: Raffles &c

Fig. 6
The Prince Regent (1762–1830),
by whom Raffles was knighted in
1817; later King George IV.
Portrait by Sir Thomas Lawrence.

Fig. 7
Princess Charlotte of Wales
(1796–1817) and Prince Leopold of
Saxe-Coburg-Saalfeld (1790–1865),
later King of the Belgians.
Contemporary print.

Although the post of Resident of Fort Marlborough (Bengkulu) was being held out to him, Raffles decided on grounds of health to postpone taking up the appointment and proceed directly to England. There, during 1816–17, much changed in his favour. He was exonerated by the Directors of the East India Company of the charges levelled against him by Gillespie as affecting his moral character,[18] and he was knighted by the Prince Regent following the publication of his book, *The History of Java* (London, 1817).[19] He also formed influential connections with Queen Charlotte,[20] Princess Charlotte and her husband, Prince Leopold of Saxe-Coburg-Saalfeld,[21] Edward Adolphus, 11th Duke of Somerset, and his wife, Charlotte, Duchess of Somerset,[22] the Whig politician, Henry Petty-Fitzmaurice, 3rd Marquess of Lansdowne,[23] William Wilberforce,[24] and prominent members of the

Fig. 8
Sir Joseph Banks (1743–1820),
President of the Royal Society.
Contemporary print after a portrait
by Thomas Phillips.

Fig. 9
William Wilberforce (1759–1833),
leading campaigner in Parliament
for the abolition of slavery.
Portrait by Karl Anton Hickel.

East India Company's directorate, including Charles Grant[25] and Hugh
Inglis.[26] He was elected a Fellow of the Royal Society[27] and became closely
associated with its President, Sir Joseph Banks,[28] and with many of the
naturalists and scientists connected with him.[29]

These were all important considerations, though Hastings may have
been influenced more favourably towards Raffles by the opinions of Sir Miles
Nightingall, who had succeeded Gillespie as Commander of the Forces in
Java, and by Raffles's successor as Lieutenant-Governor, John Fendall, who
was now a member of the Supreme Government.[30] At any rate, the conditions were favourable for a fresh start between the two men, initiated by a
letter of reconciliation which Raffles addressed to Hastings on 16 April 1818,
shortly after arriving at Bengkulu:[31]

Fig. 10
Sir Thomas Stamford Raffles (1781–1826),
Lieutenant-Governor of Java 1811–16, and
subsequently Lieutenant-Governor of
Fort Marlborough (Bengkulu) 1818–24.
Miniature portrait.

Letter 2
Raffles to Hastings
16 April 1818

Private

Bencoolen the 16ᵗʰ April 1818

My Lord,

 On my return to this Country I feel it to be my first duty respectfully to appeal to your Lordship's liberality and candour.

 In the course of my administration in Java, there were many measures which did not receive your Lordship's approbation – Some of them required explanation, others were perhaps injudicious – Your Lordship's confidence was withheld and I had the misfortune to labour under your displeasure –

 It is not my wish to agitate a retrospection of those measures – the motives and grounds of their adoption were long since submitted to your Lordship and I must be content with the decision, be it favorable or otherwise – But, now that I am entering on a new field, with the prospect of avoiding those rocks and shallows on which my little bark had formerly well nigh perished, I hope I shall be forgiven in approaching your Lordship with a hope that I may obtain your countenance and support and be allowed to look forward to your confidence and esteem –

 In this hope, and in order that I may be enabled the better to submit to your Lordship's consideration the views which I am induced to take of our Interests in the Eastern Seas, I beg leave respectfully to prefer a Request that your Lordship will grant me the honor of a personal interview and permit me to proceed to Calcutta for that purpose.

 Your Lordship's compliance with this Request will be hailed by me, as an indication of your favorable sentiments, & shall anticipate in it the accomplishment of my highest ambition –

I have the honor to be,
My Lord,
Your Lordship's
Most Obedient and
Faithful humble Servᵗ
T S Raffles

His Excellency
The Most Noble the Marquess of Hastings
&c &c &c

Hastings's reply was written from the Gogra River, during the last phase of British military operations against the Maratha Confederacy:[32]

On the Gogra
July 6ᵗʰ 1818

Sir

I have the Honor to acknowledge your Letter & offer my congratulations on your safe arrival [at Bencoolen].

It was painful for me that I had in the course of duty to express an opinion unfavorable to certain of your measures in Java. The disapprobation, as you would perceive, affected their prudence alone; on the other hand, no person can have felt more strongly than I did your anxious & unwearied exertions for meliorating the condition of the Native Inhabitants under your sway. The procedure was no less recommended by Wisdom than by Benevolence; and the results are highly creditable to the British Government.

I request you to consider yourself at liberty to carry into execution your wish of visiting Bengal whensoever your convenience & the state of affairs in the Island may afford an eligible opportunity. The means of rendering the Settlement at Bencoolen more advantageous to the Honᵇˡᵉ Company than it now appears to be[,] are certainly more likely to be struck out in oral discussion than thro' any formal correspondence.

I have &c.

P.S. Allow me to return many thanks for your goodness in sending me your account of Java which I shall read & peruse at Calcutta with great interest.

CHAPTER II

Raffles's Expansionist Policies in Sumatra

Apart from wishing to effect a personal reconciliation with the Governor-General, and to obtain recognition of his services in Java, Raffles's principal purpose in visiting Calcutta was to seek approval of the measures he had taken in Sumatra and to alert Hastings to the dangers of a resurgence of Dutch power and influence in the Indonesian islands.

Before he left England for Bengkulu late in 1817, Raffles had proposed in a paper submitted to George Canning, President of the Board of Commissioners for the Affairs of India,[33] various measures to protect British commercial interests in the Eastern Archipelago. Chief among these measures was the establishment of a British port which would serve as a resort for the independent trade and "for the protection of our commerce and all our interests, and more especially for an *entrepôt* for our merchandise". He thought that the East India Company's existing stations at Bengkulu and Pinang were too remote to serve these purposes, and he considered that a settlement should be formed on Pulau Bintan in the Riau Archipelago, which would become "a commercial station for communication with the China ships passing either through the Straits of Sunda or Malacca, [and so] completely outflank Malacca, and intercept its trade in the same manner as Malacca has already intercepted that of Prince of Wales Island". It would possess great advantages as vessels from China, Cambodia, Thailand, Patani and Terengganu "must pass in sight of that island, which forms the southern

Fig. 11
Fort Marlborough, Bengkulu, built by
the British East India Company 1713–19.
*Aquatint by Joseph Stadler after a drawing
by Andrews, 1799.*

side of the Strait of Sincapore at its opening from the China seas". If, however, this proved impossible, a British station might be established in the vicinity of Sambas or Pontianak in western Borneo.[34]

Raffles had disclaimed all intention of seeking an "extension of territory",[35] but after taking up his post as Lieutenant-Governor of Fort Marlborough in March 1818 his ideas quickly changed, at least with respect to Sumatra, because of what he regarded as the aggressive measures adopted by the newly installed Dutch Commissioners-General at Batavia. "Prepared as I was for the jealousy and assumption of the Dutch Commissioners in the East", he wrote to the Secret Committee a month after his arrival,

I have found myself surprised by the unreserved avowal they have made of their principles, their steady determination to lower the British character in the eyes of the natives, and the measures they have already adopted towards the annihilation of our commerce, and of our intercourse with the Native Traders throughout the Malayan Archipelago. Not satisfied with shutting the Eastern ports against our shipping, ... they have dispatched commissioners to every spot in the Archipelago where it is probable we might attempt to form settlements, or where the independence of the Native Chiefs offered any thing like a free port to our shipping.

These included the Lampungs in southern Sumatra, as well as Pontianak and the minor ports of Borneo, and even Bali. Moreover, a Dutch Commissioner from Batavia had recently been despatched to Palembang, "to organize, as it is said, all that part of Sumatra". Because of these activities, Britain had been left without "an inch of ground to stand upon between the Cape of Good Hope and China".[36]

Raffles wrote in even more dramatic terms to his friend, Charlotte Seymour, Duchess of Somerset, on 15 April 1818:

The Dutch are worse than I even expected, and your Grace knows that was bad enough – they are doing all they can to exclude us from the Eastern Seas altogether and have already obliged most of the Independent Ports to submit to their authority ... My arrival has I understand created the utmost alarm – I believe they look upon me as worse than Buonaparte – they say I am a spirit that will never allow the East to be quiet and that this second Elba in which I am placed is not half secure enough – The Dutch keep up a force of 3 line of Battle Ships[,] half a dozen frigates & innumerable smaller vessels to enforce their regulations, but thank god they dare not interfere with me personally – I have written home very fully on the subject and if the Government is not right down mad, Ministers & the East India Company must interfere – it will not be long I think before we come to close quarters – I am now endeavoring to establish a position in the Straits of Sunda, [and] if I succeed in this, I shall soon set up a Rival Port to Batavia & make them come down to my own terms – .[37]

This is a reference to what he described to the Secret Committee on 3 July 1818 as "a respectable Establishment" in Semangka Bay, which would secure the passage of the Sunda Straits for the East India Company's

Fig. 12
Charlotte Seymour, Duchess
of Somerset (1772–1827), with
whom Raffles maintained a
steady correspondence from
1817 until his death.
Contemporary miniature portrait.

outward and homeward bound ships and would be retained pending a reference to Europe.[38]

Furthermore, in order to induce the Dutch to withdraw from Palembang, Raffles informed the Netherlands authorities at Batavia that Padang
and Melaka would not be returned to them as provided by the Convention
of 1814. "The position I have taken up", he wrote, "is that the Dutch can
have no claim to possession where their flag did not fly on the 1st January
1803; and under this view, [their] claim to Malacca and Padang is at least
questionable, these stations having been under the English flag since 1795".
If the British were obliged to hand over Melaka, there was always the possibility of forming an establishment in the Riau Archipelago, or on some adjacent island. Moreover, if the Dutch formed a connection with Pontianak, a
rival post could be established at Sambas. This might lead to regional con-
flicts, so it would be better if the Dutch were compelled to withdraw from
Borneo altogether, or at least recognise the Equator as the boundary of their
settlements. Java was in their exclusive possession, but their pretensions to
Sumatra should be discounted and the integrity of the island maintained.
"Sumatra", wrote Raffles, "should undoubtedly be under the influence of one
European Power alone, and this power is of course the English".[39]

After establishing the small British station at Kalambajang east of
Semangka Bay, Raffles wrote to the orientalist, William Marsden:

I am already at issue with the Dutch Government about their boundaries in the Lampoon country … I demand an anchorage in Simangka Bay, and lay claim to Simangka itself. If we obtain this, we shall have a convenient place for our China ships to water; and should we go no further within the Archipelago, be able to set up our shop next door to the Dutch. It would not, I think, be many years before my station in the Straits of Sunda would rival Batavia as a commercial entrepôt.[40]

Following the arrival of a Dutch Commissioner at Palembang, and the consequent appeal in June 1818 by Sultan Ahmad Najmuddin for assistance,[41] Raffles despatched a small force of 100 men overland under the authority of Captain Francis Salmond, the Master Attendant at Bengkulu, with instructions to afford the Indonesian ruler "the protection of the British Government".[42] Salmond was placed under arrest by the Dutch Commissioner, H.W. Muntinghe, and sent as a prisoner to Batavia, eliciting from Raffles a formal "Protest" to the Governor-General G.A.G.P. van der Capellen about the treatment of a "publicly accredited and recognised"

Fig. 13
Baron G.A.G.P. van der Capellen (1778–1848), Governor-General of the Dutch East Indies 1816–26.
Portrait by C. Kruseman.

British representative, and also about the system pursued by the Dutch authorities which appeared to aim "at an absolute despotism over the whole Archipelago".[43] The object of the "Protest", he explained in a letter to Charlotte, Duchess of Somerset, on 13 August 1818, was "to bring the different questions at issue to a point – and to oblige our Ministers to come to some immediate understanding with the Dutch Authorities in Holland".[44] The "Protest", which was published in the *Annual Register for 1819*,[45] and given wide coverage in the English and Scottish press,[46] caused "a great sensation", with consequent embarrassment and annoyance to the British Government and the East India Company.

Raffles sent a copy of the "Protest", together with his correspondence with the Dutch authorities at Batavia, to the Secret Committee on 12 August 1818, under a covering letter in which he argued for the maintenance of "the integrity" of the larger islands of the Malay Archipelago: "Could the return of Banca be negociated and the integrity of Sumatra be preserved under British Protection, the greatest advantages might be anticipated".[47]

The Secret Committee replied in a despatch to the Governor-General dated 30 October 1818:

Having attentively examined the agreement concluded with the present Sultan of Palembang upon his elevation to the throne, we find no article by force whereof we are under any obligation of interference, or have any right to interfere in the manner described by the Lieutenant Governor of Bencoolen. If the Dutch, or any other European power, shall wantonly oppress that weak state, still more if their oppressions shall be auxiliary to hostile projects against the British government, there may exist a case for extraordinary interference … But it would be a strong measure to object to the establishment of a Dutch Residency or Factory in the Palembang country, merely because the ancient practices of that Nation gave us reason to apprehend that their ulterior designs may be mischievous or inconvenient to us.[48]

Raffles met with more success in extending British informal control over the region of Pasemah ulu Manna in southern Sumatra, which he visited in May 1818 ostensibly for the purpose of preventing incursions by the Pasemah people into the British Out-Residency of Manna. Before his visit, local British officials had attempted to reduce friction between the

Pasemahers and the coastal peoples by regulating trade and issuing passes to those wishing to enter the East India Company's districts; but when the contract system of supplying pepper was introduced at the beginning of the nineteenth century,[49] British supervision of the remoter districts was withdrawn, leaving the people in Manna largely unprotected against attacks by their neighbours.[50] The British Resident had concluded a treaty with Pasemah ulu Manna in 1815,[51] but according to Raffles this had been broken by British officials themselves.[52] When he visited the region in 1818, he found the people "reasonable and industrious, an agricultural race more sinned against than sinning",[53] and after consulting with the rulers he agreed to pay compensation and allow the cultivators the option of planting pepper on the same terms as those of the coast. They were also permitted to settle where they wished and the pass and the toll systems were abolished. In return, the rulers of Pasemah ulu Manna agreed by treaty to accept the East India Company's protection of their country.[54] This arrangement seems to have produced general peace and stability in the region during the remaining period of British rule, and even found favour with the Supreme Government in Bengal, which considered it to have been "well calculated to promote the welfare and happiness of the inhabitants of that part of the country", an opinion shared by the Directors of the East India Company.[55]

On returning to Bengkulu in June 1818, Raffles found a Dutch officer waiting to take charge of the settlement of Padang, which had been in British hands since 1795.[56] As the Anglo-Dutch Convention of 1814 had referred to the cession of only those colonies which had been in the possession of the Netherlands at the Peace of Amiens, Raffles refused to return Padang until the costs incurred by the British administration were settled.[57] He decided, moreover, to visit Padang himself, accompanied by Lady Raffles and the American naturalist, Dr. Thomas Horsfield,[58] and when the party travelled inland to Pagarruyung in the central highlands,[59] he concluded treaties with the Minangkabau rulers providing for the cession of Padang and the coastal regions from Inderapura to Natal to Great Britain, and for his own appointment as British "Representative in all the Malay States".[60] In this role Raffles imagined reviving the ancient authority of Minangkabau and creating a strong central government in the island under British control.[61] He accordingly stationed a British agent with a small Bugis force in central Sumatra and determined to oppose any Dutch

Fig. 14
Lady Raffles, born Sophia
Hull (1786–1858), married
Stamford Raffles in 1817.
*Miniature portrait by A.E.
Chalon, 1817.*

attempt to return to Padang. "[W]ith an influence at Menangkabau and the exclusion of the Dutch from Sumatra," he wrote to the Secret Committee on 5 August 1818,

a prospect is now held out of rendering Sumatra within a short period as valuable a possession to Great Britain as Java. It is certainly in a less cultivated state, the People less civilized, and much remains to be done, but I am satisfied that by a liberal and enlarged policy, a very few years would be necessary to draw forth most important revenues … At all events, as the British Government has now obtained the sovereignty of the country, I consider it impossible that the Dutch can be permitted to do more than re-establish a Commercial Factory there – .[62]

CHAPTER III

Hastings Favours the Southern Melaka Straits

Realising that he would require the agreement of the Supreme Government for the expansionist measures he had adopted in Sumatra, especially at Palembang, Raffles was pleased on his return to Bengkulu in August 1818 to receive Hastings's invitation to visit Calcutta. He immediately engaged the small brig *Udney* to take him and Lady Raffles, and her brother William Hull, to Calcutta, where they arrived on 29 September after transferring to another vessel when their ship ran aground at the mouth of the Hugli River.

Raffles described his reception by the Governor-General in a letter to William Marsden dated 16 October 1818:

You will be happy to hear that I have made my peace with the Marquess of Hastings, and that his Lordship has at last acknowledged my exertions in Java in flattering terms. This was one object of my visit to Calcutta, and on it depended, in a great measure, the success of the others. I am now struggling hard to interest the Supreme Government in the Eastern Islands; and the measures taken by me at Palembang, &c. will, I doubt not, lead to the advantage of some defined line of policy being laid down for the future. With regard to the Dutch proceedings at Palembang, ... Lord Hastings has unequivocally declared, that his mind is made up as to the moral turpitude of the transaction, and that he considers this but as one of a course of measures directed in hostility to the British interests and name in the Eastern Seas. My despatches are now under consideration, and it is uncertain what may be the immediate result. There is but one opinion in regard to the manner in which our interests have been sacrificed by the transfer of Java, &c. and it is clear that the government at home will be called upon from hence to interfere for the security of our trade; but in the mean time, and pending the reference to Europe, I fear that nothing decisive will be done. Lord Hastings is, I know, inclined to recommend our exchanging Bencoolen for Malacca, and to make the equator the limit.[63]

In a further letter to Marsden dated 14 November 1818, Raffles acknowledged that he had been unable to induce the Government "to enter warmly into my views with regard to Sumatra", and that Padang was to be transferred to the Dutch without delay.[64] He repeated this message in a letter to Charlotte, Duchess of Somerset, on the following day, stating that although he had received from Hastings "the strongest assurances of friendship and support", he had been unable to persuade him "to cooperate in my plans for Sumatra" and that the Governor-General was also of opinion that Padang "should be given up to the Dutch and that it is to be regretted I interfered at Palembang – My station in Samanka Bay is considered likely to excite the jealousy of the Dutch and so out of delicacy to them we must nearly sacrifice every interest in Sumatra".

Despite his evident resentment, he wrote a conciliatory letter to the Supreme Government on 16 November after receiving a formal statement of the views of the Governor-General on his political proceedings in Sumatra:

I ... regret most deeply that I should have adopted any measures not in consonance with the wishes of His Lordship. His Lordship in Council may be assured that my proceedings will be entirely influenced by the orders which I have now received and that in all future communications with the agents of the Dutch Government the most conciliatory and amicable spirit shall be manifested.[65]

Official opposition to Raffles's policies in Sumatra had been made known to him during the first week of November when he and Lady Raffles were guests of the Governor-General at his beautiful garden retreat

Fig. 15
Barakpur, garden retreat of the Governor-
General of India, where the decision was
made to pursue a mission "to the Eastward".
Drawing by Charles D'Oyly, published in
Views of Calcutta and Its Environs.

at Barakpur, sixteen miles north of Calcutta, where he spent three days
of every week escaping from the exacting duties of government business.
During these discussions with Hastings and his officials, Raffles's Sumatran
policies were completely disavowed, and the fateful decision taken which led
directly to the founding of Singapore.

Hastings, who by now had become convinced of the aggressive nature
of Dutch activities in South-East Asia,[66] decided that instead of extending
British influence in Sumatra, a better and more direct way of countering
Dutch threats to British interests, especially the China trade, was by establishing a station at the southern entrance of the Melaka Straits.[67]

Raffles reported the decision to the Duchess of Somerset on 15 November 1818:

I am now upon a new project and the object is to secure the command of the Straits of Malacca by establishing two commanding Ports at Acheen & Rhio – if the Dutch are not before hand with us, this plan offers great advantages and the civilization of Sumatra will commence from the Eastern instead of the Western side – … If I obtain the command at Rhio, which your Grace will recollect to have been one of my plans before I left England, I may eventually do a great deal – .[68]

Writing to Marsden on the previous day, he suggested that it had been owing to his own personal communications with members of the Supreme Government that they had become united "in opposing the grasping and excluding policy of the Dutch" and in keeping "the command of the Straits of Malacca, by forming establishments at Acheen and Rhio".[69] The most influential of these officials were John Adam, Private Political Secretary to the Governor-General, who became a member of the Supreme Council in January 1819,[70] and Charles Milner Ricketts, a friend, confidant and "principal adviser" of Hastings who, according to Raffles, was "the most powerful advocate" in the country "for our Javan and Malayan cause".[71] Obviously, in discussions with Hastings and his officials, Raffles expressed his earlier ideas of establishing a British entrepôt in the Riau Archipelago, although by now these ideas were widely held in commercial and political circles in Calcutta.

Indeed, as early as October 1816, the threat posed to British interests in the region by the return of the Dutch to Melaka was clearly indicated by the Resident and Commandant of Melaka, Major William Farquhar, in a "Memorandum" addressed to the Prince of Wales Island government.[72] In this, he stated that in the event of Melaka being restored to the Dutch, "it would be extremely desirable if a New British Settlement could be formed on some convenient spot near the S.E. entrance of these Straits, so as to lye as nearly as possible in the direct route of shipping passing to and from China and the Eastern Archipelago". He thought that Riau, which had formerly been under Dutch control, would be "a very desirable place for us to occupy" because it was already an important commercial centre, although

Fig. 16
Government House, Calcutta,
residence of the Governor-General,
and seat of British power in the East.
*Aquatint from J.B. Fraser's Views of
Calcutta (London, 1824–6).*

he admitted that it was "rather out of the way of ships passing to China thro' the Straits of Sincapour – but not so far as to cause any material delay in touching there". He considered that it would be less costly than establishing a new settlement and would have the advantage of preserving to Great Britain "a share at least of that influence over the Malay States, which by the restitution of Malacca will most undoubtedly fall entirely into the hands of the Dutch". After discussing the matter with the Governor of Prince of Wales Island, Colonel John Alexander Bannerman, in April 1818, Farquhar received on his return to Melaka instructions from the Pinang

Fig. 17
Major William Farquhar
(1774–1839), Resident of
Melaka 1808–1818, and
subsequently first Resident
and Commandant of
Singapore, 1819–1823.

government to conclude commercial treaties with the rulers of Riau, Lingga, Siak and Pontianak. He was forestalled at Pontianak by the return of the Dutch in the person of the Commissioner, Jacob d'Arnaud van Boekholtz, but at Pulau Penyengat in the Riau Archipelago he was able to conclude a treaty with the Bugis Yang Dipertuan Muda, Raja Jaafar, on behalf of Sultan Abdul Rahman of Johor, granting the British favoured-nation trading privileges in the ports of Johor, Pahang, Lingga and Riau, and binding the Sultan from renewing obsolete treaties with other nations. A similar treaty was concluded with the ruler of Siak in eastern Sumatra.[73]

The fact that a commercial treaty had been concluded with the Bugis ruler of Riau, while still independent of Dutch control, had an important bearing on the instructions which Raffles received from the

Governor-General on 28 November 1818.[74] Three days before they were issued, Hastings had written to the Secret Committee expressing his regret at having to adopt a "tone of censure" on Raffles's actions in Sumatra, but nevertheless expressing such "general confidence" in him that "we have actually entrusted to him the conduct of an important service to the Eastward".[75] The instructions, which according to the Calcutta merchant, John Palmer, were drafted by Raffles himself, refer initially to the Dutch exclusionist policies in the Eastern Seas, and the consequent need of the British "to secure the free passage of the Straits of Malacca" by "the establishment of a Station beyond Malacca, such as may command the southern entrance of the Straits". Riau was stated to possess "the greatest advantages for this purpose", as it effectually commanded "both the Straits of Malacca and of Sincapore", and Farquhar's recent engagement with the ruler offered "the most favourable opening for improving and confirming our connexion with the Government of the country". However, the instructions were framed on the assumption that the Dutch had not re-established their base in the Riau Archipelago, and in the event of their having done so, Raffles was ordered to "abstain from all negotiation and collision" with them.[76]

Wishing to secure the continued benefit of Farquhar's "Experience & talents", the Supreme Government on 28 November addressed a letter to him at Pinang ordering him to accompany the mission "with a view to your remaining in the local charge of the British Interests in that quarter" under Raffles's general superintendence.[77] The fact that Raffles as a relative outsider was given the superior role in conducting British policy in the Straits of Melaka was viewed with hostility by many in both India and Pinang, including John Palmer, who considered that it was "the very height of injustice" to have him benefiting from the fruits of Farquhar's earlier labours in the Riau Archipelago and at Siak. "I do hope, my Friend," he wrote to Farquhar, that you will be employed to complete and perfect the only substantially important measures which have been attempted since the Peace with Holland in these Seas; and that even Sir Stamford may not be used to diminish the value of your previous services". He urged him to "hang on another year and see the Issue of Events, big as they are likely to be, to the Eastward".[78]

Farquhar kept Raffles informed of developments in the Straits, though he was not the source of the rumours which began circulating in Calcutta early in December that the Dutch had returned to Riau. It was still un-known that a naval force had sailed from Melaka on 3 November 1818 under the command of Vice-Admiral Johan Constantijn Wolterbeek and that a new treaty had been concluded with the Bugis and Malay rulers of Riau,[79] but the rumours carried sufficient weight for Raffles to be issued with sup-plementary orders on 5 December advising him that "in the event of the previous occupation of Rhio by the Dutch, or other circumstances prevent-ing the accomplishment of our views at that port and at Lingen, it might be expedient to endeavour to establish a connection with the Sultan of Johor on the same footing as is now contemplated with Rhio and Lingen".

Clearly displaying an ignorance of the political structure of the Johor empire, the Supreme Government stated that the position of Johor ren-dered it "nearly, or perhaps entirely, as convenient a post for our purpose as Rhio; but the imperfect information possessed by the Government, both of the local circumstances of the town and harbour[,] and the condition and relations of the State of Johor, induce the Governor-General in Council to prefer a connection with the Chief of Rhio, and his immediate superior, the Rajah of Lingen, if it be practicable". But it would be necessary to obtain correct information of the "local capabilities of Johor for a British port, such as we are desirous of establishing at the mouth of the Straits of Malacca".[80]

Raffles had written a few days earlier to Charlotte, Duchess of Somer-set, stating that he had now

accomplished the principal object of my visit to Bengal and purpose embarking once more for the Eastern Islands in the course of four or five days – I yet hope to be in time to do something for the public good, but the policy of the Dutch and the unreserved terms of the [1814] Convention preclude me from being very sanguine – ... The Dutch have seized the principal parts of Borneo and declared themselves Sovereigns of the whole Island – they are also determined to have the best parts of Sumatra – my views are in consequence now turned towards Siam where I hope to have the field to myself – My next letter however will apprize your Grace whether any thing can be done against the Dutch – and until I know this myself, I can hardly speculate on my future views & plans with any certainty – if I obtain a Station at Rhio, you will hear from me very often and by every passing Ship – .[81]

CHAPTER IV

Mission to the Eastward

Raffles sailed from Calcutta with his entourage on 7 December on board HCS *Nearchus* (under the command of William Maxfield), accompanied by another Bengal vessel, HCS *Minto* (J.S. Criddle). Three days later, he wrote to the Duchess of Somerset off the Sandheads, informing her of his "unfortunate illness" in Calcutta and of his having embarked on his return to the Eastern Islands, "which I doubt not I shall find as fresh and blooming as ever except where they may be blasted by the corrupt and tainted hand of the Dutch". He again reported his success in having "at last succeeded in making the Authorities in Bengal sensible of their supineness in allowing the Dutch to exclude us from the Eastern Seas", but he feared that it was now "too late to retrieve what we have lost":

I have full powers to do all we can and if any thing is to be done, I think I need not assure your Grace that it shall be done – and quickly done – But the main questions must depend upon the Authorities in Europe and unless we can regain Banca and keep the Dutch out of Borneo & Sumatra no good can be expected – They are now almost the most powerful Nation in India – Their naval force is immense and they have 15000 European Troops besides Natives – .[82]

On his arrival at Pinang on 29 December 1818, Raffles received confirmation that the Dutch had indeed re-established themselves in the Riau

Archipelago "with a large naval and military force" under the terms of a new treaty concluded with the Bugis and Malay rulers on 27 November, the intelligence having been communicated to Prince of Wales Island by Farquhar in a letter dated 14 December.[83]

Realising the urgent need to adapt his plans to the changed circumstances, he discussed the matter with Governor Bannerman, who had been informed independently by the Supreme Government of Raffles's orders, and who at this time was not openly hostile to his mission.[84] Bannerman sent him on 31 December a copy of the correspondence between Farquhar and the Dutch Commissioners at Melaka, Jan Samuel Timmerman Thijssen and Vice-Admiral J.C. Wolterbeek, in which the latter claimed in "very strong and decided language" that the Riau Archipelago, Johor, and Pahang were dependencies of the Netherlands. But Bannerman assured Raffles that if he decided to pursue his mission, despite the Dutch return to Riau, and his own advice not to do so, he would nevertheless have "the most cordial & efficient assistance and co-operation" from the Prince of Wales Island government.[85]

However, in a private letter to Hastings dated 1 January 1819, Bannerman forcibly expressed his opposition to Raffles's mission and informed the

Fig. 18 (*left*)
Fort Cornwallis, Prince of Wales
Island (Pinang).
Aquatint by Baily, London, 1813,
after a watercolour drawing by
William Westall, 1804.

Fig. 19 (*right*)
Colonel John Alexander Bannerman
(1759–1819), Governor of Prince of
Wales Island 1817–19.
Contemporary miniature portrait.

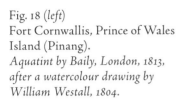

Governor-General of the "unqualified sentiments" of the Prince of Wales
Island government "against the possibility of the British Gov^t in India now
executing any advantageous political relations with the Malay states to the
Eastward" as "the period for such a measure had passed, & that any attempt
now made … to gain a footing among these States, would infalably [*sic*] produce a collision the most serious, between ourselves & the Netherlandish
authorities of Java, who seem determined to overpower all opposition by a
preponderating Naval as well as Military force".[86]

In a letter to Bannerman strongly opposing this opinion, Raffles stated
that it would be inconsistent with the British national character or interests
to yield in face of presumed Dutch rights, and when "the eyes of the whole
Malayan race are turned upon us at this moment", there was no alternative,
"in order to uphold character with the Native Chiefs", than "to make a stand
in some Port to the Eastward of Malacca where the Dutch may not have preoccupied". He admitted that it might be difficult to find "an Islet throughout
the whole range of the Archipelago, to which they will not lay claim", but so
long as "we refrain from all collision in any spot where they have Troops or
a Station, we surely may consider ourselves in common with every Malay &
Bugguese adventurer entitled to a footing on any unoccupied Territory". In

this respect, "The Island of Singapura or the Districts of old Johor appear to me to possess peculiar & great advantages ... The Carimon Islands have also advantages".[87]

In refusing to give priority to his mission to Aceh, rather than to the Eastward, Raffles soon fell out with the Prince of Wales Island government,[88] which expressed its opposition to detaching 500 men from its military establishment to support him.[89] In a heated exchange of letters, Bannerman denied that he was unwilling to cooperate with Raffles's plans, but he maintained that Raffles's instructions made Aceh the first object of his mission and he appealed to the Supreme Government on the point. He also categorised Raffles's idea of securing the island of Bangka as "chimerical" and inspired by "views of personal ambition", and claimed that Raffles's plan to establish a port in Johor or in the Straits of Singapore would frustrate the object of the Anglo-Dutch negotiations in Europe when the opportunity for direct negotiation with the Malay States had already passed. Nevertheless, if Raffles continued with his plan ("and I fear my remonstrance will have little effect on his restless, enterprising and ambitious spirit"), any settlement formed to the Eastward should be placed under the authority of the Prince of Wales Island government.[90]

Raffles, in the meantime, had informed Hastings of the return of the Dutch to Riau, and of rumours of Russian support being given to Dutch colonial activities in the region, which added urgency to the acquisition of a station commanding the southern entrance of the Straits of Melaka, despite the "hazard" of any counter-claim:[91]

Letter 4
Raffles to Hastings
8 January 1819

Penang 8th. January 1819

My Lord,

I have the honor to inform your Lordship of my arrival at this Port on 30th. Ultimo —

I am sorry to report that the Dutch have preoccupied the Station of Rhio and that there is some reason to believe they will set up a claim to extend their influence over the whole of the ancient territories of Johor. These include the Southern extremity of the Peninsula and the whole of the Islands lying off that entrance to the Straits – We are not however as yet informed of the precise nature of their engagements with Rhio – We only know that the Chief refused for a considerable time to admit them without express permission from the English, and that they at length succeeded by force – and that whatever may be the political obligations under which the Chief has been placed, he has succeeded in keeping the Dutch out of his Capital and in preserving his person free from their immediate control – The Dutch force left at Rhio consists of 30 Europeans and as many Natives and we have no reason to believe there are at present any Ships of War to the Northward of the Line –

In the present state of my information and that I may avoid all collision with the Dutch Authorities, I have thought it most prudent not to proceed further East for the present – but as it is an object to know the precise nature of the engagements which the Chief of Rhio may have entered into with the Dutch and how far we may obtain a just title to some Station in the vicinity where we may establish ourselves without collision with the Dutch, I have resolved to depute Major Farquhar on a Mission in the first instance to Rhio – where he will merely ask for information – he will afterwards according to the information he may receive proceed to obtain more detailed particulars regarding Johor – the Carimon Islands &c and act according to circumstances –

The intelligence which I have recently received from Batavia & from Malacca confirms the Reports of the Dutch having the support of Russia in their present plans[92] – Russia if not already in possession of the Sandwich Islands is openly stated to have taken measures to that effect – and a connected Chain of Ports between the Dutch Capital and the North Eastern Possessions of Russia is the declared object of policy – In two or three months the Dutch Authorities say, the Plans of Russia and the extended policy of the two Nations will be fully developed – Japan is said to be an eventual object of attack, but the conveyance of Tea from China to Malacca whence they may be smuggled into Great Britain by Free Traders and others seems to be a more immediate object with the Dutch – Speculations of this nature are already talked of and a visit to Malacca by the Governor General of Batavia on the change of the Monsoon in May or June, is the period assigned for a public declaration of the plans and prospects of the Dutch –

In short, My Lord, from every information I have been able to obtain, and my means are rather extensive, it would seem that what the Dutch have already done is only to be considered as a preliminary to some more extensive policy *not yet divulged, and when we consider the poverty of Holland, the limited extent of the Resources of Java & advert to the immense force maintained in the Eastern Seas, naval & military & to the extensive disbursements which must be occasioned by the occupation of so many Dependencies, it seems reasonable to conclude that Holland must secretly be aided by some other power –*

Should this be the case we may expect much demur on their part in acceding to any of the proposed arrangements which have been recommended to Europe, and unless in this Country we manage to command the Straits of Malacca before their ripen'd plans & policy are avowed and acted upon, we may find it too late –

My Instructions and the wishes of your Lordship are so decided with regard to my avoiding all interference where the Dutch may even set up a claim, that under existing circumstances it is very doubtful whether I can do any thing effectual – but while we carefully abstain from an interference in any Island where the Dutch may be actually established or where the Dutch flag may fly, it may be questionable whether our own safety may not dictate the propriety of establishing ourselves in an advantageous position – even at the hazard of a subsequent claim being set up by the Dutch – They can set up no claim that cannot well be contested, and notwithstanding all we have heard of their Naval and Military Force there is no chance that they would attempt to dislodge any respectable Establishment.

From every inquiry I have made I am fully satisfied of the value & importance of the Island of Sincapore which commands Johor – There is a most excellent Harbour which is even more defensible and more conveniently situated for the protection of our China Trade and for commanding the Straits than Rhio – it has been deserted for Centuries and long before the Dutch power existed in these Seas – There are about 2000 Inhabitants upon it (new settlers) under a respectable Chief – but it is probable the Dutch may say we have no right to go there as it forms part of the ancient Territory of Johor –

I have mentioned to Mr Adam[93] some particulars regarding this State & one object of Major Farquhar's Mission will be to obtain full information on the subject –

I have taken measures for surveying the Carimons – and your Lordship may confidently rely that while I omit no measure for permanently establishing our influence I shall cautiously avoid all collision with the Dutch – It would however be of much importance to me to receive your Lordship's sentiments through

M^r. Adam or otherwise whether under the alter'd state of affairs we should not act with more decision than at first contemplated – I am the more anxious to receive these sentiments as the local Government are divided in their opinions and the Majority are adverse to any Settlement to the Eastward of Penang –

I purpose proceeding in the course of a few days to Acheen accompanied by Captain Coombs,[94] whence if any essential change has taken place we shall lose no time in communicating to Bengal –

I have the honor to remain with the highest respect
Yr Lordship's most obedient & devoted servant
T S Raffles

The Most Noble
The Marquess of Hastings KG
&c. &c. &c.

The preference for a British settlement at Singapore, expressed in this private letter to Hastings written a week after arriving at Pinang, establishes beyond all doubt that this was Raffles's principal objective when he set out from Calcutta, having already suggested as much in a letter to William Marsden.[95] That it continued to be so, even after the return of the Dutch to Riau, is also clearly indicated in a despatch he addressed to the Governor-General's Political Secretary, John Adam, on 16 January 1819.[96] In this long document, he reported the information he had obtained from Asian traders and others with regard "to the capabilities of Sincapore, & other stations" in the vicinity of the ancient Malay capital of Johor Lama, and he affirmed that Singapore,

independently of the straits & harbour of Johor which it both forms & commands[,] has on its southern shores, & by means of the several smaller Islands which lie off it, excellent anchorage and smaller harbours, and seems in every respect most peculiarly adapted for our object. Its position in the Straits of Sincapore, is far more convenient & commanding than even Rhio, for our China Trade passing down the Straits of Malacca, & every native vessel that sails thro' the Straits of Rhio must pass in sight of it.

Moreover, on grounds of salubrity,

there does not seem to be any objection to a Station at Sincapore, or on the oppo-site shore towards Point Romania or on any of the smaller Islands which lie off this part of the Coast. The larger Harbour of Johore is declared by professional men whom I have consulted, and by every Eastern trader of experience to whom I have been able to refer, to be capacious & easily defensible, & the British Flag once hoisted, there would be no want of supplies to meet the immediate necessities of an Establishment. The Population here as well as throughout the Archipelago of Islands at the entrance of the Straits of Malacca, for the most part resides on the water, moving from one Island to another as their necessities and inter-ests dictate, and might be expected to flock in considerable numbers under our protection.

Raffles was unable to clarify the present political state of the Johor empire, but it had been in decline since the Dutch established themselves at Melaka. The latter had supported the nominal authority of Johor in order to prevent the ruler from ceding the Karimun Islands or other parts of his ter-ritories to the British, but "it would be absurd to suppose that 60 men sta-tioned at Rhio, are to exclude us from communication, & even from forming engagements in any of the other Islands where it may be for our interest to settle". To argue the contrary "would be to sacrifice a great national interest in deference to a principle & policy as unjustifiable as they are manifestly illiberal and injurious: it would be to give up the right of protecting our Eastern Commerce, a right for which we have been solicitous since our first Establishment in India, for no other reason but because it has pleased a subordinate Dutch authority to declare himself adverse to the exercise of it".

Raffles then gave an account of the succession dispute in the Johor empire following the death of Sultan Mahmud Shah in 1812, details of which he had obtained from Farquhar following his mission to the Riau-Lingga Archipelago in 1818, and also from his own conversations with Asian traders from Johor. He argued that if the details of the account were correct, "we may possibly find at Johor or in its vicinity, a competent authority with whom to treat, and in this case, should that position be attainable in other respects, we shall have lost nothing essential by the preoccupation of Rhio by the Dutch". Already, it would seem, Raffles had decided on a strategy of finding a Malay ruler independent of Dutch authority with whom he could make contractual arrangements for the surrender of territory, a strategy which may have been suggested to him by Farquhar, who knew of the disputed claims to the sultanate of Johor through his correspondence with Tengku Hussain Muhammad while he was Resident at Melaka.

A British port in the Lingga Archipelago, where the Malay rulers had established themselves at Daik, free from the immediate control of the Bugis regime at Pulau Penyengat, was considered by Raffles to be too far south to command the Straits of Melaka and was also inconvenient for large ships. It was therefore unsuitable as a principal British station, though it might "deserve more consideration, on account of the rank of the Chief, & its affording a secure resting place for our flag, with a view to ulterior arrangements at Sincapore or elsewhere". Therefore if there was still an opening for a British establishment in the vicinity of Johor, and should difficulties arise in procuring the required title, such a title "may be fairly expected from the Sultan of Lingin, the nominal Chief of Johor". Moreover, the vicinity of Lingga to the Karimun Islands "will at all times give us the command of such Stations, as they may afford for our shipping", and a position at Lingga, maintained with an inconsiderable force, will enable the port of Riau to be "more effectually commanded".

In conclusion, Raffles informed the Supreme Government that as the Karimun Islands had been suggested by Farquhar "as affording advantages for our proposed Port", he had requested Captains Daniel Ross and J.G.F. Crawford, commanding the Bombay Marine survey ships, *Discovery* and *Investigator*, recently arrived from Macau, to make a general survey of the islands as part of their hydrographical survey of the Straits of Melaka,[97] and report the result to Farquhar as he proceeded down the Straits. "[S]hould we fail at Sincapore", Raffles wrote, clearly indicating his preference, "these Islands may deserve immediate consideration, but for the present as they are not likely to be occupied by the Dutch, I should consider a decision upon them premature".

CHAPTER V

Establishment of a British Station
at Singapore

The following instructions issued by Raffles to Farquhar on 16 January 1819 underline the priority he gave to Singapore in his plans:[98]

Letter 5
Raffles to Farquhar
16 January 1819

To Major Farquhar
&ca. &ca. &ca.

Sir,

    Having communicated to you the general instructions, under which I am appointed to act as Agent to the Governor General, with the states of Rhio, Lingin and Johor, and placed you in possession of the views under which I consider our Interests to be placed in that quarter, I proceed to give you the following detailed Instructions for your guidance, in the Mission to which you have been deputed by me. –

    2. The Dutch having preoccupied the Port of Rhio, it would be inconsistent with my Instructions, to attempt any negociation for the Establishment of a British post at that place; but as they do not appear to have formed any establishment either at Lingin or Johor, and as a previous authority was granted to us, to survey and examine the Carimon Islands, with the view to the formation of a Settlement there; an opening may be still left, for the attainment of the main object in view, without Collision with the Dutch authorities. –

3. From every information I have received, and the result of some investigation, it would appear that Johor, or rather the Island of Sincapore, is in every respect well adapted for a British Port, such as we require. [T]he Harbour is capacious and easily defensible, and a station on Sincapore or on one of the Islands in its vicinity, would possess greater advantages than even could have been contemplated at Rhio. –

4. Should therefore the Dutch not have formed any establishment there, it is desirable that no time should be lost in selecting a proper spot for our Establishment; and in fixing our Post either at Johor itself or on the Island of Sincapore. The latter seems to offer most advantages, as it may command the Harbour and be found more salubrious than Johor, where the banks of the River are understood to be low and swampy. This however is a point that can only be determined on the spot, & after personal examination.

5. With a view to the attainment of this object, you will immediately embark on the Brig, Ganges, which has been engaged for your accommodation, and proceed to the Straits of Sincapore, communicating by the readiest means you have in your power with Captain Ross of the Discovery, who has been requested to await the arrival of a vessel off the N.E. end of the little Carimon, in order to submit his survey of those Islands.

6. Whatever may be the advantages of those Islands, and however advisable it may be to hoist the British flag & take possession of them, as soon as we have a just title to do so; it is not contemplated in the first instance to form a settlement there; at any rate not until further instructions can be transmitted to you, founded on information not yet received.

7. As the Honble Company's surveying Vessel Nearchus is proceeding down the Straits, in order to effect the [survey?] of the Straits of Sunda, Captn. Maxfield has been directed to keep company with you, & to place himself under your orders, in order that you may avail yourself of his professional judgement at Sincapore.

8. Having ascertained the capabilities of Sincapore & its vicinity, & the result being satisfactory; you will make such arrangements for securing to us the eventual Command of that important Station, as circumstances, and a deliberate consideration of the high & important interest involved, may dictate, proceeding yourself to Rhio, for the purpose of ascertaining the precise nature of the engagements which may have been entered into between the Dutch & the Chief native authority there. –

9. In the event of your obtaining an interview with the Chief of Rhio, you are authorized to state to him that the Treaty concluded by you on the part of the British Government, had met the approbation of the highest authority in India; and that in pursuance thereof, arrangements were in progress for strengthening & maintaining the good understanding thereby established: that on the arrival of the Governor General's Agent at Penang a Report was received, that His Highness had in the interim, entered into certain engagements with the Dutch, & had admitted a Dutch force into the vicinity of his Capital; that under these circumstances, His Lordship's Agent in order to avoid collision with the Dutch, with whom the English Nation are on terms of the strictest amity & friendship, has declined to proceed [to] Rhio, & that the object of your visit, is therefore to ascertain what these Engagements are; and in how far they may be considered to affect the relations existing between the British Government & His Highness, under the existing Treaty.

10. Should His Highness consider himself at liberty to respect the Treaty with the British Gov.t & to admit a British Resident; you will represent to him, that it is not consistent with the views of the British Gov.t to establish such a Resident at Rhio, lest by such an arrangement dispute & collision might arise with the Dutch who were previously established there, but that you are authorized to establish a British Post at any other place in its vicinity, which may be convenient for the protection of our Trade & in which the Dutch may not have previously formed any establishment; and if His Highness should consider himself vested with sufficient power for the purpose, it will be desirable to obtain from him his written permission for us to settle at Sincapore, the Carimons, or any other spot [which] may be selected. –

11. You will clearly understand yourself, and cause it to be equally understood by His Highness, that the object of the British Gov.t in fixing on such a Station, is not the acquirement of Territory or Revenue. The simple permission for the Residence of an Agent or Representative of the British Government, with a suitable force is all that is required.

12. The sanction of the Sultan of Lingen to this or any other arrangement that may be made, is an object to be attended to; as that state has always maintained its independence, & no Dutch factory appears ever to have been established there. *Negotiation with this Chief, should the Dutch not have formed any Establishment there, appears advisable under any circumstances, and as we have reason to believe, there is every disposition in our favour, it will be of importance to establish a small Post there, in order to support any immediate arrangements that may be made at Sincapore, or such as may eventually be decided upon regarding the Carimons.*

13. In order that you may not experience delay in carrying into effect such arrangements as may be found practicable under existing circumstances a Detachment of the strength mentioned in the margin [100 Sepoys 20 Golundaz 10 Tent & Mag: Lascars 1 Drum & fife], in addition to the party of European Artillery in the Nearchus, has been ordered on board the Mercury; & I have placed at your disposal, two public officers of distinguished merit and experience, Lieut[t]*. [Francis] Crossley*[99] *who held the most confidential situations under the British Resident at the Moluccas for seven years, and M*[r]*. [Samuel] Garling the Resident of Croee [Krui] on the West Coast of Sumatra.*[100] *I have the greatest confidence in Lieut*[t]*. Crossley's discernment & judgement, & I am desirous that you should have the aid of his advice in all points of moment. –*

14. Having thus pointed out the course which in the present state of my information it appears to me advisable you should pursue, I must next direct your attention to the importance of ascertaining, with the utmost exactness practicable, the real political state of the ancient empire of Johore: in how far it has been dismembered & in what degree its ancient capital may be considered under the immediate authority of its local Chief. It is understood, that the l[e]gitimate Chief resides in the Straits, without exercising any authority, & that he would willingly aid our views. – This is a point which may be of considerable importance in the event of the Chief of Rhio or Lingin not considering themselves authorized to grant the title we require; or of the Dutch having attempted to assume a Political influence over the whole of the Islands. –

15. In the event of your succeeding in the object of your mission you will remain in command of the Post under the appointment of the Supreme Government; and Lieut[t]*. Crossley will return to me with the Report of your proceedings[;] provisionally & until I may be able personally to visit the spot, you are authorized to engage whatever Establishment European or Native may be required and I place the most confident reliance on your rendering the proposed Post tenable, with the least delay practicable. –*

16. As soon as the service of the Nearchus can be disposed with, she is to proceed on the Survey ordered by the Supreme Government; but if you find [it] necessary, pending a reference to me, you are authorized to detain her. The Brig Ganges may also remain with you but the Mercury should be returned to Prince of Wales' Island, the moment her services can be dispensed with.

I have &ᶜᵃ.
(signed) T. Stamford Raffles,
Agent to Govʳ. Genˡ.

Prince of Wales Island
16ᵗʰ. January 1819.

Farquhar sailed from Pinang on 18 January in the 130-ton brig *Ganges*, nominally owned and commanded by his son-in-law, Francis James Bernard,[101] together with HCS *Nearchus* (W. Maxfield) carrying Lieutenant Henry Ralfe[102] and a party of 30 European artillerymen. Accompanying them was the hired ship *Mercury* (J.R. Beaumont) conveying the main company of Sepoys, the remainder being carried in the *Ganges*.

Raffles stayed behind at Pinang and, in accordance with his instructions, prepared to proceed directly to Aceh on a joint mission with Captain John Monckton Coombs to resolve a dynastic dispute in the sultanate and improve relations between Aceh and the government of Prince of Wales Island.[103]

However, as soon as Farquhar's ships had sailed, Bannerman requested Raffles to delay the Aceh mission until a reference on the subject was made to the Supreme Government in Bengal. This, according to Raffles's secretary, Dr. William Jack, was designed to keep Raffles idle, and was considered "a master stroke of policy" by Bannerman,[104] but the moment Raffles received the letter, on the evening of 18 January, he resolved to follow Farquhar's ships, which were anchored outside the harbour waiting for the tide. He accordingly ordered the ship *Indiana* (James Pearl) and the schooner *Enterprize* (Richard Harris) to prepare to sail before daybreak, and then wrote to Bannerman stating that, in accordance with his wishes, he would delay his mission to Aceh but in the meantime he would proceed on his other mission to the Eastward:[105]

Fig. 20
The *Indiana*, on which Raffles sailed
from Pinang for Singapore, January 1819.
*Oil painting, reproduced by permission of
Antiques of the Orient, Singapore.*

*Letter 6
Raffles to Bannerman
18 January 1819*

*To
The Honble Col. Bannerman
&ᶜ &ᶜ &ᶜ*

Honble Sir,
    I have the honor to acknowledge the receipt of your Letter of this date addressed to Captain Coombs and myself, earnestly entreating we will stay our proceedings and suspend the prosecution of our Mission to Acheen until a reply is received to important references made by you to the Governor General.
    Having consulted with Captⁿ Coombs, and taken into consideration the intelligence communicated in the concluding paragraph of your Letter from which

it may be reasonably concluded that there is no immediate danger to be appre-hended from the further interference of the Dutch at Acheen, it appears to me that, in deference to the high authority and earnestness of the Entreaty, I shall be justified in meeting your wishes, the more particularly as my Services in the mean time can be advantageously employed in advancing the ulterior object of my Mission –

With a view to this latter object it is my intention to embark tomorrow on the Indiana in the expectation of overtaking Major Farquhar and making such arrangements with that officer, as may facilitate our intercourse under the change of circumstances which has taken place. In according myself of the opportunity thus afforded, I shall be enabled to ensure a more immediate and active super-intendence over the objects of his Mission while I may confidentially calculate on returning to this Port in time to proceed to Acheen after affording the delay which you so urgently require –

As the Water & provisions which may have been sent onboard the Indiana will not receive any injury by remaining onboard a short time, I have not thought it necessary to desire them to be relanded, but I request that orders may be issued to put a stop to any further shipment on that Vessel.

Considering the delay which has already taken place since my arrival, I do not feel myself authorized any longer to detain the Surveying Vessel the Minto for the Mission to Acheen under the present uncertainty as to the period of its departure, and it is therefore my intention that she should follow the Nearchus without delay –

I have the honor to be &c –
(signed) T S Raffles
P. W. Island
18 Jany 1819

A true Copy
T S Raffles

The *Indiana* with Raffles on board dropped anchor off Karimun Besar on the evening of 27 January, a day after the arrival of Farquhar's ships and the survey vessels, *Discovery* and *Investigator*. The 27th of January had been spent in exploring the 20 kilometre-long island, the northern hilly side by a party including Farquhar and Captain Ross, and the southern side by Captain Crawford, Captain Maxfield and Lieutenant Ralfe. Crawford recorded in his Diary that everyone returned disgusted, having found the island "a perfect jungle, and not calculated for a settlement", but Farquhar "expressed himself delighted with this place and said that an excellent town possessing every mercantile convenience might be built, and he declared he would prefer it to any other spot".[106]

During a discussion after Raffles's arrival, Ross "pointed out on a chart a spot he considered more eligible in point of harbour, cleared of jungle, and advantageous for trade to the N.E. of St. John's Island", which he had observed on his earlier passage to China. According to Crawford, it was then agreed to examine the place, and the ships sailed for Singapore on the following morning.[107] Farquhar later claimed that it was as a result of a suggestion made by him during the voyage that it was decided to proceed to Singapore,[108] but the claim finds no support in the contemporary records, which clearly show that he wanted a British settlement on the Karimun Islands. Moreover, Ross's suggestion to examine Singapore was made long after Raffles had expressed his own opinion on the suitability of the island in his correspondence with the Supreme Government in Bengal.

The ships made Singapore around 4 o'clock in the afternoon of the same day. A few followers of the hereditary Temenggong of Johor, Abdul Rahman, immediately went on board the *Indiana* and were asked by Raffles if there was any Dutch settlement at Singapore or at Johor, or if any attempt had been made by the Dutch to establish themselves locally. According to an eyewitness account recorded many years later, and hitherto accepted as a correct version of events, Raffles and Farquhar did not land at Singapore until the morning of 29 January,[109] when they proceeded to the Temenggong's house, which stood back from the other hundred or so smaller huts on the northern bank of the Singapore River. However, Raffles makes clear in his own account that he and Farquhar went ashore and had discussions with the Temenggong on the evening of the day of their arrival on 28 January, and this fact is confirmed by another contemporary eyewitness account which states that they landed under a salute from the guns of the *Indiana* and the *Discovery*.[110]

During these discussions with the Temenggong, Raffles attempted to ascertain details of the political situation of the Johor empire, and after a further meeting on the following day, apparently on board the *Indiana*, a preliminary Agreement was concluded with the Temenggong on 30 January, which provided for the establishment of a British trading factory at Singapore, "or other place in the Government of Singapore-Johore".[111]

Farquhar was immediately despatched to Pulau Penyengat on the *Ganges*, accompanied by the *Nearchus*, *Enterprize*, and an honorary detail of European troops, for the purpose of "conciliating the friendship of the Rajah Mooda" and obtaining his agreement to the formation of a British establishment "in the Johore Dominions".[112]

On 29 and 30 January, the European artillerymen with their field pieces and the Bengal Sepoys were landed from the ships and began erecting their tents. A short time afterwards, more than 100 Chinese inhabitants and a number of Malays volunteered as labourers to cut down the grass and clear the jungle.[113]

While awaiting Farquhar's return, Raffles re-boarded the *Indiana* and sailed eastwards along the island in an unsuccessful attempt to reach Johor Lama, and the Straits separating Singapore from the Johor mainland, to investigate whether or not a small post should be established at either of these places; but he had to abandon the attempt as the passage proved too difficult and the Malays expressed a general aversion to locating a post at the old capital of Johor Lama from which they had been expelled by the Portuguese in 1587.[114]

Raffles wrote to Marsden on 31 January:

Here I am at Singapore, true to my word, and in the enjoyment of all the pleasure which a footing on such classic ground must inspire. The lines of the old city, and of its defences, are still to be traced, and within its ramparts the British Union waves unmolested ... Most certainly the Dutch never had a factory in the island of Singapore; and it does not appear to me that their recent arrangements with a subordinate authority at Rhio can or ought to interfere with our permanent establishment here.[115]

Farquhar returned to Singapore from Riau on the evening of 3 February and informed Raffles of the unwillingness of Raja Jaafar to break his treaty obligations with the Dutch or give any formal document permitting the formation of the proposed British settlement; but as he had given

Fig. 21
William Marsden (1754–1836),
the orientalist and collector.
Etching after a painting by
Thomas Phillips, 1815.

permission to the British to survey the Karimun Islands for the purpose
of forming a settlement prior to his signing the treaty with the Dutch, he
considered himself bound in the matter and "could not now object to our
using our own discretion in occupying those Islands, or such other Port in
the Straits as we might deem best adapted for the protection and convenience of our Trade".[116]

Meanwhile, on 1 February the claimant to the Johor sultanate, Tengku
Hussain Muhammad, also known as Tengku Long, the eldest son of the
late Sultan Mahmud Shah, had arrived at Singapore, having been sum-
moned by two *anak raja* from Pulau Penyengat. During a formal visit on
the following day, he confirmed the particulars regarding Johor given to
Raffles by Temenggong Abdul Rahman, and expressed "his entire acquiescence & approbation" of the preliminary Agreement concluded with
the Temmengong for the establishment of a British trading factory on the
island.

Raffles now realised that by recognising the legitimacy of Hussain's
position as Sultan of Johor, he held the key to securing the British position
at Singapore and he accordingly concluded a formal Treaty of Friendship
and Alliance with him and Temenggong Abdul Rahman on the afternoon
of 6 February. The terms of the Treaty were read out in English by Raffles's
acting-Secretary, Lieutenant Francis Crossley, and in Malay by Farquhar's

scribe, Enche' Yahya, in front of some 30 European "gentlemen" and troops drawn up in line. After the three copies of the Treaty were signed, the British flag was hoisted and salutes fired by the British field pieces and the battery of guns belonging to Temenggong Abdul Rahman, as well as by the ships off shore. The Treaty confirmed the earlier Agreement with the Temenggong permitting the establishment of a trading factory or factories at Singapore by the East India Company and provided for the annual payments to the Sultan and Temenggong of $5,000 and $3,000, with the stipulation that the port of Singapore was to be subject to the regulation of the British authorities, who would have responsibility for the collection of all port dues, except for half the duties collected on Asian vessels, to which the Temenggong was entitled.[117]

That Raffles believed he had secured a British settlement at the entrance to the Melaka Straits by a Treaty concluded with the independent Sultan of Johor is clear from the letters he subsequently wrote to the Governor-General and the Supreme Government in Bengal. The reasons for the Malay rulers agreeing to the Treaty were more complex, and directly connected with the dynastic disputes in the Johor sultanate as described in the nineteenth-century Malay text, *Tuhfat al-Nafis*.[118] While undoubtedly welcoming the formal confirmation of their respective positions by the British, and especially the financial arrangements provided by the terms of the Treaty, it is clear that Sultan Hussain Muhammad and Temenggong Abdul Rahman did not regard their new positions as being in any way independent or challenging to the unity or structure of the sultanate of Johor. They were quick to affirm this in carefully worded letters addressed to the Yamtuan Muda Raja Jaafar in Riau and Sultan Abdul Rahman in the Lingga Archipelago in which they denied prior knowledge of the arrival of the British at Singapore or of their ability "to prevent their landing" on the island. Significantly, Sultan Hussain is designated in the correspondence as "Yang di-Pertuan Singapura".[119]

Following the conclusion of the Treaty, Raffles appointed Farquhar as Resident and Commandant of Singapore with instructions prohibiting him from interfering in the affairs of the Malay states under Dutch control but encouraging him to maintain the freedom of the independent states. He was also instructed to provide watering facilities for ships, erect defences, including a small fort or commodious block-house on the Hill capable of

mounting eight or ten twelve-pounders, and barracks for the accommodation of 30 European artillerymen, as well as storehouses for ordnance and
military equipment.[120]

On the following day, 7 February, Raffles sailed from Singapore for
Pinang on board the *Indiana*. During his passage along the Straits, he
addressed a private letter to Lieutenant-Colonel James Young, Secretary
to the Military Board in Bengal, with whom he had struck up a friendship
when he was in Calcutta in the previous year based partly on their mutual
hatred of the Dutch. He had already written to him on 12 January 1819 from
Pinang complaining about the "determined obstruction" by the Prince of
Wales Island government to his mission,[121] and now, after repeating this
complaint, he gave Young one of the earliest accounts of the founding of
Singapore:[122]

Letter 7
Raffles to Young
12 February 1819

Straits of Malacca
12ᵗʰ February 1819

My dear Sir,

*I have the pleasure to inform you that notwithstanding the obstacles thrown
in my way and the uncheering prospect at one period afforded – I have been
abundantly successful in the accomplishment of the main object of my Mission
– a British Station has been established in a position commanding every possible advantage that could be required and the object has been obtained without
collision or interference with the Dutch Authorities –*

*After detaining me at Pinang for upwards of 20 days and insisting upon
my going to Acheen in the first instance, I no sooner reported my intention of
proceeding there the next day, than Colonel Bannerman pounced upon me with
a Letter requiring me to stay proceedings until answers were received from Bengal
protesting against my employment at Acheen at all – Much as I regretted this
useless detention & the unhandsome manner in which I was requested, I was
glad of the opportunity to go in person to the Eastward – and I accordingly
embarked without a moments delay – and the result is what I now report to
you – This letter is written at sea on my return to Pinang –*

*The place in which I have fixed our Establishment is Singapour the ancient
Capital of the Malay Kings and the Rival of the great State of Menangkabau in*

Sumatra – Here I found an Authority competent to treat, a Harbour in many respects superior to Rhio, and every facility for the protection of shipping &ᶜ – a more admirable situation for our purposes under every point of view in which it can be considered cannot well be conceived – The Harbour has been regularly surveyed and our Fortifications are already commenced, and in the course of two or three years it may be expected to become one of the principal Ports of Trade to the Eastward – Cast your eye on the Map where you see the Straits of Sincapore marked – our Station is four miles to the S. of St. Johns and altho the Map from being altogether erroneous in detail will give you some idea of the Harbour, the position of the place will at once shew how well it is calculated for commanding the Straits of Malacca on one side and the whole European & Native Trade of China[,] Cambodia[,] Siam &c. on the other.

If you can get a sight of my Despatch or of the Plan forwarded with it you will be able to form a correct judgment of the footing on which we stand –

The Dutch will no doubt view our Establishment with jealousy & as they are not very scrupulous, they will I doubt not make some violent Representations against me – but we have justice and equity on our side and have in fact treated them with ten times more respect & delicacy than they demand[.]

I hope I may warmly urge your support and patronage of our infant Establishment – My determination is to keep it a free Port – there are no duties and every thing shall be done to invite and encourage the resort of the Merchants & Capital – Do all you can at Head Quarters to uphold what has been done & to prevent undue impressions – & Believe me

Always sincerely yrs
T S Raffles

Colonel Young

CHAPTER VI

Raffles's Official Account of the Founding of Singapore

The "Despatch" referred to in his letter to James Young was addressed by Raffles to John Adam, Political Secretary to the Governor-General, and dated 13 February 1819, the day he arrived back at Pinang from Singapore. Despite its historical importance in recording his official account of the founding of Singapore, including an interesting reference to a small Chinese resident population on the island engaged in gambier cultivation and the smelting of tin ore, the despatch has escaped general notice. Given its date and length, one must assume that Raffles drafted the despatch during his voyage along the Straits of Melaka in the *Indiana*, although because of stylistic imperfections it is perhaps more likely that it was dictated to someone travelling with him or to a clerk after he arrived at Pinang. The original despatch may survive in the Government records in India, but the present transcription is from the copy in the British Library sent from Calcutta to London in 1819:[123]

To J. Adam, Esq*ᵣ*.
Chief Secy. Supreme Gov*ᵗ*. – Fort William

Sir,

On the 19*ᵗʰ* ultimo, I had the honor to advise you of the circumstances under which I was enabled to accompany Major Farquhar, in prosecution of ulterior objects of my Mission. –

2d. I have now the satisfaction to report, for the information of the Most Noble the Governor General in Council, that those objects have been fully and substantially accomplished; & that a British Station commanding the Southern entrance of the Straits of Malacca, and combining extraordinary local advantages with a peculiarly admirable Geographical position, has been established at Singapore the ancient Capital of the Kings of Johor, on terms and conditions, which I trust will meet the approbation and confirmation of His Lordship in Council.

3d. In my dispatch under the date the 16*ᵗʰ*. ulto. I expressed an opinion that altho' the occupation of Rhio by the Dutch might exclude us from that Port, yet there was still a prospect under the additional Instructions which I had the honor to receive from you under date the 7*ᵗʰ*. [sic] Decr., of obtaining our object at Johore – With this impression I was desirous, previously to any further communication with Rhio or any other of the Malay States, to ascertain the situation, which on a comparative view of all the material considerations and circumstances belonging to it, possessed the greatest local capabilities and advantages for our proposed Establishment – The Carimons having been recommended by Major Farquhar, and Capt. Ross having undertaken a general survey of them, I thought it advisable, as they lay in the route to Johore and Rhio, to proceed in the first instance to these Islands –

4*ᵗʰ*. Geographically the Carimons seem to be well situated for giving to a strong Naval Power the Command of the Straits during War; but they are yet uninhabited, and are covered with an almost impenetrable forest – The Northern part of the larger Island is mountainous, but to the Southward, a portion comprehending at least three fourths of its extent, it is low and apparently swampy – The only harbour the Carimons possess is formed to the North East, by the position of the lesser Island, and altho' there is a sufficient depth of water on one side of *this harbour to enable Ships to approach the Shore in the event of their finding it necessary to seek protection from a battery, yet when this advantage is afforded, the mountains rise abruptly from the Sea, and the Settlement must necessarily be established at a considerable distance, where level land may be found – the nature of this land is such as to justify a doubt of its salubrity, and on the whole, the position did not appear to me to be sufficiently inviting to be made our Chief object of attainment; the uncertainties & difficulties attendant on the first clearing of a primitive forest, & the establishment of a distance Colony in an unknown & unfrequented Island, surrounded and out flanked by the commanding Stations of our Rivals at Banca, Rhio & Malacca, would have demanded countervailing advantages which are not possessed by the Carimons, & it appeared to me that the views & wishes of His Lordship in Council would be more adequately fulfilled by our Establishment in a Situation which had previously acquired a name, where Commerce and population had already resorted, & where in alliance with the Native Authorities and on terms of friendship with the people we might hope to obtain all the advantages of a Military and Commercial Station without incurring the uncertain hazard and the certain expense which the Colonization of a new Country necessarily involves. –*

5ᵗʰ. I accordingly proceeded to Singapoor where the Chief Authority of Johore proper and the adjacent Islands was reported to have fixed his Residence – This town which was founded in the 12ᵗʰ Century is situated on the Northern side of the Straits to which as well as to the Islands it has given its name, and at the bottom of a harbour which I believe is unrivalled in these Seas either with reference to its extent or to the Shelter and safety which it affords – The Port of Rhio I have reason to believe will not bear any comparison with it on these points or in the more essential one of Geographical situation, as it lays in the direct route of our China Trade and all other Ships passing through the Straits – In the neighbourhood of the Town there is cleared ground sufficient for the immediate accommodation of our Settlement and Troops – The surface of the Country in the Vicinity and generally throughout the Island is elevated without being Mountainous, the Soil and the Water are excellent and I am justified by the concurrent opinion of all the Naval and Military Officers who accompanied the Mission in reporting it to be a Station admirably adapted in every essential circumstance for our proposed Establishment. –

6ᵗʰ. On my arrival off the Town a deputation came on board with Compliments and congratulations of the Chief Native authority and a request to know the object of my visit – Having enquired whether there was any Dutch Settlement, or flag here or at Johore and whether the Dutch had by any means attempted to exercise an influence or authority over these ports, they replied that Johore [L]ama or old Johore had long been deserted; that the Chief authority over it and all the adjacent Islands, (excepting those of Lingin and Rhio) now resided at the ancient Capital of Singapore where no attempt had been made to establish the Dutch Power and where no Dutch Flag would be received – After this explanation I stated my intention of visiting the Chief in the course of the Evening when the object of my visit would probably be more fully explained. –

7th. On landing I was received by His Highness with every mark of personal attention, and every demonstration of respect and attachment to the British Govt. – The principal object of my visit being to obtain information on the present political State of Johore, the relative condition and power of its princes and the connection existing between the different States of the Empire, I found means to lead to these points, and obtained the following intelligence in reply to my enquiries which has since been confirmed by universal testimony and which combined with the information I previously possessed on it, will I hope place the subject in a clear point of view. –

8th. The Kings of Johore trace their descent through a line of Twenty-five Sovereigns commencing from the first Hind[u] Prince who established himself at Singapoor in the year 1160; after various vicissitudes in consequence of which they removed the Seat of their Government first to Malacca and subsequently to Johore, they were ultimately obliged by an invasion from Menangkabow to abandon Johore, in the early part of the last Century. – The Sultan fled to Pahang where he died, but his Bandahara or first Officer of State proceeded to Malacca and other places on the Coast where he engaged several Bugguese Chiefs in the Service of the King – with these auxiliaries the Bandahara sailed for Rhio, where after some time the Heir of the deceased was proclaimed Sovereign of Johore – This Prince in reward of the services eventually rendered him by the Bugguese (Natives of Celebes) ordained and determined that the Rajah Moodah or Vizier of Rhio should always be a Prince of Bugguese extraction, and should be charged with authority over all the Bugguese and other Traders resorting to it – The Sultan himself generally resided at Rhio or Lingin and exercised a general control over the States of the Empire, which with those already mentioned, comprehended also the separate Government or rather Kingdoms of Pahang and Johore. –

9th. Conformable to the long established usage of the Empire, founded perhaps originally on the natural divisions of the States composing it, the great Council of Johore was constituted as follows. –

First – The Eldest Son of the reigning Monarch, who was also the legitimate successor to the Throne. –

Second – The Bandahara and Chief of Pahang. –

Third – The Tummungung and Chief of Singapore and Johore proper which comprehended the Island and the Southern extremity of the Peninsula; and

Fourthly – the Indrabongso whose title is now extinct – The Great offices of the Bandahara & Tummungung have never ceased to exist and when the number of the Princes of the Blood has admitted to it have always been filled by the Sons of the Sultan. If on the contrary he had no male offspring, the title of Bandahara was conferred by his pleasure and carried with it the right of succession to the Crown while the other offices were either filled up by his warrant or descended by Inheritance from the previous occupant. –

10th. It may be material to observe that the Rajah Moodah of Rhio had only a local jurisdiction; being necessarily a Bugguese, he had no voice in the Govt. & was particularly excluded from all affairs which had a reference to the political Interest of the Malayan Empire. –

11th. The tranquillity of these States had long been disturbed by the restless ambition of the Dutch Company and the Intrigues of the Bugguese, when on the Establishment of the British at Malacca in 1795, one of His Majesty's Ships conveyed the legitimate sovereign Sultan Mahummud Shah to Rhio and established him in the independent Government of his dominions from whence he had been in temporary exile – The acknowledgement of his independence by the English, the personal Character and talents of the Sultan and the attachment of the Malays to their ancient constitution and to their legitimate Sovereign soon reorganized the Empire and consolidated the power of this Prince whose reign was in general tranquil and prosperous – He died about six years ago universally respected, and according to the Constitution and Custom of the State he previously declared and installed his Eldest Son Tuankoo Loong as his Successor to the Throne of the Empire – This Prince has since assumed the title of Sultan Hussain Mahummud Shah. –

12th. The death of the late Sultan unfortunately took place at a period when his Successor was absent from the Seat of Govt., on a visit to his relation the Bandahara at Pahang; between this place and Lingin communication can only be held in the favourable Monsoon, and nearly a year had elapsed from the *father's death, before his Son arrived to take possession of his hereditary rights, and to assume his legitimate authority. During the interregnum however the Chieftains who possessed the local authority both at Lingin and at Rhio had found means to extend their influence and to throw obstacles in the way of the regular Succession, which either by subverting the constitution or dismembering the Empire, would tend to perpetuate their independent power – The Heir to the Throne was poor and had no means of assembling a Force to support his rightful claim while the Bugguese Chief of Rhio was rich and surrounded by his Tribe. – Under the pretence of waiting until all the distant Chiefs were assembled the installation of the new Sultan was deferred sine die and a small part of the Port duties of Rhio was assigned for his subsistence. The Second Son of the late Sultan who is understood to be of an easy disposition and of weak intellect continued in the meantime in the nominal exercise of authority at Lingin and it ultimately accorded with the policy of the Bugguese Chief at Rhio to consider this person as his immediate Superior; the empty allegiance and honors necessary to a chief of his own creation being more easily rendered than the substantial rights of the legitimate Sovereign to the established portion of the Revenues of Rhio and to the undivided authority of the States. –*

13th. Affairs remained in this State for about four years antecedent to the Mission of Major Farquhar to Rhio and Lingin – The Govt. was considered to be in an unsettled State and was in fact so anomalous that while the Chief of Rhio held from the rightful Sultan the exercise of his authority at these Islands the justice of his Claims were universally and unequivocally acknowledged and a certain portion of the Revenues were set apart [?] of his duty to enter into the local politics of the Govt., but it is to be remarked that when he addressed the person called Sultan by the only title of Sultan known to us, that Chief distinctly stated to him that he was not Sultan of Johore, & requested Major Farquhar would not address him by that Title – If after this any doubt remained on the Subject, the Document given by this Chief to Major Farquhar and transmitted by him to the Government of Prince of Wales's Island would be conclusive of the Question – It is declarity [sic] of the authority which had been assumed by the Rajah Moodah – it is not attested by the Seal of the Sultan of Johore, and it expressly states that the Rajah of Lingin had never at any period asserted or assumed the Sovereign power, the words of the translation are "I have never from the first to the present time been in the habit of discussing or settling any State Affairs" and again "no matters of business have ever yet appertained to me". –

14*th*. The Treaty which Major Farquhar as Agent to the Penang Govt. entered into at Rhio, and which is attested by the Seal of the Rajah Moodah as Vizier of Rhio was, it is true, executed by the parties, in the name of Abdul Rahman Sultan of Johore, Pahang, Rhio and Lingin. The introduction of this title was probably a designed stroke of policy on the one part, and the admission of it was perhaps inconsiderate on the other; but if, under any circumstances, a mistake of this nature could affect the just rights of the Constitutional Chief, or be considered as an acknowledgement by our Govt. of an usurped authority, that consequence would in the present instance, be happily obviated, by Abdul Rahman's previous abrogation of the title so gratuitously conferred upon him. –

15*th*. During the period which intervened between the conclusion of this Treaty and my return to these Seas[,] [t]he Dutch arrived at Rhio & demanded the renewal of their ancient but now obsolete rights – This was firmly and positively refused, and they then brought forward proposals for a new Treaty. For several weeks their admission into Rhio on any terms was vigorously opposed, but at length the blockade of the Port by a line of Battle Ship[s] and Frigate[s] and his apprehension from the powerful military force on board the Netherlands Squadron, prevailed over the wishes and the opposition of the Rajah, who was finally obliged to admit them into Rhio and to enter into such terms as they were pleased to dictate – The Dutch authorities now endeavoured to assemble the Chiefs of Lingin[,] Pahang, and Singapore, but of these the latter only attended the Convocation, and he boldly opposed their establishment at Rhio on the terms of the treaty by which the long established and lucrative right of himself and other Chiefs to a participation in the Commercial Revenues of Rhio was usurped & appropriated by the two contracting parties. – His remonstrances were of course unavailing nor did he deny the right of the Rajah Moodah to make such arrangements with regard to Rhio as suited his present circumstances however inconsistent they might be with his former engagements – he however declared that he would never for himself or the absent Chief of Pahang submit to any terms which could compromise the independent authority which they exercised in their respective States, until the legitimate Sultan assumed the general Government of the Empire [nor] would he ever admit the Settlement of the Dutch nor the interference of their Ally the Rajah Moodah in his own Territories. –

16*th*. Subsequently to this declaration the Tummungung was requested by the Dutch authorities to affix his Seal to the Treaty which they had concluded with Rhio as a mark of his friendship and good will towards their Nation – To this *application the Tummungung replied that he was desirous of always remaining on terms of amity with the Subjects of His Netherlands Majesty with whose Power he was well acquainted – he had however been always more intimately connected with the English, and provided a compliance with the request did not tend to interrupt that intercourse and could not be considered to commit him with regard to that Nation or to his own Sovereign he could have no objection to attest the deed which they had executed and he accordingly affixed his Seal to it in compliance with their request – He did not however consider himself by any means a party to the Treaty in question. His Name and that of Singapore is not mentioned in it to his knowledge, he did not then nor has he since received any Copy nor has he had any communication verbal or written from the Dutch regarding it.*

17th. The legitimate Sultan of Johore was at this period in the Straits but it did not [accord] with the Interests of the Rajah Moodah to invite him to the conference and on the other hand this Prince was probably satisfied with the opportunity thus afforded him of preserving his independence of Dutch Authority. –

18th. The person whom I found in the exercise of Sovereign power at Singapore and its dependencies is the Tummungung to whose spirited and independent conduct in support of the rights of his State and of his Sovereign I have already adverted – The division of the Empire under his authority descended to him from his ancestors and he holds his warrant from Sultan Mahummud Shah to govern the lands of Singapore and its Dependencies with the title of Sree Maharajah Datoo Tummungung – On the death of Mahummud Shah, he was at Rhio where he remained for above a year after that event in the hope of assisting in the Instalment of the Successor; but finding his hopes disappointed and that measure retarded by the intrigues of the Bugguese, he quitted Rhio in disgust and returned to his Govt. at Singapore where in concert with the Rajah of Pahang he still continues to hold out hopes to the Sultan Hussein Mahummud Shah of extending his rule over the other States – Thus the only two duly constituted authorities of the Empire who have a voice in the affairs of Govt., the Bandahara & the Tummungung, are decidedly favourable to the legitimate Sovereign and a local intrigue of the Vizier of Rhio who can never himself aspire to the Crown, is all that impeded his succession to the inheritance of his ancestors transmitted to him through a line of twenty-five Monarchs and through a period of Six Centuries. –

19*th*. It is proper to observe that from the period of the late Sultan's demise until the Establishment of the Dutch at Rhio an argument subsisted between the Chiefs of the separate States by which the Division of the Revenues arising from the Port Duties at Rhio, that is to say the principal productive source of Revenue now existing, was regulated in certain proportions. – In their Treaty with the Rajah Mooda the Dutch overlooked this circumstance and by appropriating a moiety to themselves & another to the local Chief have disunited all the previously existing relations –

20*th*. Finding that the object of my Mission might be adequately obtained at Singapore in the event of any circumstance of difficulty at Rhio which the occupation of that Island by the Dutch rendered extremely probable, but desirous nevertheless of effecting that object with every possible degree of delicacy and attention as well to the neighbouring States as to the prejudices and feelings of their Chiefs, I dispatched Major Farquhar to Rhio according to my original intention and with the additional instructions of which I have the honor to enclose a copy for the information of His Lordship in Council – In these instructions the attention and efforts of Major Farquhar were principally directed to conciliating the friendship of the Rajah Moodah and to obtaining his concurrence, however unnecessary on a general view of the Subject that concurrence may be considered, to our Establishment in the Johore Dominions – Major Farquhar was also particularly directed to avoid all collision with the Dutch Authorities. –

21*st*. At this stage of my proceedings it appeared to me to be advisable and proper to enter into some terms with the Tummungung by which he might be engaged and secured to our Interests and I have the honor to transmit a copy of Preliminary Articles of agreement which I accordingly entered into with that Chieftain on the 30*th*. Ulto.,[124] by which I obtained his permission to establish a British factory on any part of the Dominions subject to his Authority – My object being so far secured I deferred the ulterior arrangements until the return of Major Farquhar from R[h]io and the arrival of His Highness the Sultan Hussein Mahummud Shah who was absent from Singapore at this period but whose authority and sanction I considered indepensible [sic] to any definite agreement. –

22*nd*. The Troops having been landed on Singapore I availed myself of the leisure afforded me by the circumstances which I have already stated to proceed further to the Eastward for the purpose of Surveying the Port of Johor and the Northern side of Singapore as well as for determining on the necessity of *placing any small post in either of these Situations – as I found the access to them however to be difficult and as I discovered a very general prejudice to exist among the Natives to any Establishment on the unfortunate site of old Johore[,] which having been three times destroyed had received the malediction of the late Sovereign[,] I did not consider it necessary to persevere in this object. –*

23d. On the 1ˢᵗ. Instant His Highness Sultan Hussein Mahummud Shah arrived at Singapore and on the following day he paid me a formal visit, during which I explained to him the object of my Mission – His Highness confirmed the particulars of the intelligence I had previous received from the Tummungung, expressed his entire acquiescence & approbation of the Agreement which that Chief had concluded with us, and requested in return to be taken into the alliance and protection of the English Nation. –

24ᵗʰ. In replying to His Highness's request and in explaining to him the terms on which we [were] desirous of establishing a permanent Station at Singapore under the sanction of his authority, I was careful to impress on his Highness's mind our fixed determination to avoid all interference in the political concerns of his Empire and to take no active share in asserting or maintaining his power over any portion of his States: I would nevertheless willingly stipulate to afford to His Highness personal protection from all Enemies while he resided in the vicinity of our Factory and taking these principles for a Basis I informed His Highness that I would be happy to enter with him on the consideration of the articles of a defensive Treaty between His Highness and His Excellency the Most Noble the Governor General. –

25ᵗʰ. On the following day [3 February] Major Farquhar returned from Rhio and delivered to me the accompanying Report of his Mission[125] *from a perusal of which His Lordship in Council will perceive that the result is as favourable as could be reasonably be [sic] expected, under existing circumstances, without committing and involving the Native Authorities with those of His Netherlands Majesty now established on that Island – while the Vizier regrets his incapacity to fulfill the Commercial agreement into which he entered, he declares his friendship and attachment to our Nation and it is satisfactory to find that the Dutch have received no authority from him supposing him for [a] moment competent to grant it – The Dutch possess no authority by virtue of the new Treaty concluded with him even to exercise any power or to establish any Settlement either at Pahang, Lingin or elsewhere, and in short have no pretension derived even from the Vizier to any other position than that of Rhio –*

26th. *Under the circumstances I had no hesitation with regard to the pro-priety of immediately concluding the requisite definitive arrangements for the Establishment of a British Factory at Singapore and having delivered to the Sultan under appropriate Honors the letter containing my Credentials with which I had the honor to be charged by the Most Noble the Governor General, I proceeded to discuss with their Highnesses the Sultan and the Tummungung the terms of the projected Alliance. –*

27th. *On the 6th Instant a Treaty, of which I have the honor to transmit one of the original Copies in the Malayan and English Languages[,]*[126] *was executed in Triplicate by their Highnesses and by me in the capacity of Agent to the Govr. General – The British Flag was hoisted at the same time on Singapore under a Royal Salute from our Garrison, from all the Shipping and from the Tummungung's Battery. –*

28th. *As the Provisions of this Treaty include all those which formed the substance of the preliminary Articles of Agreement, the explanation which it is necessary I should enter into on the Subject of them will [be] common to both – You will observe that after the preamble and the confirmation by the Sultan of the agreement concluded on his part by the Tummungung on the 30th. Ultimo the 2nd. Article of the Treaty proceeds to the Grant on the part of the [East India] Company of a compensation to the Sultan for such advantages as might be lost to him now or hereafter in consequence of the Establishment of our Factory which the 3d. Article authorizes and confirms, or the regulation and command of the Harbour which is ceded to us by the Eighth. –*

29th. *In determining the amount of this Compensation which I trust will appear to His Lordship in Council to be but a moderate return for the transfer to our Authority of the best port in His Highness's Dominions, I was influenced partly by a consideration of the reasons which the Article holds out[,] but chiefly by the knowledge that the Sultan was excluded, both by the Vizier's Cession of half the Revenues of Rhio to the Dutch and by His Highness having entered into a Treaty with us, from all hope of the further payment to him from this Source of the small share which had been assigned for his subsistence and which amounted to about 4,800 Dollars per Annum. –*

30th. *The allowance of Sp. Drs. 3,000 pr. Annum to the Tummungung appeared to me a fair compensation for the sacrifice to us of his immediate authority over the harbour and as a ground rent for the Post occupied by our Troops and establishment, now placed in the lines which surrounded the ancient*

Capital, containing a considerable portion of the cleared and consequently most productive land, and on the most commanding situation which the Island affords. In addition to the reasons which I have adduced and which apply to their Highnesses individually, some weight is due to the consideration of their having both deprived themselves by the 5th. Article of their Treaty, of all the advantages which might eventually have been derived from an union or alliance with other Nations. –

31st. His Lordship in Council will observe in the conclusion of the 2nd. Article which as well as the 3rd. and 4th. relates to this Subject, the caution with which I have assiduously avoided all occasion of interference in the political relations or affairs of these States which could possibly compromise our tranquillity, by any Collision with the subjects of His Netherlands Majesty, or by any discussions with the Chieftains of the Empire who have assumed an independent Authority – personal protection to their Highnesses or a reciprocally defensive alliance, was a stipulation however of indispensible [sic] necessity to these Chiefs, who are sensible that by an alliance with us they have exposed themselves to the ill offices of our Rivals in peace and to the attacks of our Enemies in War; and every consideration of sound policy of what [was] due to our Character and to the dignity conferred by our Alliance would have forbad me to deny to their Highnesses as long as it suits their convenience or policy to remain in its vicinity, the protection of the Flag which we have pla[c]ed in their Dominions.

32nd. The 6th. and 7th. Articles which relate to the Jurisdiction and to the Administration of Justice and the 8th. and 9th. regarding the regulation of the Port and the duties which may hereafter be derived from it will form the subject of a future communication when the progress of the Settlement may naturally lead to it, and furnish the foundation to which the future edifice is to be adapted. In the meantime I entertain a confident hope that on a Review of the Treaty, His Lordship will be of opinion that while the British Interests have been fully provided for, those of the Native Authorities have been considered with justice and liberality; and that in conformity to my instructions every precaution has been taken for preventing the necessity under any circumstances of involving ourselves in any political question whatever. –

33rd. In order to afford to His Lordship in Council a general idea of the nature of our position at Singapore, I have the satisfaction to forward by [the] Bearer of this Dispatch a regular Survey of the Harbour[127] with a description and Instructions for Shipping, executed at my request by Captain Ross of the

Honble Company's Bombay Marine – This Survey is purely Nautical, but it will nevertheless serve to shew the Site of our Establishment, the nature of the Harbour and the general Capacity of the whole for defensive operations – the sketch on a larger Scale which accompanies it,[128] *the corresponding points of which can be easily found on the general map, is intended to shew the facilities of defence afforded by the nature of the ground contiguous to and forming our principal position. –*

34th. The point marked <u>A</u> is [the] apex of a hill rising about 100 feet from the level of the plain which extends itself to a considerable distance to the Northward, and commanding every circumjacent Situation; the ascent is an inclined plane of about 30 degrees from the Sea face, … the whole extent of which could if it were necessary, be strengthened by a wet Ditch constantly supplied from the River which washes its base towards the South – On the top of the Hill there is abundant space for the construction of a small Fort or blockhouse and between the base and the Sea on the lines and ditch which formerly surrounded the Capital of Singapoor inclosing a considerable space cleared and level on which the British Troops are now encamped. –

35th. To the Northward of the point marked <u>B</u> and between it and the Malay Village a Battery under the Command of the Fort or blockhouse and containing 2 or 3 heavy Guns and Mortars might be advantageously constructed to serve as a point d'appui to another Battery on Sandy point; the last of which would have the anchorage for all Vessels of a moderate size within the range of its Guns and would also possess the command of the Inner Bay marked <u>C</u> which both for extent and depth as well as for the conveniences of wood and water is admirably adapted for the reception and shelter of the Native trade – As the ground in the vicinity of this point[,] as well as in general throughout the [h]arbour is soft mud, and as the soundings are inserted in the Chart of the lowest range to which they fall in [?] and spring tides, whips of the greatest burthen might in any future circumstance of necessity find Security under its Guns[.] It is the opinion however of all the professional men whose judgement I have had an opportunity of consulting that a Martillo Tower on Deep Water point would be the most efficient, eligible, and ultimately the cheapest mode which could be adopted for the defence of the harbour – It would require but a few men – it would altogether supersede the necessity of Batteries and the consequence subdivision of the Garrison, whilst it would fully Command and protect within a distance of a few hundred yards an extensive anchorage where the heaviest Vessels would be in the most perfect *safety – As their arguments appear to me to be reasonable, I take the liberty of suggesting the proposal to the consideration of His Lordship in Council, and in the Event of its being honoured with His Lordship's approbation, of recommending that prepared timber and frame work, Guns and traversing Carriages, be forwarded from Bengal by any convenient opportunity – The construction of the Tower will, as soon as the proper materials can be collected, be readily undertaken by Lieut^t. Ralfe of Artillery,[129] whom I have provisionally appointed Assistant Engineer, under the Superintendence of Major Farquhar. –*

36th. With reference to the foregoing observations as well as to the Military force requisite under existing circumstances for the Garrison of Singapore, my judgment has been directed in a great measure by that of Major Farquhar with which it entirely coincides, and I should have had the official expression of that Officer's professional opinion had not the shortness of the period which intervened between his return from Rhio and my departure, and the numerous avocations by which that period was occupied, deprived him of the means of entering fully into the Subject – I shall hereafter have the honor of supplying this deficiency but in the mean time I am justified by a knowledge of his sentiments in reporting for the information of His Lordship [in] Council that the number and description of Troops mentioned in the Margin [3 Companies Sepoys 30 European Artillery 70 Golundauze] is in our opinion adequate for all probable exigencies – I have accordingly requested the Governor and Council of Prince of Wales's Island to detach 2 Companies of the 20th Native Regiment in addition to the Company which accompanied me, and have been disembarked at Singapore, to complete the requisite proportion of that description of force – The Artillery and Lascars now at Singapore are also detailed in the Margin [30 E. Artilly 20 Golundauze 10 Lascars] and I beg leave to recommend that fifty Golundauze be embarked from Fort William by an early opportunity to complete the proposed Garrison. –

37th. Having determined on the nature and extent of the Military defences to be immediately constructed, my attention was next directed to the formation of the necessary provisional Establishment for conducting the various Civil and Military duties of the Settlement – For the necessary information on this Subject I take the liberty of referring you to the accompanying Copy of the Instructions with which I furnished Major Farquhar previously to my departure, and which I trust will meet the approbation of the Most Noble the Governor General in Council – The establishment which I have provisionally authorized while it ought to ensure an efficient discharge of the duties confided to it, has been limited by a due attention to œconomy and the Public Interests, and the contingent expense attending the construction of Works & Buildings, will I have reason to believe be limited in its amount, and be applied with integrity & ability – It may be necessary to observe that under the circumstances of the moment and of the new Settlement, no Estimate of that expense could possibly be obtained. –

38*th*. In appointing an assistant to Major Farquhar in the Civil Duties of the Residency, I have availed myself of the Services of Lieut*t*. Crossley of the European Regt.,[130] who has been under the necessity of leaving Bengal on sick certificate[.] This officer held for seven years the most responsible and confidential situations under the late British Government at the Moluccas, and from his knowledge of the Character and language of the Natives, as well as of the duties which he will be required to perform[,] is peculiarly qualified for the Situation – In a new Establishment, where so much depends on the ability, character, and application of the persons employed, and where there are few precedents for the guidance of the Public functionaries in the details of their duties, the Services of such an Officer are peculiarly valuable, and I earnestly hope His Lordship in Council will do me the honor to confirm a nomination, which has been dictated by the strongest sense of what is to the Public Interests. –

39*th*. I have the honor to transmit an Indent for the Ordnance and Military Stores required for the Batteries and Garrison, which I request may be furnished with the least delay practicable; as well as the Articles of provision necessary for the use of the Troops during a period of one year, for which I have also the honor to transmit an Indent with this letter – As Rice is procurable here on cheaper terms than it can be freighted from Bengal and as I may also have an opportunity of transferring a part of the very large quantity in store at Bencoolen, I have not thought [it] necessary to include it in the Indent; I beg leave however to observe that the Stores at Penang and Bencoolen being an extent too limited to permit the supply of any other articles required by us, and the importance being so great of rendering our Establishment at Singapore respectable and efficient at any early period, I would on no account recommend the modification of the Indent now transmitted, under an expectation of finding means of supplying them to the Eastward – and I hope that it may be found practicable to dispatch them before the failure of the present monsoon, may render the transport tedious and expensive –

40*th*. As it is my intention after my Services at Acheen can be dispensed with to proceed to Bencoolen by the route of Singapore, an opportunity will be

*afforded me of making such additional arrangements and of issuing on the spot,
such further Instructions to Major Farquhar, as longer experience and more
particular local information, may render necessary and proper – In the meantime I trust I shall stand excused in anticipating some of the leading advantages
which will in my judgment necessarily result from the permanent Establishment
of the British in this quarter, and for pointing out the features and circumstances
by which Singapore is peculiarly adapted and recommended for the purposes of
such an Establishment. –*

*41ˢᵗ. The short experience which has been afforded us of the bold and vigor-
ous policy of the Dutch since the restoration to them of our Conquests in these
Seas, has been sufficient to demonstrate the spirit of exclusion and encroachment
which characterizes and animates their rising power; & the comprehensive and
enlightened views of the Governor General in Council have been directed and
have foreseen the necessity which was thereby imposed on His Lordship's Govt.
of guarding against the abuse on the part of the Dutch authorities of the gener-
ous policy of His Majesty's Ministers, and of securing the means of protecting
our Commercial and political relations before the maturity and consolidation
of their arrangements, should have deprived us of the power of averting the evil
consequences which might arise from their success. –*

*42ⁿᵈ. With this view, it was of primary importance to obtain a post which
should have a Commanding Geographical position at the Southern entrance of
the Straits of Malacca; which should be in the track of our China and Country
trade; which should be capable of affording them protection and of supplying their
wants; which should possess capabilities of defence by a moderate force; which
might give us the means of supporting and extending our Commercial intercourse
with the Malay States; and which by contiguity to the Seat of Dutch power,
might enable us to watch the march of its policy and if necessary, to counteract
its influence. –*

*43ʳᵈ. To prove that the position now occupied by our force at Singapore pos-
sesses the means, and affords the greatest comparative facilities to the attainment
of the important objects contemplated by His Lordship in Council; and to demonstrate, I trust to the satisfaction of His Lordship, that the measures which I have
taken to secure it, have been regulated by just and honorable principles, is the
object which I shall endeavor to attain in the concluding paragraphs of this letter. –*

*44ᵗʰ. Owing as much perhaps to the Bankrupt state of the Dutch East India
Company, and to its having subsequently been under the immediate authority of*

our Settlement at Prince of Wales Island – as to the want of a harbour for the protection or convenience of Trade, Malacca has long been on the decline; but the new Establishment at Rhio, and the energy which now animates the Dutch into [sic] would have probably soon raised it to its former importance – a glance at Singapore on the Map, is sufficient to shew that it as completely commands the Straits of Malacca and of Rhio, the last of which is in sight of our Settlement, as it does those which bear its name[.] It is also obvious that while the occupation of it by the British, destroys the Political importance of Malacca, by giving us the power of interrupting at any time its connection with the Chief Govt. and the other Dutch dependencies, it paralyzes all plans, which may have been in progress for the exclusion of our Commerce and influence with the Malayan States – Our Station at Singapore may therefore be considered as an effectual check to the rapid march of the Dutch over the Eastern Archipelago, and whether we may have the power hereafter of extending our Stations or be compelled to confine ourselves to this Factory, the spell is broken, and one independent Port under our Flag may be sufficient to prevent the recurrence of the System of exclusion [and] monopoly which the Dutch once exercised in these Seas, and would willingly re-establish. –

45th. Situated at the very extremity of the Peninsula, all Vessels to and from China via Malacca, are obliged to pass within five miles of our Head Quarters, and generally pass within half a mile of St. Johns, a dependent Islet forming the Western point of the Bay on which I have directed a small post to be fixed, and from whence every ship can be boarded if necessary, the water being smooth at all Seasons – The run between these Islands and the Carimons, which are in sight from it, can be effected in a few hours, and crosses the route which all Vessels from the Northward must necessarily pursue which are bound towards Batavia and the Eastern Islands. –

46th. As a Port for the refreshment & refitment of our Shipping and particularly for that portion of it engaged in the China trade, and [sic] it is requisite for me to refer to the able Survey and Report of Captain Ross[131] and to add to it, that excellent water in convenient situations for the supply of Ships, is to be found in several places; and that industrious Chinese are already established in the interior, and may soon be expected to supply vegetables &ca. &ca. equal to the demand. – The Port is plentifully supplied with Fish and Turtle, which are said to be more abundant here than in any other part of the Archipelago. Rice, salt and other necessaries, are always procurable from Siam[,] the Granary of *the Malay Tribes in this quarter – Timber abounds on the Island and its vicinity; a large part of the population are already engaged in Building Boats and Vessels, and the Chinese of whom some are already employed in smelting the ore brought from the Tin Mines on the Neighbouring Islands, and others employed as Cultivators or Artificers, may soon be expected to encrease in a number proportionate to the wants and Interests of the Settlement.*

47th. The Capability of affording protection to Ships and of their being defended by a moderate force has been already adverted to, and for any further information which may be necessary I beg leave to refer you to the Instructions of Major Farquhar. –

48th. A measure of the nature of that which we have adopted was in some degree necessary to evince to the varied and enterprising population of these Islands, that our Commercial and Political views in this quarter, had not entirely sunk under the vaunted power and encroachment of the Dutch, and to prove to them that we were determined to make a stand against it. – By maintaining our right to a free Commerce with the Malay States and inspiring them with a confidence in the stability of it, we may contemplate its advancement to a much greater extent than has been hitherto enjoyed – Independently of our intercourse with the Tribes of the Archipelago, Singapore may be considered as the principal Entrepot to which the Native Traders of Siam, Cambodia, Champa, Cochin China and China will annually resort. – It is to the Straits of Singapore that their Merchants are always bound in the first instance, and if on their arrival they can find a market for their goods and means of supplying their wants, they will have no possible inducement to proceed to the more distant, unhealthy and expensive Port of Batavia – Siam which is the Granary to the Countries North of the Equator, is rapidly extending the Native Commerce, nearly the whole of which may be expected to enter at Singapore – The passage from China has been made in less than six days and that number is all that is requisite in the favourable Monsoon for the passage from Singapore to Batavia or Acheen while two days are sufficient for a Voyage to Borneo. –

49th. The justice and legitimacy of the title under sanction of which, we have established ourselves at Singapore, may be summed up in a few words, by a short Statement of Facts, none of which can be denied, and is such, as cannot in my judgement be disputed, with any shadow of reason or degree of plausibility – From the detail which is included between the 8th. and 23rd. Paragraphs of this dispatch, I think it will appear evident, that the Sultan of Johore and the

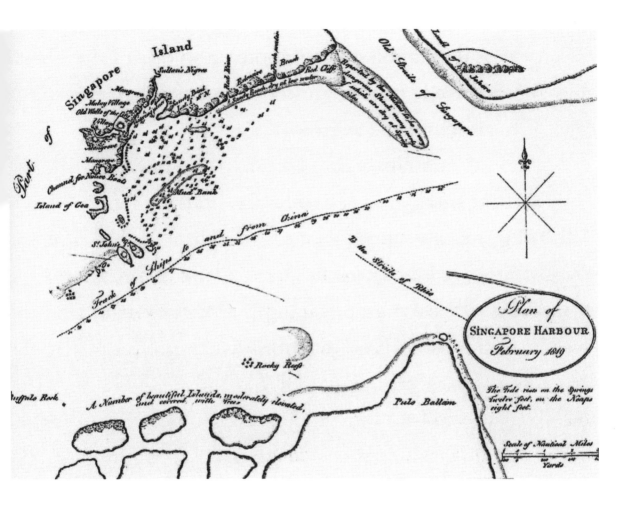

Fig. 22
Plan of Singapore Harbour, February
1819, by Captain Daniel Ross.

Tummungung of Singapore, are competent to the conclusion of a treaty and the transfer to the British of ground sufficient for our Factories – That we are even justified by the example of the Dutch at Rhio, to consider the Tummungung alone, as a competent authority for these purposes – That we have for adequate considerations procured the grant of the Sultan and Tummungung for our Establishment at Singapore – That the Dutch flag has never been planted on that

Island – That we are not aware of the existence of any Claims now or heretofore on the part of the Dutch to any authority over Singapore or its Chiefs – That we have the authority of the Rajah Moodah of Rhio, who has lately concluded a treaty with them, for believing that the said treaty relates solely and exclusively to Rhio. – That on the visit [of] Major Farquhar to that Island, it was not concealed from the Dutch that a British force was then at Singapore; and that no intimation of a claim to it on their part or protest against the occupation of it on our's, was made by their authorities – On a review of the whole I trust it will appear to His Lordship in Council that the Dutch have no just reason to complain, that far from interfering with them at Rhio, we, as soon as we found they were established there, submitted to be excluded from that Port, rather than incur the hazard of any Collision with them; and that if they possess any shadow of a claim on Singapore, it must be founded on some ancient or obsolete treaty by virtue of which, as Sovereigns of the Eastern Seas, they might as reasonably hope to exclude us from the Archipelago altogether. –

50th. It is hardly necessary to anticipate the assertion of a Claim so puerile, but I nevertheless take occasion to observe that there is less reason to suppose the States of Johore can be subject to such a claim, than almost any other in the Eastern Seas; as it appears from a Notification addressed to the Sultan of Johore by the Commanders of the British Sea and land forces at the capture of Malacca in 1795, that they had the authority of the Dutch Govt. of Malacca for declaring the Agreement between the Governor General of Batavia and the Sultan of Johore to have ceased, and that the States of the latter were independent. – As a reference to this Document may be desirable I do myself the honor of transmitting a Copy of it enclosed in this letter. –

51st. In conclusion it may be satisfactory to His Lordship in Council to be informed, that no connection having ever existed between the States of Siam and Johore, our establishment at Singapore can have no possible influence on our political relations with the former people, beyond the means which it may ultimately afford us of observing their Character and Cultivating their friendship. –

I have &ca
(signed) T.S. Raffles

Prince of Wales' Island
13th. Feby. 1819

CHAPTER VII

Raffles's Private Reports on the Founding of Singapore

Two days after completing his official despatch to the Supreme Government, Raffles addressed a private letter to the Governor-General relating to other matters connected with his mission to Singapore, including the lack of co-operation he had received from the Prince of Wales Island authorities and their unwillingness to provide military support for the new settlement:[132]

Private

Penang — February 15th 1819

My Lord,

It is with much satisfaction that I now have the honor to inform your Lordship of the full accomplishment of the ulterior object of my Mission — a British Station has been established in the Straits of Singapore in the vicinity of Johor in a situation combining every advantage geographical and local which we could desire, and I have had the good fortune to effect the arrangement without immediate collision or interference with the Dutch authorities and on terms and conditions which I can with confidence submit for your Lordship's approbation and confirmation.

The Dutch having previously occupied Rhio, my first object was to ascertain whether they had still left at our command any other Port that would answer our purpose and if so whether we could establish ourselves in such [a] Port with the consent of the Native Authorities and in justice to the Dutch claims and rights – and the Port of Singapore offering itself on every account as exactly suited to our purpose I was happy to find that not only the Authority with whom the Dutch treated at Rhio was incompetent to make arrangements for any of the States beyond the Port of Rhio, but that such States were not even included in his Treaty with the Dutch – Rhio alone being referred to –

At Singapore I discovered a most superior Harbour and found an Authority both competent and willing to treat for our establishment and that we might not want the highest sanction to our arrangement the legitimate Sultan of Johor became a party to our Treaty – and now resides under our protection –

As I have endeavor'd in my Despatch to afford your Lordship the fullest information on every point, I will not intrude on your Lordship's valuable time by a repetition of the advantages which the Station affords or of the arguments on which I found our right to maintain and enjoy those advantages – but as it may be convenient for immediate reference I have taken the liberty to forward to your Lordship under a separate Envelope a Sketch of the Harbour of Singapore shewing the position with relation to the China Trade[133] –

In the execution of the duty which I have had the honor to perform as your Lordship's Representative, I am confident that every liberal and indulgent consideration will be given to the peculiar and delicate situation in which I have been placed – I have never lost sight of the high importance of the object to be attained nor of the necessity of attaining it without collision – but it was impossible from the first not to foresee that in prosecution of the avowed policy of the Dutch they would attempt to dispute our right to any interference whatever in the Eastern Seas – They will probably appeal in the present case against our Establishment at Singapore, but I trust the grounds on which we maintain our rights in that Station will furnish a fair answer with which their arguments may be successfully combatted[134] –

It is impossible also for me to conceal from your Lordship that I have not met with that cordial cooperation and assistance from Colonel Bannerman in which I had a right to expect from the local Government or from the assurances of Colonel Bannerman himself on my first arrival[135] – I have throughout met with nothing but obstruction and a determination by every possible means to prevent my interference either to the Eastward or at Acheen – I can assure your Lordship that on my part every degree of conciliation and respect has been evinced, and that it is with the deepest regret I have found them unavailing to secure me against the intemperate Conduct of the Chief Authority at this place – Your Lordship will perceive that in the first instance my proceeding to the Eastward at all was violently opposed, and that I was informed it was my duty at any rate first to go to Acheen – desirous of meeting the wishes of the local Government I agreed to do so, but after a detention of twenty days by frivolous & unnecessary delays, just as I was on the eve of embarking I received a requisition to stay my proceedings and not to visit Acheen until a reply to some Despatches sent to Bengal was received – I also met this wish and in the interim proceeded to the Eastward & accomplished the main object of my Mission – On my return I naturally requested Colonel Bannerman to afford me two additional Companies of Sepoys to complete the number he had promised should be held at my disposal – He now says he is not justified in giving me any further assistance and without knowing on what grounds the arrangements to the Eastward have been made declares a judgment against them – and in order that they may be annulled exposes the Station to insult and our interests to hazard – It is in vain that I urge these arrangements as made in your Lordship's name, and that what-ever differences of opinion there may be, these arrangements considering how much is at stake they ought to be supported until the final orders of the Supreme Government are received – The local Government are determined to oppose all interference on the part of your Lordship except it be communicated in the shape of a positive order, and I should make but a bad return for the confidence with which your Lordship has honoured me, if I did not apprize your Lordship of this circumstance –

I hope it will be clearly understood that I make no complaint against the local Government – it is not my wish to agitate any question in which they are concerned, but as I fear the same delicacy will not be observed on their part, I deem it necessary to say this much in explanation and in my own defence.

Fortunately for the public interests I have still the command of a sufficient amount of Troops and Stores at Bencoolen to complete the Garrison of Singapore to the requisite strength until your Lordship's further orders are received[136] *– and however much the disappointment in receiving this expected reinforcement from Penang is to be regretted on account of the delay and expense it may occasion, it forces me to the adoption of an alternative which has some advantages – namely* the gradual transfer of our Establishment from Bencoolen to Singapore – knowing the sentiments of your Lordship on this subject I shall not hesitate to carry into effect this arrangement as far as may be safe & practicable – and I shall in all probability be myself as much at Singapore as Bencoolen –

In the detailed arrangements for our defences and for the Establishment at Singapore I trust your Lordship will find nothing to disapprove – I have directed Major Farquhar to collect materials and to construct a Blockhouse on the principle which your Lordship did me the honor to suggest[137] and I have no reason to believe that our Fortifications will involve any considerable expence – The Establishment is moderate but sufficient to secure efficiency in the first instance – I am particularly anxious to solicit your Lordship's favorable consideration of Lieutt Crossley[138] who I have appointed to assist Major Farquhar – the services of an officer possessing the peculiar qualification of Lt Crossley are most essential on the first establishment of the Settlement, and altho' I have great reliance on Major Farquhar's well known character and mildness, I have no reason to expect from him any knowledge of the details of business or any very great personal energy in case of emergency[139] –

I have signified to Captain Coombs my desire of proceeding to Acheen without delay, and whatever may be the arguments brought forward to oppose our progress I shall certainly persevere in the execution of the high trust reposed in me – Your Lordship will be happy to hear that the Report of the Dutch having made an offer to the ExKing[140] is altogether unfounded – No attempt at negociation has ever been made by that Power and there is no reason to believe they contemplated any thing of the kind – Since my arrival in this quarter I have received much information from Acheen but until I can write to your Lordship from the spot I should not feel myself justified in hazarding an opinion beyond my conviction that nothing is to be so much depreciated as our interference in any manner in the domestic politics of the Country – it will involve us in troubles not less than those which have occurred at Ceylon, and I hardly know what corresponding advantage could be contemplated –

While I feel the utmost anxiety to know your Lordship's sentiments on the arrangements which have been concluded, I place the fullest reliance on your Lordship's gracious assurance of support, and I can assure your Lordship that the first and only object of my ambition was to effect what would redound to the honor and credit of your Lordship's unrivalled administration, & by a *devotedness to your interests to prove myself in some degree worthy of the con-fidence reposed.*

I have the honor to remain, with the highest respect,

Your Lordship's most obedient &
most devoted humble S^t
T S Raffles

The Most Noble
The Marquess of Hastings K.B.
&c &c &c

Four days later, Raffles wrote to John Adam, Political Secretary to the Governor-General, repeating his complaints about the opposition of the Prince of Wales Island government to his mission to the Eastward:[141]

Private

Letter 10
Raffles to Adam
16 February 1819

Penang 16th. February 1819

My dear Sir,

The immediate departure of the Hope does not admit of my doing more than closing my despatches and referring you generally to their contents for the result of my Mission to the Eastward, which I am happy to say has in every respect been most successful – Singapore possesses advantages far superior to Rhio and I think you will admit that the ground on which we stand is perfectly secure –

I have been placed as you will perceive, in a very delicate and responsible situation and while I kept the main point in view, namely the attainment of our Station to the Eastward, have had to contend with other opponents besides the Dutch – Where such great national interests were at stake it is to be regretted that the local Government did not abstain from gratuitous opposition – I regret this opposition the more as it may annoy his Lordship who could not do otherwise than look for active cooperation and zeal in the prosecution of his plans – I trust however I shall have the credit for not having provoked this opposition & for having exercised every possible forbearance –

I have this instant since closing my Despatch received a Letter from Colonel Bannerman calling upon me still to stay my proceedings and not to go to Acheen until replies to his Letter are received from Bengal – and should I persist he states his determination of sending over the Troops, alludes to accompanying them himself, and if they are not wanted, adds his intention of sending them to Bengal – thus depriving himself of the only means of supporting our Establishment to the Eastward –

I shall persevere steadily in the accomplishment of the objects entrusted to me, and you may rely on my using every caution not to involve the Supreme Government unnecessarily in any question with the local Government – Fortunately I can support my Station at Singapore without the immediate aid of this Gov^t., but it is of importance that the early orders of the Supreme Government should be received with regard to the force to be permanently set apart for the Station –

It is probable the local Government here may request that the new Station be placed under their orders[142] – this would be tantamount to withdrawing it at once, for it has already their valediction – I can assure you I have no personal feeling in the question, but so much is involved in the proper management of a new Settlement for the first few years that I am most anxious to keep it under my wing – where by the bye it can only legally be protected, for by the Company's Charter all to the southward of the Town of Malacca can only be administered in the Company's name in connection with Fort Marlborough which is made an exception to the general rule –

I have just received your Letter respecting Mr Napier & shall be most happy to shew him every attention & to forward his views to the utmost of my power[143] –

Yrs very sincerely
T S Raffles

Pray excuse the haste with which this is written

John Adam Esq
&c &c &c

Under the same date, Raffles wrote to Colonel Young of the Military Board in Calcutta, again complaining about the unwillingness of the Prince of Wales Island government to supply adequate military support for the new settlement of Singapore:[144]

Letter 11
Raffles to Young
16 February 1819

Private

Penang 16: February 1819

My dear Sir,

*I wrote you a few lines from onboard ship on my return from Singapore to this place and I must confess I expected to meet a different reception to what has been offered – Before I went to the Eastward I had the repeated and public assurances & pledges of this Gov*ᵗ*. that tho' they differ'd in opinion they felt it their duty to afford me every cooperation – that 340 Sepoys & on the arrival of the returning Battalion a much larger force as I might require should be at my disposal for operations to the Eastward, & on this solemn pledge I acted – I have established my Port with only one Company – I require two more to support it – this they decline to give me – and say as I appear in their judgment to have violated my Instructions from the Supreme Gov*ᵗ*. they will give me no assistance whatever until the further orders of the Supreme Gov*ᵗ*. are received – Shame on such conduct! They are so mortified that against their predictions I have succeeded they stop at no point to distress me – It is in vain I urge the arrangement is made in the name of the Gov*ʳ*. General – that the flag as it now stands is exposed to insult – No say they, we form our own Judgment, a Copy of the Instructions given to you were sent to you & we are the competent local authority to form such judgment –*

Fortunately I am independent & can support my Port by transferring my Establishment from Bencoolen coute qu'il coute – but no thanks to them for that –

*As they advocate the cause of the Dutch, & have publicly declared their opposition to the Settlement, I earnestly entreat of you at the present moment to represent this in a true light in a proper quarter – the disrespect is to the Gov*ʳ* General.*

I rely more on what you may do in ten minutes than on all the personal influence I have elsewhere – in return command [?] me – The object I have obtained is great – let it not be thrown away –

The Court of Dir[ectors] are said to have given up Java because they feared the establishment of a King's Gov^t. there – In the same spirit Col. Bannerman once a Director would give up all our Eastern & China Interests – to maintain his little authority at Penang against my interference further East –

I am ashamed to send this Letter which I now for the first time discover to have been commenced at the other end – it is late at night – the ship sails before day light therefore excuse it

Sincerely yrs
T S Raffles

Col. Young

On the following day, 17 February 1819, Raffles informed the Dutch Governor of Melaka, Jan Samuel Timmerman Thijssen, that acting on instructions from the Supreme Government and as agent to the Governor-General, the Marquess of Hastings, he had "entered into and concluded a treaty and defensive alliance" with Sultan Hussain Muhammad Shah and Temenggong Abdul Rahman by which "a British factory [had] been established at Singapore, and the port and island placed under the protection of the British flag".[145]

Fig. 23
Jan Samuel Timmerman
Thijssen (1782–1823), Governor
of Dutch Melaka 1818–23.

Five days later, he informed Charlotte, Duchess of Somerset, of his success in establishing a British station at the entrance of the Straits of Melaka:[146]

I have ... to communicate to you a political event of great import – namely the accomplishment of the great object I have always had in view by forming a permanent British Establishment in the Malayan Archipelago, by which the progress of the Dutch Supremacy may be checked and all our Interests political and commercial, secured. It has been my good fortune to establish this Station in a position combining every possible advantage geographical and local, and if I only meet with ordinary support from the higher powers I shall effectually destroy all the plans of the vile Dutchman – That I may be sure of success I hope I may be permitted to place the new Settlement under the immediate patronage of your Grace – With such a patroness we cannot fail – I must however tell you where you are to look for it in the Map – Follow me from Calcutta within the Nicobar & Andaman Islands to Prince of Wales Island, then accompany me down the Straits of Malacca, past the Town of Malacca, and round the South Western Point of the Peninsula – You will then enter what are called the Straits of Sincapore and in Marsden's Map of Sumatra you will observe an Island to the North of the Straits called Singapura – this is the spot or the site of the ancient Maritime Capital of the Malays and within the walls of their fortifications raised not less than six centuries ago, I have planted the British Flag where I trust it will long triumphantly wave in spite of the Dutch and to the utter ruin of their despotisms and monopolies – The situation has every possible advantage for all the political advantages we desire – ... The Dutch view our Settlement not only with jealousy but with a determination to destroy it by all possible means fair or unfair – and therefore I am desirous that its value to us should be duly known and appreciated – Almost all that I have attempted in Sumatra has been destroyed from a delicacy towards the Dutch – if this last effort for securing our interests also fails, I must be content to quit politics and turn Philosopher – but how can it fail under such a Patroness?

Raffles wrote again to the Marquess of Hastings from Pinang on 28 February 1819, giving him news he had received from Farquhar in Singapore and details of the Treaty concluded by the Dutch with Riau, which was more inclusive of the Johor empire than he had expected:[147]

Private

Penang 28*th* February 1819

My Lord,

I had the honor on the 15*th* Instant to inform your Lordship of the success which had attended my proceedings at Singapore, and I have now the satisfaction to add that the accounts which I have since received from Major Farquhar are in every way satisfactory – every necessary arrangement had been made for the comfort of the Troops and considerable progress had been made in the collection of materials and otherwise for the several works directed to be executed – Native Traders were arriving from all the neighbouring Ports and the best understanding prevailed –

At the period when I closed my Letter to your Lordship as well as my general Despatches by the Hope I had not received the Dutch Treaty with the Chief of Rhio – and this is the first opportunity which has since offer'd for my correcting a mistake which I find I was led into by the Native Chiefs – This Treaty was certainly intended to include the whole of the ancient Empire of Johor and it is therefore rather upon the incompetence of the party who recorded it than upon the Treaty itself that our argument must rest – The Tommengong of Johor seems also to be included in a manner different from what would be inferred from his Statement to me, but I have no reason to believe that Statement incorrect, and am rather inclined to believe that the Dutch used his name as best served their purpose and without his knowledge or authority –

I am not aware however that this mistake in any way affects the ground on which our title stands – The basis on which our Treaty rests is perfectly independent of any thing contained in that of the Dutch – being made with an independent Prince who was no party to the Dutch Treaty and has no connection with them, whose right to the Throne is unquestionable & who if the point were agitated would prove to be the Superior and Sovereign of those with whom the Dutch have treated –

It is impossible the Dutch can justly maintain any right to exclude us from the Territories of Johor by virtue of their ancient Treaties with that State, for altho' it is acknowledged Rhio was once dependent on their Government of Malacca, it did not remain so permanently, and when the English took possession of Malacca in 1795, no jurisdiction was exercised over it – The Naval and Military Commanders of the expedition demanded of the Dutch Governor whether Rhio was a Dependency or not, and the reply was that all Agreements between Rhio and the Government of Batavia had ceased – The consequence was our acknowledgement of the Chief as an Independent Prince and as such he has ever since been considered –

It may be expected that our new Establishment will be viewed with great jealousy by the Dutch – but it is impossible for them to prevent its rise – and while we confine ourselves to one Station there is no probability of collision – We do not interfere with their authority at Rhio, neither do we dispute the power of those Chiefs to make engagements for Rhio and Lingen – The legitimate Sovereign is contented with a fourth of his dominion and we are contented with one Station within this – The communication which I have made to the Dutch Governm^t. in reply to their protest, will I have no doubt leave the question to be discussed, as far as may be necessary, between your Lordship and the Supreme Government of Batavia and prevent all measures of opposition or collision on the part of the local authorities –

The orders of your Lordship respecting Acheen having been received by this Government, it is our intention to proceed thither without delay and I hope in the course of a fortnight or three weeks to report to your Lordship the result of the Mission to that State –

I have the honor to remain, with
The highest respect,
Your Lordship's
Obliged and very
faithful humble serv^t
T S Raffles

The Most Noble
The Marquess of Hastings KG
&c &c &c

After his return to Pinang from Aceh on 29 April, Raffles worked on his long report of his mission which, he informed the Chief Secretary of the Supreme Government, George Dowdeswell, in a private letter dated 5 May 1819, had occasioned initial "trouble and annoyance" with the Prince of

Wales Island government and his fellow Commissioner, Captain Coombs. He continued, with regard to Singapore:[148]

I have the pleasure to inform you that our Settlement at Singapore is making great progress – The arrival of the three Company's of Sepoys from Bencoolen has set at rest all questions regarding the insufficiency of the Garrison, and every thing is going on harmoniously even with the Dutch – I much fear the account of their violence was in the first instance much exaggerated and that it may have occasioned undue alarm in Bengal – It was natural that the Governor of Malacca should feel annoyed at a blow which destroyed all his prospects & reduced to a nullity the Settlement of which he had charge – but this has now gone by, and he is as desirous to withdraw every hasty expression as perhaps he was at first ready to make one – The Port of Singapore is already crowded with Native Vessels – The batteries and other defences are nearly completed and the Population is most rapidly increasing – Major Farquhar informs me that the Dutch are talking of withdrawing from Rhio and it is now generally believed the Dutch will willingly cede Malacca for a pecuniary equivalent – If there should be any hesitation on this subject why not transfer Bencoolen in exchange? The Dutch would gladly accept the offer & further accede to the Equator being the Boundary of our respective States[149] –

Having now, I trust satisfactorily accomplished all the objects of the two Missions on which I had the honor to be employed, it is my intention to leave this Place as soon as our Report is dispatched – at Singapore I shall await for a short time the arrival of the further orders of the Supreme Government, and thence proceed to Bencoolen, returning to Singapore whenever my presence there may be necessary –

On 19 May 1819 Raffles wrote privately to the Governor-General informing him of the completion of his report on Aceh, and of his reconciliation with his fellow Commissioner, Captain Coombs, and the Prince of Wales Island government concerning their differences over Aceh.[150] He also noted that as a result of Hastings's instructions to Bannerman, adequate military reinforcements had now been sent to Singapore:[151]

Letter 13
Raffles to Hastings
19 May 1819

Private

Penang 19ᵗʰ May 1819

My Lord,

We have now the satisfaction to forward by the Stanmore, under charge of the Lord Bishop who has kindly offered to deliver them, our Report and Proceedings on the Mission to Acheen.

We can hardly expect that our very voluminous proceedings, consisting of not less than a thousand pages, should undergo a detailed examination, but in our Report I have endeavor'd to bring forward all the leading points, and marginal references are made to the proceedings in support of the information which it conveys – I trust therefore considering all circumstances that your Lordship will be able to obtain an insight into this very troublesome question as it has appeared to us on the spot, without much trouble or inconvenience –

I am happy to inform your Lordship that since I had the honor to write by the Boyne the unpleasant feeling excited by the result of the mission has in great measure subsided, and that by conciliation & temper much has been effected – Captain Coombs on explanation has been induced to withdraw his application to resign his Appointments and Governor Bannerman seems satisfied in the communication to Captain Coombs that his services at Acheen are unnecessary – I have myself had the satisfaction of personally communicating with the Governor and Mr. Phillips on the subject of our Interests at Acheen, and if the orders from Bengal are decisive I yet trust every thing may go on favorably – an early and direct communication from your Lordship to the King, ratifying the Treaty would I think be extremely advantageous.

On the conclusion of this very unpleasant but important duty, I hope your Lordship will perceive throughout the whole of my proceedings, that I have studiously avoided all reference to the local Governmᵗ. or the former Commission under its authority; and I believe there is not one point throughout the whole of our very voluminous record which can be attacked on this score – the result is not only accorded in by my Colleague, but I have now the satisfaction to find that it is nearly the same as that to which Governor Bannerman looked on his first arrival, and as it was on the opinion of Captain Coombs that he was induced to consider another result more advantageous, it is reasonably to be expected that in the course of a very little time, the change which was effected in the opinion of Captain Coombs will have its due and natural effect with the higher authority –

Since the result of your Lordship's Instructions I am happy to say that every aid has been tendered for our Garrison at Singapore – I have availed myself of the offer to effect the relief of the Troops and to send down by the Transports 16 heavy Guns for our principal Battery which is nearly completed –

We have just received accounts that the Rajah Mooda of Rhio has left that place for Lingen alledging to us that he will no longer live under the Tyrannical rule of the Dutch – What may be his story to them I know not, but it is rumoured that the Dutch will either be left entirely to themselves at Rhio or withdraw altogether, the latter is said to be in contemplation – So far therefore from there being cause to apprehend attack, we find our Rivals moving further from us – As I purpose leaving this place for Singapore in a few days I shall not trouble your Lordship with further particulars until I can send a more detailed report from the spot –

In closing my immediate duties with this Government, it is my study to conciliate and quiet all unpleasant feelings and I am not aware that it will be necessary for me to make any further public Representations than I have done – I must however solicit your Lordship's particular consideration of the two points to which I have been under the necessity of requesting the attention of the Supreme Government, because they are somewhat of a personal nature to the parties, and connected with the dignity and authority of your Lordship's Representative – I allude to the extraordinary communication to Major Farquhar that he was not in honor and much less duty bound to obey my Instructions,[152] and to the intimation to Captain Lumley that his ship was solely appropriated for my accommodation – In the former Major Farquhar has been involved in the necessity of perhaps personally offending Governor Bannerman, and in the latter, I felt it my duty personally to remove all unpleasant feeling from the mind of Captain Lumley.

I fear that a very considerable & unnecessary expense has been incurred in consequence of the opposition I have met with – the detention of the Transports and other heavy charges, cannot fairly be attributed to your Lordship's Agents who certainly did their utmost to keep down every charge as far as the prevailing judgment of the Mission could interfere –

I was in hope to have had the honor of forwarding by the present conveyance a companion for the Tapir,[153] but I have been disappointed – and my influence at Malacca where they most abound, is not at present very great – I hope however to be more successful in Sumatra, and in the mean time, I request respectfully to refer your Lordship to the Lord Bishop for an account of our more general researches in Natural History[154] –

I have the honor to remain with the highest respect and consideration your Lordship's most obliged and faithful humble S^t T S Raffles

The Most Noble
The Marquess of Hastings KG. KGCB
&c &c &c

CHAPTER VIII

Rapid Progress of the Settlement

Raffles sailed from Pinang for Singapore on 22 May 1819 on board the *Indiana* and arrived there nine days later. He spent nearly four weeks in the island completing the necessary administrative arrangements and issuing Farquhar with instructions for the future governance and layout of the settlement.[155] On 26 June he made specific "Arrangements" with the Sultan and Temenggong, "for the better guidance of the people of this Settlement", by indicating "where all the different castes are severally to reside, with their families, and captains, or heads of their campongs".[156]

Earlier, on 8 June, he had written to Hastings giving him a summary statement of the progress of the settlement:[157]

Private

Singapore 8th. June 1819

My Lord,
  I have the honor to inform your Lordship of my return to this Station on my way to Bencoolen, and to report the general prosperity and rapid advancement of our new Establishment. The exertions of Major Farquhar during my short

absence have been indefatigable – the Country has assumed a new appearance, the Harbour is filled with shipping and our defences are already very respectable – a Population of not less than five thousand souls has accumulated under our protection and the number is daily increasing – Ambassadors and Chiefs from the different Native States in the Vicinity have been deputed to court our friendship and alliance and upwards of two hundred Native trading Vessels have arrived since our first Establishment – The principal Battery has been compleated and the Guns mounted – The Cantonments are spacious and the Troops healthy – Provisions in abundance and labour cheap – in a word, as far as the time has admitted every object has been accomplished which could have been expected – Confidence has been reestablished and it is no longer in the power of the Dutch to deprive us of our due share in the Eastern Commerce –

I shall have the honor to address your Lordship more fully by the Transports now under dispatch – by them I shall also forward my official despatches – and in the mean time it may be satisfactory to your Lordship to know that I shall be able to reduce the Military Establishment to the standard first contemplated, namely three Companies of the 20th. Regiment with a small party of Artillery – the four relieved Companies are now under orders for embarkation for Bengal, and on my arrival at Bencoolen I shall lose no time in sending from thence to Penang two of the Companies now stationed there, so as to divide the 10 Companies of this Battalion equally between my authority and that of the Government of Prince of Wales Island –

I have the honor to remain,
with the highest respect,
your Lordship's
most obliged and
very obedient humble St
T S Raffles

The Most Noble
The Marquess of Hastings K.G. KGC
&c &c &c

On the following day, 9 June 1819, Raffles informed his London agent, John Tayler,[158] of his founding of Singapore:

You will I am sure be happy to hear that the Settlement I had the satisfaction to form in this very centrical and commanding Station has had every Success, and that our Port is already crowded with shipping from all the Native Ports in the Archipelago – We only require confidence in the permanency of our tenure [for it] to rise rapidly into importance – My proceedings have met with the unreserved approbation of Lord Hastings[159] and altho I have had much to contend with from the narrow views of the Penang Government there is little reason for apprehension provided we can manage the Dutch – .[160]

Two days later, he gave Charlotte, Duchess of Somerset, a more detailed account of Singapore's rapid progress:[161]

Your Grace has been fully apprized of my anxiety to establish a British Station in this neighbourhood, and I am sure it will delight you to hear that I have been in every way successful – The situation I selected proves to be most eligible in every respect and my new Colony thrives most rapidly – We have not been established four months and it has received an accession of Population exceeding five thousand souls, principally Chinese and their number is daily encreasing; it is indeed with difficulty we find room for them – Native and other vessels from all parts of the East already frequent our Harbour, and if the authorities at home only confirm and support what I have done, Singapore bids fair to become the great commercial Emporium of this part of the World – It is not necessary for me to say how much interested I am in the success of the place – it is a Child of my own – and I have made it what it is – You may easily conceive with what zeal I apply myself to the clearing of forests, cutting of Roads, building of Towns, framing of Laws &c – I am literally as the Malays say 'making a Country' and to give you an idea of its importance I need only tell you that I have this morning given audience to one Sultan and received Ambassadors from four other neighbouring Kings courting my alliance – ...

Our capital is situated on the Island usually called Sincapore in the Straits of the same name – and we are not distant from China above a weeks' sail and less from Siam – ... All our differences with the Dutch are referred to Europe – they are greatly enraged against me and declare they can have no peace while

I am allowed to remain – I hope our Ministers will at last think it worth while to consider the numerous interests involved in the question which is left to their decision –

In a further private letter to Hastings from Singapore dated 17 June 1819, Raffles reported his engagement in Calcutta of the two French naturalists, Pierre Diard[162] and Alfred Duvaucel,[163] to accompany him to Bengkulu to undertake research into the fauna of Sumatra on the same basis as Dr. Horsfield had conducted his natural history researches in Java:[164]

Letter 15
Raffles to Hastings
17 June 1819

Private

Singapore 17*th* June 1819

My Lord,

*I have taken the liberty to forward by the present opportunity a Representation respecting the two French Naturalists who were introduced to me by M*r *Ricketts and who at his suggestion accompanied me to the Eastward*[165] *–*

*The extensive Collections and interesting discoveries they have already made and the zeal and devotion with which they are forwarding their labours, promise very important results to Science and Knowledge in general, and I sincerely hope that in the Request I have made to consider them on the same footing in Sumatra that D*r*. Horsfield*[166] *was considered in Java will not be thought unreasonable – The arrangements made with regard to D*r*. Horsfield were entirely approved by the Court of Directors who now possess in their Museum the whole of his Collections while D*r*. Horsfield has himself proceeded to Europe for the purpose of superintending the publication of such Selections as may be thought fit to be generally communicated*[167] *– Sumatra and the adjacent Islands, properly Malayan, offer a more novel and extensive field – The Island of Java had already been partially explored but the larger Island of Sumatra, with the exception of its Coasts remain[s] to this day almost unknown –*

One of these Gentlemen is the Stepson of M. Cuvier,[168] *and they are both eminently qualified for the task they have undertaken as set forth in an Address which I received from them some time since, and which I do myself the honor to enclose for your Lordship's perusal –*

The encouragement which has always been held out to similar pursuits by the Honble Court of Directors emboldens me to hope that they will not object to what is proposed, but I am more prompted to make the request on the grounds of your Lordship's established Reputation as the Patron of every undertaking calculated to extend the sphere of human knowledge and improve the condition of Society – Humble as our pretensions may be, we trust that our labours may be found not altogether undeserving of notice, and honored & encouraged by such illustrious patronage, it would be our study to render them as extensively useful as possible –

The Botanical Department is under the immediate direction of Dr Jack who is attached to me as a Medical friend,[169] and in Mineralogy we all occasionally assist – My object is to collect during my residence in these Islands materials for the Natural History of Sumatra and the adjacent Countries, and the leisure which may be afforded from the limited nature of the duties of Bencoolen, promises me sufficient time for the general Superintendence of such an undertaking – In my public application I have not represented the extent of the interest which I take on the occasion, because I have not yet proceeded sufficiently far to authorize the expectation of any defined plan, and more particularly because I am not yet assured how far I may calculate on your Lordship's approval and patronage, without which, all my views must necessarily be foregone – Animated and encouraged by your Lordship's exalted protection and support, many difficulties which now lie in our path would be removed, and no exertion of human labour mind or body wanting to render the results in some degree worthy of the patronage under which they would be obtained –

> I have the honor to be, with the
> highest consideration and respect,
> Your Lordship's
> most obedient and
> devoted humble Serv[t]
> T S Raffles

The Most Noble
The Marquess of Hastings K.G. KGCB
&c &c &c

Fig. 24
Dr. Thomas Horsfield (1773–1859),
the pioneering American
naturalist in the East Indies.
Portrait by J. Erxleben.

On 17 June 1819 Raffles informed Hastings of the despatch to Calcutta of three companies of the 20th Regiment of the Bengal Native Infantry which he had earlier ordered to proceed from Bengkulu by way of Singapore in case they were needed to reinforce the local garrison. As he had issued this order to the officer in charge immediately on his departure from Calcutta in December 1818, it resulted in his being severely reprimanded by Hastings for interfering in military matters while still within the jurisdiction of the Supreme Government.[170]

Letter 16
Raffles to Hastings
17 June 1819

Private

Singapore 17th. June 1819

My Lord,

    In dispatching for Bengal the three Companies of the 20th. Regiment lately relieved from Bencoolen, I feel myself called upon in a particular manner to communicate to your Lordship the obligation under which I feel myself to Captain Manley[171] for his zealous cooperation and ready attention to my views and wishes as well at Bencoolen as in coming round to this Station – and as that officer has for some years commanded at Bencoolen and has since had an opportunity of estimating the comparative advantages of his position in a military point of view, I take the liberty of referring your Lordship to him for any further information that may be required beyond what is communicated in my public Despatches –

At the urgent request of Captain Manley and in consideration of the unexpected delay the Native Troops have already met with in their passage from Bencoolen, I have authorized Major Farquhar to order the Transports to proceed direct to Calcutta, instead of touching at Penang as originally intended – a measure which as it originates in an attention to the Military Department, and in an obvious saving of time and expense, will I trust meet your Lordship's approbation –

On my arrival at Bencoolen it is my intention to despatch from thence to Prince of Wales Island one or two of the Companies now stationed there, so as to divide the ten Companies equally between the respective authorities – under this arrangement I propose that three Companies should still continue and form the permanent Garrison of Singapore, [and] that of Bencoolen being gradually reduced as low as practicable –

From the experience and peculiar qualifications of Captain Manley I regret that the rules of the Service did not authorize my detaining him in this Command; but in the event of any change being contemplated, I take the liberty of pointing him out to your Lordship, as an officer in every respect worthy of confidence and attention –

> I have the honor to be, with
> the highest consideration and respect,
> your Lordship's
> most obedient & faithful
> humble servant
> T S Raffles

His Excellency
The most Noble the Marquess of Hastings
KG. KGCB &c &c &c

In a final private letter to Hastings from Singapore dated 22 June 1819,[172] six days before leaving the island, Raffles wrote of the defences of the settlement, and, irresistibly for him, considering his recent founding of Singapore, of "an opening", he perceived, "for the establishment of the British influence in Borneo", the details being included in an official letter he wrote to the Supreme Government on the same day.[173]

Letter 17
Raffles to Hastings
22 June 1819

Private

Singapore 22^d June 1819

My Lord,

My official despatches will convey to your Lordship every information on the progress and present state of this Establishment, but as Major Farquhar is not yet prepared with the detailed Plan of the defences, I do myself the honor to forward under a private cover a rough Sketch shewing the position and division of the Town &c and the disposition of the principal works proposed for its defence – This Sketch does not include a considerable Native Establishment to the Westward of the River nor any part of the Eastern Bay & is perhaps more calculated to shew the situation of our present Head Quarters than to convey an adequate idea of the extent to which the Town is already spreading[174] –

It is impossible to conceive a Situation better calculated for Military defence, the position is only open to attack in one direction, and the natural advantages even in that quarter are very great – If the proposed Fort on the Hill were of sufficient magnitude to justify such an appropriation, I should have ventured on the liberty of dignifying it by the appellation of "Fort Hastings" and if I may be permitted to estimate the importance of the Work rather by its political consequences than the value of the materials by which it may be composed, I would still hope that the success which has hitherto attended the enlightened plans of your Lordship's Government, even in this remote quarter of our Indian Empire, may be crowned by the auspicious application of a name as immortal as it is revered and respected –

The extreme caution with which I have confined all our present views to the immediate interests of this particular Station, will I hope prove to your Lordship that my first and only object is to act in strict compliance with your Lordship's wishes, and to devote the humble portion of my Services in aid of the great and enlightened views which distinguish your Lordship's brilliant & unparalleled administration – Moderate and limited as your Lordship's views may at present be in this quarter, the conduct of other Nations and the general interest of benevolence and humanity may eventually lead to their extension, and at all events the World will have to thank your Lordship for the establishment of at least one Station beyond the Ganges whence the Arts and Improvements of Civilized life may be extended to the largest portion of Mankind, and where the British Interests may advance with their natural impulse without any of the obstructions and disabilities which have so unfortunately marked our previous Establishments to the Eastward –

These considerations induce me to solicit your Lordship's attention to the command which our present position affords us over Siam and Borneo, countries hitherto most imperfectly known but interesting and important in the highest degree in every point in which they can be viewed – Reserving such observations as occur to me for improving our relations with the former State, until the further progress of this Establishment may authorize such an extension of our views, I take the liberty of submitting to your Lordship the present situation of the principal States on the West Coast of Borneo – and I am the more anxious to do this on the present occasion, because in my official communications to the Supreme Government I have avoided further allusion to the subject than was indispensably necessary –

The three States in which the Dutch have attempted to establish an influence are Pontiana [Pontianak], Mempawa [Mampawah] and Sambas – at each of these places they have a Resident and a small force, the total amount of which does not at present exceed 300 men – At Pontiana the recent death of the Sultan and the disputed succession to the Throne, has occasioned the greatest confusion, and the party opposed to the Dutch which appears to include nine tenths of the Population are on the eve of removing to some place where they expect to find an asylum from the oppressions they have recently experienced – At Mempawa, the country is equally unsettled and at Montradak [Monterado] where the principal Chinese population under Sambas reside, not only has the Dutch Flag been several times pulled down and rent in pieces, but very recently the Amboinese Guard were made Prisoners and disarmed & the Resident and his Writer wounded – The general opinion is that unless a force of nearly two thousand men is sent from Batavia, the Dutch will not be able to subdue the refractory

Chinese, whose numbers are estimated at not less than a hundred thousand, principally miners and labouring People – The Expense of these Establishments to the Dutch is so great, and their failure to enforce a corresponding Revenue so general, that considering the urgent demand for their Troops in the Moluccas, where a new Insurrection is stated to have broken out, it is very probable they will be rather inclined to abandon their plans on Borneo than to extend them with the efficiency that is indispensible for their safety –

But whatever may be their policy in this respect, an opening appears to be still left for the establishment of the British influence in Borneo, should such a measure be deemed advisable – The Messenger or Deputy who has visited this place from Pontiana, while he is authorized to inform me that the principal Chief of that State and a large proportion of the population of the other places which have fallen under the sway of the Dutch are anxious to remove under our protection, is accompanied by a respectable Chieftain of the Matan Empire who is entitled by inheritance, if not to the Government, at least to the principal influence at Kadawang, a province situated on the large River of that name which disembogues between Succadana and Banjar Masin – This part of Borneo, never fell under the Dutch authority at any period of their History, and the Sultan of Matan in consequence of his residence in the interior has hitherto escaped their notice and policy –

The object of these Chiefs is to obtain the alliance of our Government under which they propose opening the Trade of the River and establishing a Port of general commerce – Without this security, they are justly apprehensive that their efforts will no sooner be attended with success than they will be paralized by Dutch interference – With it, they feel that their proposed Establishment will soon become the most important in Borneo – It is situated to the Southward but in sight of Caramata, there are several Islands lying off the mouth of the River which cover the anchorage and as far as their statements can be depended upon, as a Port, it has greater natural advantages than any place yet known on the West Coast, it is within three days sail of this place, and exactly in the position that would be convenient for our China ships passing through the Straits of Sunda, being not very distant from Point Sambar or what is generally considered the South Western Point of Borneo –

The Residence of the Sultan of Matan is at a considerable distance inland, where the Population in Dayaks or Native Borneans is said to be more dense than any other part of the Coast – The produce of the country Gold and Diamonds with the usual productions of the Malayan Islands – and the interior penetrable in most directions by navigable Rivers, on the Banks of which cultivation has been considerably extended – Were our protection once afforded, the influx of Chinese and the produce of the mines might of course be extended ad infinitum –

I will not however detain your Lordship by further particulars at present on a subject on which you may not be desirous to enter – but in stating my conviction that the Dutch have no claims whatever to oppose to our Establishment in that quarter, request your permission, should the subject be considered of sufficient interest, to submit to your Lordship at an early period such connected observations in the shape of a Memoir, as may enable your Lordship to judge of the practicability and advantage of the measure – If in a general and more extensive political view, your Lordship's attention should be directed to this vast and hitherto unexplored Island, it will afford me the highest gratification to submit such detailed information and suggestions as may be convenient for reference – In the mean time I shall privately as well as publicly refrain from encouraging any expectations of our interference or assistance[175] *–*

Having requested Major Farquhar to state explicitly the nature of his communications with the Dutch Commissioners at Malacca with regard to the Dependence of the Islands to the South of the Straits on the Dutch continental possession I do myself the honor to enclose for your Lordship's perusal the Letter which he has addressed to me on the occasion – and which I hope will prove satisfactory –

Since I had the honor to acknowledge the receipt of your Lordship's Letter of the 6th. April, it has occurred to me as possible that in attending to my acting under a modification of my official Instructions Colonel Bannerman may have referred to the discretion which I stated to him I understood to be personally given to me of proceeding to the Eastward in preference to Acheen, in the first instance should circumstances authorize such a measure – This I certainly did state to him both personally and in my official correspondence because I had so understood your Lordship and Mr Ricketts – but this did not imply any modification or alteration in the Instructions themselves; I had the honor to be deputed on two Missions and I conceived it to be left to me to enter first on that which was most pressing – but in deference to the opinion and wishes of Colonel Bannerman I consented to waive my own judgment on the occasion –

It is my intention to proceed from hence to Bencoolen in the course of a few days – and I trust the arrangements which have been made for the duties of this

Station and the prosecution of your Lordship's views, will have been such as to meet your approbation and ensure a continuance of the prosperity which has hitherto attended our efforts – The expences attending the first Establishment, have been in some respects heavier than I could have wished, but yet will I trust be considered small compared with the advantages obtained – the Establishment is on the most limited scale, and I can assure your Lordship that while my first and principal attention has been devoted to the main object of success, I have not been inattentive to the importance of the strictest economy –

Your Lordship will perceive that on my departure from Singapore I leave a Balance in the local Treasury of upwards of a lac of Rupees to answer the demands of the current year – This will of course render it unnecessary for Major Farquhar to draw on Bengal for some time, but as money can always be obtained from the shipping touching at the Port cheaper than it could be forwarded, I have thought it advisable to authorize him eventually to draw when the state of the Treasury might require it –

> I have the honor to be, with the
> highest respect and consideration,
> your Lordship's
> most obliged and
> devoted humble Servt
> T S Raffles

The Most Noble
The Marquess of Hastings KG. KGCB
&c &c &c

[Enclosure: Major William Farquhar's letter to Raffles dated 22 June 1819.[176]]

To
The Honble Sir Stamford Raffles
&c. &c. &c.

Letter 17 encl.
Farquhar to Raffles
22 June 1819

Honble Sir

In reply to your note of this morning wishing to know whether the Dutch Commissioners at Malacca did ever specify to me the Islands at the mouth of the Straits as Dependencies on their Continental Possessions, I beg leave to *inform you that to the best of my recollection during the whole course of our official Proceedings, the Commissioners never once particularized the Islands in question as such Dependencies. At the opening of the Commission a question was put to me by Admiral Wolterbeek relative to what I considered to be the Dependencies of Malacca and whether Rhio and Perak were not so. My reply was decidedly in the negative with respect to those places, and I further stated that Malacca had no other dependency than the inland district of Nanning, when the conversation dropped. The Admiral some time afterwards in speaking of the Carimon Islands, observed that he considered the Rajah of Rhio as a vassal of the King of the Netherlands, and all the Johore dominions as falling under the control of the Dutch.*

It does not occur to me that any thing further took place on this subject, than what has already been stated in my official Correspondence with the Dutch Commissioners.

I have the honor
To be
Honble Sir,
Your most obedient
Humble Servant
Wm Farquhar
Resident

Singapore
June 22nd 1819

Raffles sailed from Singapore for west Sumatra on 28 June 1819 aboard the *Indiana* and arrived at Bengkulu on the evening of 31 July. He reported his arrival in a private letter to Lord Hastings three weeks later, declaring at the same time that in accordance with his instructions he had handed over the former Dutch settlement of Padang to the Netherlands authorities and withdrawn the British posts from the Minangkabau highlands and Semangka Bay. This represented a humiliating end to his attempts to extend British power and influence in Sumatra, although in his letter to Hastings he attempted to put a more positive gloss on the matter:[177]

Letter 18
Raffles to Hastings
20 August 1819

Duplicate

Private

Bencoolen Augt 20th. 1819

My Lord,

I have the honor to inform your Lordship of my return to this Settlement on the 1st Instant.

After so long and unexpected an absence it was natural for me to find some arrears and irregularities but I have much satisfaction in reporting that nothing essential has occurred out of the usual course and that in a very few weeks every thing will be again in order –

The Settlement of Padang was duly transferred in May last,[178] but from what I can learn the Dutch have not met with a very welcome reception on the part of the Inhabitants – They have doubled the duties and in some instances raised them still higher, which has had the effect of transferring some of the trade to this place – where under the sanction of your Lordship's authority all Custom Duties have been abolished – It will be satisfactory to your Lordship to know that no difficulty was experienced in explaining to the Native Chiefs of Menangkaboo the circumstances under which my previous engagements with them could not be approved[179] – They had considered them entirely provisional and subject to your Lordship's approval or rejection, and we were able to withdraw without any compromise of character – The Native Chiefs are satisfied that I did my utmost to save them from the blow which has fallen upon them, and that I did not succeed they consider more as their misfortune than my fault –

No time was lost in withdrawing the Establishment from the Straits of Sunda[180] – and since the 1st. of January last when a communication and agreement on the subject of boundaries took place between one of our Parties in the Hills and the Dutch Authority at Palembang – no intercourse or interference has existed in that quarter – About that period a Report had gained circulation that I had proceeded to Palembang from Bengal and the person in charge of the Interior was anxious to ascertain the fact and effect a communication with me – This brought him in contact with the Dutch Authority at the head of the

Palembang River, and the result was an Agreement on both sides that neither of them should pass certain boundaries than previously defined.

I am particular in mentioning this occurrence to shew that in the more recent occurrences at Palembang and which have terminated so much to the disgrace of the Dutch, they cannot lay the blame on us –

It is with extreme regret that I find since my arrival, by the recei[p]t of letters from England down to the beginning of March and even the Public Prints to February, the part which has been taken by Opposition in consequence of my Protest which it appears had then been received from Java – Nothing could have been further from my intention or indeed my interest than a public discussion of the kind – and I feel it particularly unfortunate for personal considerations that the part I had taken should have been unexpectedly espoused by the Party adverse to Ministers –

Your Lordship is already aware of the situation in which I was placed and the difficulty of remaining neutral with any feeling of patriotism or public spirit – I may have done wrong, but my motives cannot be questioned and in the kind and indulgent consideration of your Lordship I received the most liberal judgment – On this kindness I still rely, and I can with the utmost sincerity assure your Lordship that I would willingly suffer any pain or privation rather than be supposed for one moment to abuse it –

I have the honor to remain
With the highest respect & consideration
your Lordship's
most obliged and
devoted humble Servt
T S Raffles

His Excellency
The Most Noble the Marquess of Hastings
KG KGCB &c &c &c

CHAPTER IX

Raffles as a "Political Agent" in the Malay Archipelago

One can detect in the final paragraphs his letter to the Marquess of Hastings of 20 August 1819 Raffles's increasing embarrassment at the publicity given in England to his "Protest" of 12 August 1818 to the Netherlands authorities. In January 1819 *The Times* and other London newspapers, as well as the provincial and Scottish press, printed the "Protest" or its principal contents in full.[181]

The Foreign Secretary, Lord Castlereagh, who was strongly critical of Raffles's activities in Sumatra, confided to the Netherlands Ambassador in London in January 1819 that the actions had gone *ultra crepidam* (beyond the limit) of his powers as Lieutenant-Governor of Fort Marlborough.[182] This view was shared by the President of the India Board of Control, George Canning, who instituted enquiries by the Secretary of the Board, Thomas Courtenay, with the Secretary of the East India Company, Joseph Dart, to ascertain if the Court of Directors had any knowledge which justified the style adopted by Raffles in his proceedings "to countenance a belief, that he had been invested with some public character on the part of the British Government, in addition to that which belongs to him as a servant of the Company". Dart stated in his reply on 23 January 1819 that "no instructions have been given to Sir Thomas Raffles, nor is there any on the Records of the Company beyond what have been officially transmitted to the Board for approbation".[183] This information was passed to the Secretary of State for War and Colonies, Earl Bathurst, who, in a debate in the House of Lords on 29 January 1819, explained that a few days before Raffles's departure for Sumatra,

> *he represented, that if he went out only as head of the residency in the neighbourhood of another of which he had been governor, he would be placed in a disagreeable situation, as it might appear to many that the charges against him [by Major-General Gillespie] had been thought well founded. Upon this representation it was agreed that he should have the nominal appointment of lieut-governor, but he was expressly to consider himself in fact as merely the commercial resident, and as having no political authority whatever.*[184]

Bathurst's statement, which was widely reported in the British press, represented a public humiliation for Raffles, who reacted by criticising Bathurst and refuting the accuracy of his statement in correspondence with his friends. In a letter to his brother-in-law, Peter Auber, Deputy Secretary of the East India Company, dated 14 July 1820, Raffles wrote:

> *I never was instructed to consider my office as purely commercial, so much for my Lord Bathurst's assertion; this is a question of fact, and if disputed, the onus probandi [burden of proof] must remain with his Lordship. It is true, I was first appointed Resident; and afterwards informed, that I was allowed the same rank I had enjoyed in Java, but expressly that it was to occasion no additional expense to the Company – this was the only reservation, the only condition. I afterwards received a commission from Government giving me full authority as Lieutenant-Governor to do all acts of government, the words being the same as in the commissions to Penang, Madras, and Bombay, with the single exception of what related to a council being struck out, thereby giving me more power than either of those Governors.*[185]

Raffles believed that a political role had been conferred upon him as a result of his discussions in London with the Chairman and Deputy Chairman of the East India Company, John Bebb and James Pattison, and by a letter from the Secretary of the East India Company, James Cobb, dated 5

Fig. 25
East India House, the London offices
of the East India Company.
Engraving c 1799.

November 1817, which he had received shortly after his arrival at Bengkulu. In this letter he was informed that it was "highly desirable that the Court of Directors should receive early and constant information of the proceedings of the Dutch and other European nations, as well as of the Americans, in the Eastern Archipelago", and that the Court therefore "desire that you will direct your attention to the object of regularly obtaining such information, and that you will transmit the same to them by every convenient opportunity, accompanied by such observations as may occur to you, whether of a political or commercial nature". Moreover, if, in his opinion, these communications were deemed to be of a secret nature, he was instructed to address them to the Secret Committee.[186]

Fig. 26
George Canning (1770–1827),
President of the India Board
of Control 1816–21, and later
Prime Minister of the United
Kingdom, 1827.

When he was in Calcutta in November 1818, Raffles attempted to justify his actions in Sumatra to both Hastings and the members of the Supreme Government by explaining that when asked in England if he would accept the post of Lieutenant-Governor of Fort Marlborough, he had replied that he would, "provided the political agency in the Archipelago were attached, but not otherwise". According to him, it was then proposed to designate him Commissioner to take charge of British interests in the Malay Archipelago from the time he ceased to be Lieutenant-Governor of Java. He was aware, he informed the Supreme Government, that Fort Marlborough was dependent on Bengal, but on his return to Asia he "had in view a more important duty and responsibility than under any circumstances could have been called for in the limited concerns of Bencoolen", and that he "considered it the wish of the authorities in England that I should as far as possible check the Dutch influence from extending beyond its due bounds". He believed that he would receive detailed instructions to this effect, but when they arrived they had not gone as far as he expected,

but yet they gave me the range of the Archipelago for which I had all along been desirous, and which I may indeed say was a condition of my appointment. ... I left England under the full impression that I was not only Resident at Bencoolen, but in fact Political Agent for the Malay States, on the same footing as Mr [Robert] Farquhar held that appointment as Lieutenant-Governor of Penang after the Peace of Amiens.[187]

It is surprising that Lord Hastings accepted this far-fetched explanation of Raffles's unauthorised actions in Sumatra as "perfectly satisfactory", especially Raffles's supposed conditional acceptance of the post of Lieutenant-Governor of Fort Marlborough. Raffles's long-standing wish to have overall political authority in the Malay Archipelago was expressed in a revealing letter to his friend, William Ramsay Jr., as early as 5 August 1815, when he was still Lieutenant-Governor of Java:

Should Java be after all given up to the Dutch – I have expressly stated my wish, to be appointed Political Agent on the part of the British Gov^t. for the Eastern Seas – this appointment would be very agreeable to me as Resident of Bencoolen, and I think I would manage e'er long that my Empire taking root on Sumatra should soon extend it's [sic] branches through the Eastern Islands, and tho' secondary in the commencement, should in the end become Supreme – .[188]

This was written a month before he learned of the decision of the Court of Directors to remove him from his post in Java, but when he did receive this official notification he wrote to Ramsay in September 1815 in a markedly different tone, stressing the fact that his "reversion to Bencoolen, is now the point on which my public & private Character so much depends that it must be secured",[189] without any mention of conditions being attached to the appointment. It is clear that the political powers which Raffles believed went with his appointment as Lieutenant-Governor of Fort Marlborough had more to do with his hopes and desires than what was actually accorded to him during his discussions with the Directors of the East India Company. In any case, as George Canning at the India Board of Control pointed out to Hastings in a private letter dated 30 January 1819, such political powers, by Act of Parliament, could not be conferred by the East India Company, but only by the Crown:[190]

I trust, your Lordship will have given me credit for not having intended to set up, within the limits of your jurisdiction, an authority so great & so formidable as that which Sir T. Raffles has assumed, & affirmed, himself, to be. But I repent me, that I had not the precaution to communicate to your Lordship some of my apprehensions and misgivings as to the scope which this gentleman seemed to be disposed to allow himself in the Eastern Seas. ...

Mr Raffles presented himself here two years ago in a character the most favourable for obtaining confidence, & good will; – that of a man who had been accused of enormous & disgraceful misconduct; & who was pronounced entirely guiltless of the charge. Hence, when the question of his departure for Bencoolen ... arrived, he easily prevailed with the C^t. of Directors that, in order not to return with disgrace to the Eastern Archipelago, he should return there not lowered in title, but still L^t. Governor though only at Bencoolen. – I was sufficiently alive to the inconvenience of this change of title, not to give the necessary consent of the Board of Commissioners to it, without stipulating that it would not be understood to make any change in the character of the Residency, of Bencoolen, to convert it from a commercial into a political Establishment. I was sufficiently aware of Mr Raffles's propensity to politicks to stipulate – when I consented to his sending directly home intelligence of the Dutch & American proceedings in the Indian Seas – that this direct communication should not be in lieu, but merely in duplicate, of his correspondence with your Lordship in Council – ...

But I repent me that I did not express still more strongly, than by these implications my distrust of the lengths to which Mr Raffles's enterprising spirit might carry him when he found himself once more within sight of the theatre of his former greatness. What he has been doing, your Lordship knows. – The despatches of the Secret Committee will shew you that he has done every thing without the slightest authority from home. From the Court of Directors he has, & he can have, by act of Parliament, no other than the <u>commercial character</u> of Resident, tho' decorated ... with the style & title of L^t. Govr. – From the Crown he has <u>no commission of any kind</u> – nor by my advice, will he have any – His treaties & his acquisitions of territory, therefore, & all the pretensions to "agency in the Eastern Seas", are wholly of his own mere notion: the latter entirely self assumed & with the former word <u>by statute</u>. That he is therefore wrong in all his views, & that the Dutch are right in all their doings, by no means follows. But it follows that Sir T. Raffles has brought us into the most inconvenient discussions, in the most precipitate & perplexing manner, – and making us clearly in the wrong in modo, & rendering it rather an uphill labour to set ourselves right in re [in fact or reality].[191]

CHAPTER X

Proposal for the Amalgamation of Pinang, Singapore and Bengkulu

Because of the political controversy stirred up in England by his "Protest" to the Netherlands authorities and by his other unauthorised activities in Sumatra, Raffles considered it advisable to remain quietly at Bengkulu pending a final decision on the retention of Singapore.

The situation changed at the end of September 1819, when the brig *Favourite* (under J. Lambert) arrived at Bengkulu from Calcutta with news of the death in Pinang of the Governor, John Alexander Bannerman, and that of his son-in-law, William Edward Phillips, the senior member of the Prince of Wales Island Council.[192] Though the news arrived at an inconvenient time, it was more than welcome to Raffles, who had been told by Hastings in Calcutta that he thought the administration of Pinang, Bengkulu and Singapore should be placed under a single head, and that as no one was better qualified for the situation than Raffles, he would recommend the measure on the removal or departure of Bannerman.[193] Raffles therefore wrote immediately to Hastings, soliciting his support for his "pretensions to the Government of Pinang", at the same time pointing out the advantages which would result from uniting all British interests to the Eastward under a single authority:[194]

Private

Bencoolen 29th. Sept 1819

My Lord,

I have just received authentic intelligence of the death of Colonel Bannerman on the 8th. of last month, and also a Report that Mr Phillips who provisionally succeeded to the Government died some days after.

This unexpected change induces me most respectfully to solicit your Lordship's favorable consideration of my pretensions to the Government of Pinang, and the advantages which must result from uniting the charge of all our Interests to the Eastward under one authority.

Should the Report of the death of Mr Phillips prove true, I am by my standing in the Service and the terms of my appointment in 1805, the next in succession and entitled to claim the provisional charge, Mr Erskine[195] being absent and altogether incompetent from debility of body and mind – this circumstance I take the liberty of mentioning, not with the view of preferring any right to the succession, but simply to place your Lordship in possession of the arguments which may be used in my favor.

Had not Colonel Bannerman, a Director of the East India Company, stood in my way, I have every reason to believe that on M^r. Petrie's Death[196] my claims & services would have been attended to by the Court above all others – and it was under this conviction and knowledge of your Lordship's favorable disposition and general views, that while in Bengal, on the advice of M^r. Ricketts I lost no time in pointing out to my friends at home the importance of my obtaining the succession even some years hence when it might be vacated by Colonel Bannerman.

What may have been the result of this application I know not, my reliance was mainly on the influence of M^r. Ricketts and the favorable opinion of your Lordship –

The vacancy in the Government of Pinang at this moment, offers so favorable an opportunity for uniting the two Establishments, and for adopting some more consistent and advantageous plan for the management of our more Eastern Possessions, that I am led to hope considerations of economy and policy will favor my pretensions – But it is to your Lordship's kindness – to your Lordship's *patronage that I alone look for the accomplishment of my wishes – Whatever may be your decision I shall be satisfied and gratified for the confidence already reposed in me –*

I have succeeded in reducing and simplifying the Establishment at Bencoolen so far that without risk or inconvenience to the Public Interests I can quit the place at any time and be responsible for the due performance of the duties under a more general superintendence[197] – The immediate departure of the Vessel which will convey this Letter does not admit of my preparing official despatches in time, but I am anxious to apprize your Lordship that it is my intention to forward by an early opportunity a full and detailed Report of the result of the changes which have been effected and the actual state and value of Bencoolen – The information which this Report will afford will only serve to confirm the sentiments already entertained by your Lordship, of the comparative insignificance of the place and the uselessness of maintaining for its management any but a very limited Establishment.

From the full and unreserved communications with which Mr Ricketts honoured me while in Bengal and the confidence your Lordship was pleased to place in me I am inclined to hope that I have rightly conceived the views and principles on which your Lordship is desirous, that in the event of my succeeding to the Government of Pinang, our Settlements to the Eastward should be administered – They have hitherto been a burden & in many instances defeated the object of their Establishment, and their proper regulation on some fixed principle must form an important epoch in the general administration of our Indian Possessions – fortunately the subject has attracted your Lordship's attention, and I shall be proud if I can be rendered the humble Instrument in effecting the improvements your Lordship's wisdom may suggest. If further personal communication is deemed advisable I will not lose a moment in proceeding to Bengal – or otherwise, should it be agreeable to your Lordship, I will take the liberty of submitting such details for consideration as I conceive to be most consonant with the just and enlightened principles of your Lordship's Government.

I have the satisfaction to add that by the latest accounts from Sincapore every thing was going on well – the Enclosed Extract from a Letter I have just received from Batavia will shew that however unfortunate I may have been in my discussions and proceedings with the Dutch, it seems probable that I shall have it in my power by a trifling concession in point of courtesy, whenever good policy may recommend it, to bring about a reconciliation and good understanding – I shall not fail to cultivate the feeling which exists on the part of Baron Van De Capellen, and in the event of your Lordship being disposed to acquiesce in the advantage of my proceeding to Batavia, I shall not hesitate to do so in the confidence that the personal influence which I may exert will tend to restore that harmony which, it must be confessed, I have been the means of disturbing —

I have not yet received any communications from Bengal on the result of the Acheen Mission — I need not however point out the advantage which may result to our Interests in that quarter from my succession to the Government of Pinang —

I have the honor to remain with,
the highest respect and consideration
your Lordship's
obliged and very
faithful humble Servt

T S Raffles

His Excellency
The most noble the Marquess of Hastings
KG. KGCB &c &c &c

Raffles appears to have had doubts about the accuracy of the report of Phillips's death, which indeed had been confused with that of John Lyon Phipps, Accountant and Auditor of Prince of Wales Island,[198] and with the prospect of his old enemy having already succeeded to the temporary charge of Pinang, he was inclined to wait upon events at Bengkulu.

However, his aide-de-camp, Captain Thomas Otho Travers, pointed out to him that it would require "the exertion of much interest" to remove Phillips, and that as Raffles had few friends in Calcutta, his only chance of success was to press his claim directly with the Governor-General in person.[199] Raffles accepted this advice and wrote to Hastings on 5 October 1819, stating his intention to proceed immediately to Calcutta on the brig *Favourite*:[200]

Fig. 27
William Edward Phillips
(1769–1862), Lieutenant-Governor
of Prince of Wales Island 1820–24.

Fig. 28
Captain Thomas Otho Travers
(1785–1844), Raffles's aide-de-
camp in Java and West Sumatra.
Miniature portrait c 1817.

*Letter 20
Raffles to Hastings*
5 October 1819

Bencoolen 5ᵗʰ. October 1819

My Lord,

 An opportunity of proceeding direct to Calcutta having offered since I had the honor of addressing your Lordship on the subject of Colonel Bannerman's death, I have resolved to profit by it and it is my intention to embark for this purpose on the Brig Favorite in the course of tomorrow.

 In adopting this measure I have been influenced, not only by a consideration of the immediate measures which may become necessary at Penang, but the probability that by the period of my reaching Bengal, your Lordship may be apprized of the views and disposition of the Authorities at home with regard to our more Eastern Interests generally –

The possibility that further information and explanation may be required respecting Sincapore and Acheen, has also had its weight, and the advantage of personal communication may also be felt on some of the leading subjects of reference from Bencoolen.

Under these circumstances and considering that in the present settled state of Bencoolen no inconvenience is likely to arise from my absence, I trust that the measure will be approved.

I have the honor to be, with the highest consideration and respect, your Lordship's most devoted and obedient humble servant T S Raffles

His Excellency
The Most Noble the Marquess of Hastings
KG. KGCB &c &c &c

The *Favourite* was a small ship, but as there was no prospect of another vessel appearing on the west coast of Sumatra so late in the season, Raffles had to make do with what available space there was.[201] No accommodation could be provided for Lady Raffles, but he took with him his secretary, Dr. William Jack, and his former aide-de-camp, Thomas Watson, who was proceeding to India on private business.[202] Despite the cramped conditions, Raffles and Jack spent six weeks on board writing official papers and reports, Jack in particular completing an important report on the local population of Bengkulu[203] which, he informed his parents, Raffles was "well pleased with", and had forwarded it to Calcutta "with a very high recommendation".[204] He also told them that he and Raffles had been employed during the voyage in drawing up papers for Lord Hastings "on the future government of the Eastern Islands, proposing great reforms and alterations", as well as suggesting "the propriety of establishing a native college at Singapore".[205]

The first of the papers, which was later printed privately in London as *Substance of a Memoir on the Administration of the Eastern Islands,*[206] was

Fig. 29
Suffolk House, Pinang, built by
W.E. Phillips in 1809, served as the
residence of several early Governors.
*Aquatint by William Daniell after a
painting by Captain Robert Smith.*

handed to Hastings by Raffles shortly after his arrival at Calcutta on 17
November 1819. It proposed, among other things, a reduction in the burdensome and costly administrative structures of Pinang and Bengkulu and their
replacement by "commercial stations, similar in principle to what has lately
been adopted at Singapore".

The reforms had been proposed on the assumption that both Bannerman and Phillips were dead, but by the time of his meeting with Hastings,
Raffles knew that Phillips had assumed temporary charge of Prince of
Wales Island and that his appointment as Governor was likely to be confirmed by the Supreme Government. Raffles wrote privately to Hastings on
25 November stating that while he understood these arrangements would

be an obstacle to the immediate and full implementation of the proposals made in his paper, especially with respect to Pinang, his own personal wish was "to secure the eventual succession to the general charge of our interests to the Eastwards" rather than the immediate appointment to Pinang on its present footing, and he therefore wondered if the interests of all parties might be resolved if a date were fixed for the introduction of the reforms and Phillips permitted to remain in charge of Pinang until then:[207]

Letter 21
Raffles to Hastings
25 November 1819

Private

Calcutta 25th. November 1819

My Lord,

When I had the honor to submit to your Lordship the suggestions which had occurred to me on the subject of the future management of our Eastern Establishments, I took the liberty of stating that the paper was drawn up under an impression that the death of both the parties immediately interested in the continuance of the present System had created at Penang an emergency which called for the interference of your Lordship's Government.

Since my arrival however, I have found that the information on which I proceeded was in part incorrect, and that the obstacles which I did not then suppose to exist may in consequence be in the way of the immediate and full adoption of the plan suggested, at least with reference to Penang.

In making these propositions I trust it is unnecessary to assure your Lordship, that I was not actuated by personal motives – A natural ambition to render myself instrumental in carrying into effect a plan which appeared to be calculated to promote the public interest, and extend the sphere and influence of your Lordship's enlightened administration was the principal and I may add the only inducement – I was not aware that I should interfere or come in competition with the personal interest of any person whatever, or that by advancing my Claims, they would have clashed with the pretensions of any other Individual.

If the general principles of the plan suggested, should coincide with your Lordship's views, it may perhaps remove embarrassment and tend to its ultimate accomplishment, to shew that the public advantage and private interests of all parties are not incompatible – I beg to state candidly and fairly to your Lordship that my object is rather to secure the eventual succession to the general charge of our interests to the Eastward, than to obtain the Government of Penang on its present footing. The more extensive and important charge which your Lordship has already confided to me, renders that in some measure a secondary object. The interference of your Lordship's Government seems indispensable and in that portion of the Eastward which is more directly under your Lordship's control, no obstacle of moment appears to oppose the immediate adoption and declaration of the principles on which the changes at Bencoolen and its dependencies have been made – A decision at this moment is called for, and if those principles are approved and assumed as the basis of a general plan such as I have had the honor to propose, Penang must and will sooner or later fall naturally into the general arrangement – If on the contrary, the present emergency is allowed to pass without an opinion being expressed as to the line of policy advisable, it may be apprehended, that in ignorance of the true nature and objects of our connection with the Eastern Islands, the continuance and extension of the Government of Penang on its present footing may be authorized at home, and the present System, so universally condemned, be accidentally perpetuated, to the possible prevention of your Lordship's arrangements.

*Whatever may be the decision of the Authorities in Europe on the questions which have arisen with the Dutch Government, I am not aware that they can in any way interfere with the consideration of the nature and principle of our own Establishments, and it is essential to the economy efficiency and due administration of these, that some defined principle be adopted and acted upon. If that which I have taken the liberty to submit is assumed, Bencoolen and Tappanooly may forthwith be placed on the same footing as Singapore, and the economy of these arrangements eventually extended to Penang whenever the concurrence of the Authorities at home and the personal interests of individuals may admit – Under any circumstances it might not perhaps have suited your Lordship's views to enter on the immediate reform proposed at Penang, but the necessity of the change being pointed out by your Lordship and elsewhere acted upon would naturally ensure its eventual adoption – With regard to M*ʳ*. Phillips, the gentleman now in temporary charge of Penang, it is understood that it is by no means his intention to remain in this Country beyond a definite period, and perhaps, the interests of all parties might be sufficiently consulted, if a date were fixed at which the reform might be acted upon, and until which he might retain the Government* *on its present footing. By such an arrangement, the danger which might arise to the public welfare by the clashing of personal interests at home might possibly be in a good measure avoided.*[208]

I have to offer an apology to your Lordship for this intrusion; I am actuated by a desire to relieve your Lordship from any embarrassment which might arise on the question, and I have conceived that a communication in this form might be more convenient to your Lordship than to have requested a personal interview, knowing the numerous and important demands on your Lordship's time.

I have the honor to remain,
with the highest respect,
your Lordship's most
obedient & faithful
humble Servant
T S Raffles

His Excellency
The Marquess of Hastings KG. KGCB
&c &c &c

Hastings replied two days later, on 27 November 1819, and without committing himself to the details of Raffles's letter, expressed his general approval of the proposal to amalgamate Pinang, Singapore, Bengkulu and Tapanuli. At the same time, he pointed out that the matter could not proceed until the conclusion of negotiations in Europe between the British and Netherlands governments:[209]

Letter 22
Hastings to Raffles
27 November 1819

Calcutta, November 27th, 1819.

My Dear Sir,

The consolidation of our Eastern possessions into one government, subordinate to the supreme authority, would unquestionably be a desirable arrangement. I think it likely to strike the Court of Directors, in consequence of the various documents which have within the last two years been transmitted to them. Their judgment possibly may not determine the point, for the consideration of the subject will be complicated with the result of discussions between the Courts of London and Brussels. I fear we shall have put a patched determination. Till a decision shall be signified to us, it would be premature to fashion, even provisionally, any plan; but it is always expedient to scrutinize, in the interval, all particulars, so as to be prepared to act upon the principle which may be dictated to us.

I am, &c. [Hastings]

CHAPTER XI

Raffles and Singapore

With his ambition of succeeding to the governorship of Prince of Wales Island thwarted, and the prospect of returning to Bengkulu empty-handed, Raffles's usually buoyant spirits flagged, and he expressed his despondent feelings in a letter to Charlotte, Duchess of Somerset, on 27 December 1819.[210] He had written to her in the previous month on board the *Favourite* in the Bay of Bengal stating that he saw an opening for extending his "views and plans to the Eastward", but that it would be the last effort he would make: "if I succeed I shall have enough to occupy my attention while I remain in the East – and if I do not I can only return to Bencoolen and enjoy domestic retirement in the bosom of my family".[211] Having failed to secure the Governor-General's support for these plans, and nursing a bitter disappointment at not having succeeded Bannerman at Pinang, he now wrote to her:

I have had enough of sorrow in my short course, and it still comes too ready a guest without my bidding – but I drive it from the door whenever I can and do my best to preserve my health and spirits that I may last a few years longer and contribute as far as I can to the happiness of others – But away with this melancholy strain, I fear I am getting almost as bad as those to whom I would preach, and in truth I am at this moment heavy and sick at heart; I could lay me down and cry – and weep for hours together and yet I know not why except

Figs. 30, 31
Captain William Flint (1781–1828), married to
Raffles's sister, Mary Ann (1789–1837), became
the first Master Attendant of Singapore.

that I am unhappy – but for my dear Sister's arrival I should still have been a
solitary wretch in this busy Capital – .

He sent the Duchess a copy of the paper he had prepared for Hastings
on the administration of the Eastern settlements, but added that he did not
set his heart on achieving his objective, "or indeed on any thing else, except
returning to England as soon as possible; I am almost tempted to say that
this is becoming every day more and more the sole object of my desires".[212]

Raffles suffered from "a severe and trying illness" in Calcutta, and
during the last month of his stay he was confined to his bed and forbidden
to write letters.[213] This contributed to his general sense of depression, but
he was cheered by the arrival of his sister Mary Ann, her husband, Captain
William Flint, R.N., and their child, William Charles Raffles Flint, on the
private ship *Rochester* (D. Sutton).[214] He immediately arranged for them to
accompany him back to Bengkulu on the *Indiana* (James Pearl), along with
Lady Raffles's younger brother, Robert Hull,[215] and Dr. William Jack.

During the voyage his health improved. "The sight of Sumatra and the health-inspiring breezes of the Malayan Islands", he wrote to the Duchess of Somerset on 12 February 1820, "have effected a wonderful change and tho' I still feel weak and am as thin as a scarecrow I may fairly say that I am in good health and spirits".[216] The *Indiana* reached Bengkulu on 11 March and, judging by an entry in the Journal of Captain Travers, Raffles appears to have exaggerated his achievements in Calcutta:

From his own account it would appear that the Supreme Government entirely approved of the plan of placing all our Eastern possessions under one Government and giving it to him, and the business had been recommended in the strongest terms to the authorities in Europe. But it would, of course, take considerable time before any decision from home could be received, and during this time it was Sir Stamford's intention to remain quiet at Marlbro.[217]

Laying politics entirely aside, Raffles threw his energies into assembling large natural history collections for shipment to England, and in encouraging agricultural pursuits at Bengkulu. "As I have left the Dutch and our wise Ministers to settle their disputes as well as they can", he wrote to the Duchess of Somerset on 2 June 1820,

my time is now principally occupied in agricultural pursuits, and if I don't move to Singapore, I hope to do much for the advantage of this part of Sumatra – I have established an Agricultural Society which is in full activity and our Waste Lands are gradually coming into cultivation – a new Spirit has been infused into the population and I really begin to have some hopes of the place – .[218]

He wrote to her again on 9 October 1820:

After having drawn together all the wild animals of the Forest and … collected the rich plants of the mountains I am now endeavouring to tame the one and cultivate the other and have undertaken the arduous task of converting a wilderness into a garden – … I am making new Roads and Water Courses, regulating the police of my villages, abolishing Slavery and Bond Service, forcing the idle to be industrious and the rogues to be honest …

Fig. 32
Henry Petty-Fitzmaurice
(1780–1863), 3rd Marquess of
Lansdowne, Chancellor of the
Exchequer 1806–1807, and later
Lord President of the Council;
introduced to Raffles by the
Duchess of Somerset in 1817.

However, he admitted that he seriously felt the effects of the climate, and that if there were no other inducements he would return home:

In a public point of view all I wish is to remain long enough to see my new Settlement at Singapore firmly established, and lay something like a substantial foundation for the future civilization of Sumatra – .[219]

In the previous April, he had informed her that he had received "a very kind letter" from the Marquess of Lansdowne, and that he had taken the opportunity "of sending his Lordship a slight sketch of my political views" and would "be happy to learn that he generally concurs in them".[220] She had been responsible for introducing him to Lansdowne in 1817, and he had been invited to his seat, Bowood House in Wiltshire, on 11 September, shortly before his departure for Sumatra. He seems to have impressed Lansdowne sufficiently for him to defend his Sumatran policies in a debate in the House of Lords on 1 February 1819, when he criticised the Government's decision to restore Java to the Netherlands and praised Raffles's administration of the island: "That gentleman established wise regulations, by which industry and commerce were protected and full security given to the natives".[221]

On 15 April 1820 Raffles wrote to him:

I feel much flattered by your Lordship's kind notice of my exertions in the interior of Sumatra – they were well intended, and at one time promised very satisfactory results but the check which I have received from the Ministry and the occupation of Padang by the Dutch has thrown a damp over all the fair prospects which I had once indulged for the improvement and civilization of this noble Island – Not having met with that support for the extension of our influence in Sumatra which I had calculated upon, my attention has for some time turned in another direction and your Lordship will doubtless have heard of the important position I have been fortunate enough to establish at Singapure[,] the ancient Maritime Capital of the Malays – The rapid rise of this important Station during the year that it has been in our possession is perhaps without its parallel – When I hoisted the British flag the population scarcely amounted to 200 souls, in three months the number was no less than 3000, and it now exceeds 10,000[,] principally Chinese – No less than 173 sail of vessels of different descriptions, principally Native, arrived & sailed in the course of the first two months, and it already has become a Commercial Port of importance – .[222]

In a further letter to Lansdowne dated 19 January 1821 he repeated the story of Singapore's success as a free port:

Singapore which instead of a minor Station has turned out on experiment to be the most important in the Eastern Seas, ... and I am happy to say our Establishment there has succeeded beyond all possibility of calculation – In point of Commercial importance it already rivals Batavia, and its whole charge scarcely exceeds £10,000 a year, ten times which amount might be collected were I to allow of the Collection of even moderate duties – but I am so satisfied that all our more Eastern Settlements should be in the strictest sense of the word free Ports that I will not admit of even the shadow or supposition of a Custom House restriction or duty – The fate of Singapore however now rests with abler heads and no doubt in better hands than mine, and we must trust to the Wisdom[,] foresight and energy of H M. Ministers to retain for us what to the Dutch is of no value but to us is invaluable indeed – .[223]

In March of the following year he again described the continuing progress of Singapore:

I have much satisfaction in reporting that my Settlement of Singapore still continues to advance, steadily but yet rapidly – The certainty of its permanent retention by us is alone wanting to ensure its prosperity – ... hitherto it has been merely a Port for Barter and Exchange, and Merchandize has not been stored on the Island to any extent, but as Capital accumulates and Mercantile Establishments are formed, Store Houses will be built & the Trade of course encrease in proportion to the additional facilities that will be afforded – It is my intention to go round to Singapore in the course of a few months in order to make such general arrangements as will admit of the expansion and rise of the Settlement without endangering the principle on which it is established – .[224]

CHAPTER XII

The Resident of Singapore

Raffles longed to visit Singapore, but with its future uncertain he decided that it was better not to do so. He had raised the matter in 1820 after Farquhar's repeated requests in the previous year to be relieved of his post as Resident and Commandant of Singapore, and having informed the Supreme Government of Farquhar's wishes on 24 March 1820,[225] he reported to Hastings on the following day that he had provisionally appointed Captain Travers to succeed him.[226]

Letter 23
Raffles to Hastings
25 March 1820

Private

Bencoolen 25th. March 1820

My Lord,

I have the honor to inform your Lordship that in consequence of the repeated and earnest solicitations of Major Farquhar I have acceded to his request to be allowed to proceed to Europe by one of the Ships of the present Season – Captain Travers my acting Second Assistant has been provisionally appointed to succeed, and as this officer belongs to the 20th. [Regiment of the Bengal Native Infantry] on duty at Singapore and is otherwise in every respect qualified, and competent to the trust, I hope your Lordship will be pleased to approve and confirm the arrangement –

I have lost no time in reducing and confining the Establishment at Singapore to the lowest possible standard, and I think it will be satisfactory to your Lordship to know that the monthly Expenses of this highly important Station will not in future exceed 5,000 Dollars a month –

The general tranquillity and confidence which prevail have justified my reducing the strength of the Military force to two Companies of the 20th. which will be fully equal to all the duties –

There are several questions particularly those relating to Police and the Administration of Justice which will require attention immediately, and whenever a favorable decision may be received from Europe I hope your Lordship will approve of my visiting Singapore & remaining there some months – The character & eventual prosperity of our Establishment depends so much on the precedents and principles established in the first two or three years that I think my presence may be very useful particularly as I am not aware of any necessity for my constant residence here – Singapore has already risen into far higher importance than Bencoolen can ever attain and on this account may be the most appropriate residence for the Chief Authority –

The Dutch Authorities at Batavia and Padang are very conciliatory in their present Conduct, and on this Coast the utmost harmony prevails.

I have the honor to remain
your Lordship's most obedient &
faithful humble Servant
T S Raffles

I trust your Lordship will approve of my having selected Captain Flint for the Post of Master Attendant at Singapore – Your Lordship is aware of his very peculiar claims on the [East India] Company and it will conduce much to the value & character of the Port that an Officer of rank and experience superintends its details – I have been sorry to learn that many complaints have been made against Mr Bernard[227] who was at first placed in provisional charge of this Office, but I may confidently assure your Lordship that under the arrangement now made irregularities of the kind cannot recur –

His Excellency
The Marquess of Hastings
&c &c &c

The fact that as early as 1819 Farquhar had made several attempts to resign his post as Resident and Commandant[228] diminishes his claims to be considered an equal with Raffles in the founding of Singapore since he was willing so early to abandon responsibility for the infant settlement.

Raffles's letter to Travers appointing him Resident stated: "Major Farquhar having earnestly requested to be permitted to avail himself of his leave of absence from the Madras Government to proceed to Europe, I have thought it expedient to appoint you to succeed him provisionally as Resident & Commandant at Singapore, and you will accordingly be pleased to proceed to that station without delay".[229]

Travers was delighted with the appointment,[230] and sailed from Bengkulu with his wife and child on 26 March 1820 on the *Coromandel*, arriving at Singapore on 8 April. He carried a letter to Farquhar from Raffles announcing his replacement as Resident:

I have the honor to inform you that in consequence of your repeated & earnest request to be relieved in the charge of the Settlement of Singapore in order that you may avail yourself of your former permission from the Madras Government to proceed to Europe, and the impossibility of my visiting Singapore myself for some months, I have appointed Captain Thomas Otho Travers[,] my Acting 2nd Assistant, to succeed you as Resident & Commandant, and that officer has accordingly been directed to proceed to Singapore forthwith … On the occasion of your relinquishing the charge of Singapore, I again request to offer you my warmest acknowledgements for the zeal and ability with which you have devoted yourself to the prosperity of the Establishment and for the prudence and judgment which you have displayed under circumstances of considerable difficulty …[231]

However, instead of relinquishing his post, Farquhar complained of the difficulty of securing a passage to Europe so late in the season, and expressed his regret to Travers "at being thus compelled to postpone the delivering over charge of the Residency into your hands until the usual period of the H[on]: C[ompany]: ships passing for China – in one of which it is my intention to embark and shall at all events hold myself in readiness to resign the rein of Govt. to you on or before the 1st Septr next".[232]

Travers accepted this arrangement and expressed his "readiness to afford … every assistance in my power and to be employed in any way you may deem best to promote the interests of the Settlement",[233] an offer gratefully accepted by Farquhar, who appointed him to take charge of the Pay Department "during the few months I have still to remain at Singapore".[234]

On 18 August an "unpleasant correspondence" commenced between the two men with a letter from Farquhar stating that as he had received no reply from Calcutta or Bengkulu on the subject of his intended resignation on 1 September, he was unwilling to transfer the charge of the settlement to Travers, "until such time as answers to the Dispatches in question shall have come to hand", or at least for a limited period of "say another month", but if Travers did not agree he would "deliver over charge on the day specified in my official Letter to you of the 13 April".[235] This was followed by another letter to Travers on 4 September giving as a further excuse for not resigning a statement in a letter from Raffles to the effect that the longer his departure was delayed "the more gratifying it will be to him".[236] The ensuing correspondence on the subject does not reflect well on Farquhar,[237] Travers attributing Farquhar's change of mind to his realisation that the increasing prosperity and growing importance of Singapore afforded him the means "of providing for his large native family".[238] Unwilling to face a further delay in referring the matter to Calcutta, Travers decided to proceed immediately to Europe, leaving Farquhar in charge.

Raffles, who was unaware of these proceedings, was under the impression that Travers had been in provisional charge of the administration of Singapore since April. He therefore wrote privately to Hastings on 12 August suggesting that he should be replaced by his Second Assistant, Captain William Gordon Mackenzie, who had recently arrived at Bengkulu from the Cape of Good Hope.[239]

Letter 24
Raffles to Hastings
12 August 1820

Duplicate

Bencoolen 12th. August 1820

My Lord,

My 2nd Assistant Captain Mackenzie having arrived from the Cape, I have the honor to introduce him to your Lordship as an officer whom, on many accounts, I have selected for the charge of Singapore should such an arrangement meet with your Lordship's approbation.

Independently of a wish expressed by Captain Mackenzie to proceed in the first instance to Bengal after his long absence from India, I am chiefly influenced by a most earnest desire to evince to your Lordship by every possible means, my extreme anxiety to suspend the adoption as far as possible of any measures without your previous approbation, and which might in any way interfere with or embarrass your Lordship's ulterior views and arrangements. The expectation which may naturally be entertained of an early decision from Europe has been a further inducement to this step.

The arrangement made at Singapore by the provisional appointment of Captain Travers will afford every accommodation to Lieu^t Colonel Farquhar, and prevent any inconvenience to the service, in now sending Captain Mackenzie to receive your Lordship's commands.

The unparalleled advance and prospects of this rising Establishment under numerous difficulties and obstructions which in the first instance conspired against it, will I have no doubt be as satisfactory to your Lordship as they are consolatory to myself, and it is but natural I should watch with peculiar anxiety over the future destinies of a place which I was the humble instrument of founding in furtherance of the extended and enlightened views of your Lordship for the protection of British Interests to the Eastward. Were I therefore to consult my own wishes and what I cannot but consider the interest of the place, I should have been happy to have relieved Lieu^t Col. Farquhar myself, particularly as the arrangements now introduced at Bencoolen have so simplified the establishment that my change of residence would not have occasioned inconvenience here, and the urgent request of L^t. Col. Farquhar and of the Chiefs that I would visit Singapore, were it even for a day, would at any rate have induced me to have done so at the present moment were I not apprehensive of exciting unnecessary jealousy and observation which might possibly lead to annoyance and embarrassment; I of course allude to the construction it might receive at Pinang & Batavia —

It is not to be denied that notwithstanding my efforts at conciliation, an extreme degree of jealousy exists on the part of the prevailing authorities at Penang towards me as well as towards the Settlement I have been the means of establishing; and in attempting to obtain the superintendence of that Settlement to my prejudice, it is probable that not only my movements and actions but the state & interests of the new Station may be liable to misrepresentation. If the sacrifice of my personal claims would in any way conduce to the further advantage, or tend to relieve your Lordship from any embarrassment or difficulty, I would not hesitate one moment, but I am fully convinced that were the Station of Singapore placed under the Penang Government, as at present constituted and with its present feelings, such a step would ruin all that has been done, and tend not only to frustrate the plans and views under which it was originally established by your Lordship, but to cast a blight on the rising prospects of the place, and involve with it a serious injury to the commercial interests of the Nation.

With regard to the Dutch authorities, I defy them to call in question upon any just grounds any part however minute of my proceedings or movements since the occupation of Singapore. I have felt it equally my duty and interest studiously to keep myself as quiet as possible and to confine myself to objects altogether unconnected with politics – Notwithstanding this the policy of the Dutch seems to be that of encouraging an impression that I am interfering to their further annoyance. The object of this policy is obvious, as in separating me from the general proceedings of the British authorities, the whole weight of their opposition may be made to fall on an Individual, who standing alone would find it difficult to maintain himself. There can be no doubt that the most exaggerated accounts are encouraged on their part in order to shew that our Establishment at Singapore was an act of aggression and calculated to injure their possessions, instead of being one of mere protection to ourselves without any views adverse to the right or legitimate possessions of that power – They have no cause whatever for alarm except from their own misgovernment, and their trade can only be affected by their adherence to Regulations which are intended for the manifest injury of that of other Nations –

I have only on this head to request that if any such representations either have been or may be made to this effect, your Lordship will place a full reliance on my assurance that as far as I may be concerned, all such complaints are utterly groundless and unjust –

In conclusion I will take the liberty of observing that I can have no personal interest or view to patronage in any arrangements that may be adopted with reference to Singapore. I am solely influenced by public motives, and a laudable ambition to act in the strictest accordance with the spirit and letter of your Lordship's views, & wishes.

I trust the time is not far distant when the real value and object of the Settlement at Singapore will be fully and justly appreciated, by all parties, and that in the completion of these legitimate objects your Lordship will derive satisfaction from the contemplation of the important benefits conferred on the

*Commerce of Great Britain at a period when it stood so much in need of effectual
aid and support; and that amid the numerous benefits and splendid successes
which have so eminently distinguished your Lordship's unequalled administration, the establishment of this small port (the key however to the commerce with
Countries whose population have been estimated at a third of that of the Globe)
will not be considered by your Lordship as the least of them; an expectation
which the importance that the place has already assumed in public estimation
fully justifies my entertaining –*

*I have the honor to be, with the highest
respect and consideration,
My Lord,
your Lordship's
most obedient
humble servant
T S Raffles*

*His Excellency
The Marquess of Hastings KG KGCB
&c &c &c*

It is appropriate that these memorable words should conclude Raffles's
private letters to Hastings on Singapore. His decision not to prejudice the
future of Singapore by undertaking the early administration of the settlement and incurring the hostility of the authorities in Pinang and Batavia
was entirely laudatory. Farquhar had written to him on 16 April 1820 stating
that news of his own imminent departure from Singapore had

*excited a very general feeling thro' out the various classes of Inhabitants ... as
well as the Sultan and Tummongong to solicit that I would convey to you their
united request that you would if possible gratify them with a visit previous to
the period fixed on for my departure, in which solicitation I most cordially join
them from a conviction of the Public benefit likely to accrue in the present stage
of this rising Colony, by your personal presence, even for so limited a time[,] as
it becomes a duty of the first importance to endeavour to strengthen by every*

possible means the present ardour of feeling, increasing confidence and attach-
ment towards the British Government and Nation which has hitherto so hap-
pily prevailed in the minds of all classes of Native Inhabitants, not only in this
Settlement but throughout all the surrounding countries.[240]

This invitation to visit Singapore must have had an overwhelming appeal to Raffles whatever political objections he felt stood in the way of its acceptance. He replied to Farquhar on 16 August 1820 expressing his regret that

circumstances do not admit of my meeting your wishes & those of the Chiefs by
proceeding to Singapore at the present moment, and I have in consequence the
honor to enclose a short letter to the Sultan and Tumongong stating my intention
of visiting the place at a future period – In the meantime I have no doubt that
the same confidence in the protection & measures of the British Government will
continue to exist among all classes of the inhabitants.

He then added an interesting statement reflecting his own concerns about the future of Singapore:

The peculiar political circumstances in which the Settlement is at present placed
in regard to the Dutch Authorities, render the most extreme caution necessary in
our communications with the surrounding Countries, and it is prudent to avoid
adopting any measures which may create a greater degree of confidence in the
permanence of the Establishment than those circumstances warrant.[241]

CHAPTER XIII

Final Exchanges and Hastings's Death

Raffles addressed two further brief private letters to Lord Hastings from Bengkulu in October 1820 and May 1821,[242] the first relating to the death of his brother-in-law, Captain Robert Hull,[243] and the other to a locally printed work by the Baptist Mission Press.[244] No other private letters appear to have passed between them, Raffles relying instead on his official despatches to the Supreme Government to keep Hastings informed of Singapore affairs even during the period when he was in charge of the administration of the settlement between October 1822 and June 1823.

At the time of his final departure from Singapore, Raffles received from the Governor-General in Council a welcome and possibly surprising endorsement of his administration:

On the occasion of relieving Sir Stamford Raffles from the superintendence of Singapore, the Governor-General in Council deems it an act of justice to that gentleman to record his sense of the activity, zeal, judgment, and attention to the principles prescribed for the management of the settlement, which has marked his conduct in the execution of that duty.[245]

Yet, even with this pleasing recognition of his services, and his own public acknowledgment of Hastings's important role in the retention of Singapore, Raffles harboured a sense of grievance against the Governor-General.

From their first meeting in Calcutta in 1818 he was critical of Hastings's flamboyant style of government and his "regal state", which he thought exceeded "all the Nonsense I have heard of".[246]

Also, Hastings's refusal to support his Sumatran policies, or honour his promise to appoint him to the governorship of Prince of Wales Island after Bannerman's death, seems to have fed a bitter feeling of resentment, which he expressed in a letter to Charlotte, Duchess of Somerset, in 1823 on the occasion of the arrival at Calcutta of Lord Amherst as Hastings's successor:

He is likely to prove a very different Character to our last Governor General whose pomp and vanity exceeded all belief – He was undoubtedly extremely fortunate and by good management continued to obtain the <u>public</u> approbation of most parties – <u>privately</u> the best informed seem to doubt the justness of his Claim to such high approbation and I should not be surprised if at no distant date many of his measures are proved to be as hollow and unsound as he is himself – for certainly the high varnish with which he has covered them cannot last long and never was there a man less sincere than Lord Hastings – .[247]

Given these opinions of Hastings, there is undoubtedly a degree of hypocrisy in Raffles praising Hastings and his achievements in his private

Fig. 33
William Pitt Amherst (1773–1857),
1st Earl of Amherst, Hastings's
successor as Governor-General
of India, 1823–28.
*Engraving by S. Freeman after a
portrait by T. Lawrence.*

Fig. 34
The Marquess of Hastings, after
his term in India, was appointed
Governor of Malta in 1824, serving
there until his death in 1826.

Fig. 35
Sir Thomas Stamford Raffles.
Portrait by George Francis Joseph, 1817,
reproduced by permission of the
National Portrait Gallery, London.

letters to him, certainly to the extent that he did, and then on his return to England soliciting Hastings's support for his claim for compensation from the East India Company for his losses in the fire on the ship *Fame*.[248] Writing to him in Malta, where Hastings was serving as Governor and Commander-in-Chief, he requested a testimonial in support of "the general character" of his administration, which he might communicate to the Chairman of the Directors or any other person involved with his claim:[249]

Letter 25
Raffles to Hastings
9 October 1824

Cheltenham 9th. Oct 1824

My Lord

The dreadful loss which I sustained by the destruction of the Fame by fire, on which ship I was returning from India with my family, has obliged me to throw myself on the liberality of the Court of Directors for such compensation as they may think due; but before I can expect a decision on my Claim it is necessary that my whole public conduct should pass under review –

Your Lordship cannot be ignorant of the base assaults which may be made on my public character or the mede [meed] of fair praise which may be withheld – In the course of my administration as well in Java as in Sumatra and Singapore, it was my misfortune to suffer occasional and sometimes severe censure even from your Lordship's Government, and this condemnatory matter may I fear be brought forward to my prejudice, altho I think I may fairly say it related principally to minor points & for the most part applied exclusively to cases in which I had unfortunately allowed my zeal to overstep my prudence –

My object therefore in addressing your Lordship on the occasion is to prefer a respectful request that you will favor me with such a general testimonial as the general character of my administration may have appeared to merit, and in such a shape, (a Letter for instance) that I may if I find it necessary communicate its contents to the Chairman or other public Authority with whom the question may rest.

In making this Request I feel considerable reluctance in making the intrusion on your time and attention, and nothing but the known liberality and magnanimity of your Lordship's character and the extent to which you have already extended your kindness to me personally, would have induced [me] to take the freedom which I have done – Few of the Company Servants have been placed in such difficult, untrodden, scenes and Countries, and I trust that in appealing to your Lordship I am not saying too much when I add that few have endeavoured to do so much good for their Country and Employers and for those who have fallen under my Sway both Europeans and Natives – How far my Endeavors were prudently directed or successful is a question which others must decide – but this at least I may say that my intentions have been always upright and pure.

I take the liberty of bringing myself to the recollection of Lady Hastings and of tendering my best respects – & Lady Raffles unites with me in the most fervent wishes that you may long enjoy health[,] prosperity and that high renown so justly your own and which every honorable mind declares to be your due.

> *I have the honor to be, with*
> *the highest respect*
> *your Lordship's*
> *most devoted & obed^t*
> *humble S^t*
> *T S Raffles*

The Marquess of Hastings
&c &c &c

Hastings's reply was probably not what Raffles expected.[250] It expressed the undoubted truth regarding the Supreme Government's repeated censures on many of his policies in Java and Sumatra, and conveyed a realistic appraisal of Hastings's own loss of influence with the Directors of the East India Company following his much criticised actions relating to the loans of William Palmer & Company to the Nizam of Hyderabad:[251]

Letter 26
Hastings to Raffles
5 December 1824

Malta, Decr. 5th 1824.

My Dear Sir
The Letter dated the 9th of October, which I have had the Honor to receive from you, puts me into great embarrassment. You will not, I am sure, doubt the satisfaction I should have in bearing the fullest testimony to your Zeal &

Exertions. The doing so, however, in general terms would appear irreconcilable to the Records which exhibit instances where the Indian Government, whilst I was at the head of it, had not approved some of your measures. On the strange terms existing between me & the India House, such an inconsistency would not fail to be taken up & distorted. At the same time, there would be singular awkwardness & apparent invidiousness did I state those points as exceptions. It would rejoice me to be serviceable in any way not involving this dilemma, tho' I fear that I have at present little influence capable of being so employed. The calamity you suffered would be a spur to that disposition were any necessary. Believe that I lamented it deeply, as being not less a Loss to Science than to you; a feeling which I am sure has been universal.

> *I have the Honor, my dear Sir, to remain*
> *Your very obedient &*
> *Humble Servant*
> *Hastings*

Sir Stamford Raffles

Hastings's own claims on the East India Company in respect of his services in India were more deserving than those of Raffles, and his personal financial circumstances were certainly more distressing. Having spent during his life-time an enormous fortune by over-indulgent generosity to members of the French *émigré* nobility, the Prince Regent, and similar undeserving causes, he left his own family in straitened financial circumstances. Instead of an honourable retirement on his return from India, he was obliged to accept the relatively minor appointment of Governor and Commander-in-Chief in Malta. He died on 28 November 1826, four months after Raffles, on board HMS *Revenge* in Baia Bay off Naples. His body was returned to Valletta where, before it was interred, Lady Loudoun had his right hand removed and preserved. This remaining relic of her husband was later buried with her in the family mausoleum at Loudoun Castle in Scotland following her own death on 9 January 1840. Hastings's remains rest in a marble sarcophagus in a garden named after him in Valletta.[252]

Fig. 36
View from Government Hill
(Singapore Hill), Singapore.
Coloured lithograph by Langlume
after Deroy, Paris, 1828.

When Sir Walter Scott learned of his death, he wrote in his *Journal* on 22 December 1822:

Poor old Honour and Glory dead – once Lord Moira, more lately Lord Hastings. He was a man of very considerable talents, but had an overmastering degree of vanity of the grossest kind. It followed of course that he was gullible. In fact the propensity was like a ring in his nose into which any rogue might put a string. He had a high reputation for war, but it was after the pettifogging hostilities in America where he had done some clever things. He died, having the credit, or rather having had the credit, to leave more debt than any man since Caesar's time. £1,200,000 is said to be the least. There was a time that I knew him well, and regretted the foibles which mingled with his character, so as to make his noble qualities sometimes questionable, sometimes ridiculous. He was always kind to me.[253]

It is perhaps to be regretted that Singapore Hill was never named Fort Hastings by Raffles. He had at one time considered honouring the Governor-General in this way, and the designation would have been appropriate in recognising that modern Singapore owes its existence to the decision taken by Hastings at Barakpur in November 1818 to establish a settlement at the southern entrance of the Straits of Melaka in order to outflank the Dutch and protect the China trade. Raffles had the vision to see that the small settlement he founded would grow into something of great importance, but neither he nor Hastings could have imagined Singapore as it is today. That particular miracle is the work of the thousands of Asian immigrants who flocked to the new settlement after it was founded in 1819.

Additional Letters of Raffles

Appendix I
Letter from Raffles to Lieutenant-Colonel James Young from Penang,
12 January 1819 (referenced on p. 49).

Penang 12th Jany 1818 [1819]

My dear Sir,

I wrote you a few words by a small Brig which left this some days ago – if you were able to make out what I intended to say, you will have perceived that I do not quite draw with this Government – They are vehemently opposed to all my proceedings – My Mission to Acheen on one side & to Rhio on the other, is not inaptly compared by Colonel Bannerman to cutting off his right hand & his left and the result is nothing but the most determined obstruction – but I shall steadily persevere in the service I may have to perform say & do what they will – The Council is divided in itself and the minority has the public voice unanimously in its favour.

There is still a hope of doing something and even of effecting the grand object to the Eastward – I yet think the Coast is clear but before I venture upon it I am desirous of a little examination & enquiry – I shall not on any account involve myself with the Dutch, and so far do I think the plans I have in view practicable without Collision with them that I shall not hesitate if I can carry them into effect, to go in person to Batavia to communicate the result – &ᶜᵃ

You know something of Acheen affairs from Johnson – The Ex-King's cause[254] has since been in some degree strengthened by the offer of the Dutch who consider him as the legitimate Monarch – I shall however keep my mind unbias'd except by information which I receive & not made up till we investigate the affair on the Spot –

May I beg of you to impress on Adam[255] & in such other quarters as you may think useful, the importance of not listening to the exaggerated Reports & representations that may be made, but to leave me free to act unencumbered by further restriction – I feel the full weight of the responsibility on my shoulders – I shall be cautious & I hope prudent – but I will not lose the main object in one Mission if attainable by fair & proper means, nor in the other allow the National honor to be sacrificed nor any Individual to complain of manifest injustice.

Sincerˡy Yʳˢ
T S Raffles

Letters will reach me here under cover to Carnegy Hˢᵉ for the next two or three months.

Col. Young

Appendix II
Two Letters from Raffles to the Marquess of Hastings from Bengkulu,
23 October 1820 and 15 May 1821 (referenced on p. 132).

Bencoolen 23ᵈ October 1820

My Lord,

It is with much pain I have to report to your Lordship the death of Captain Robert Hull of the 10ᵗʰ Bengal Native Infantry[256] occasioned by the excessive fatigue and exposure he underwent while in pursuit of the Peshwa and at the Siege of Chandah,[257] from which he never recovered. – He died on the 21ˢᵗ Instant.

Considering the claims which this sacrifice may have established & your Lordship's kind disposition towards his Brother Lieuᵗ John Hull of the same Corps,[258] as intimated to me by Mʳ Ricketts[259] and Mʳ Adam,[260] I hope I do not intrude too much on your indulgence in soliciting your Lordship's patronage in his favor for the Staff appointment that will be vacated by an older Brother.

The appointments to which I allude are I believe those of Barrack and Post Master at Hussingabad.

I have the honor to remain with the highest respect

*Your Lordship's
most faithful and
obedient humble servant
T S Raffles*

*His Excellency
The Marquess of Hastings
&c &c &c*

Bencoolen 15ᵗʰ. May 1821

My Lord,

I take the liberty of presenting to your Lordship the First Volume of the proceedings of our Agricultural Society, a few copies of which have been printed for the convenience of the Members and for circulation among those interested in the fate of the Settlement.[261]

As our exertions have hitherto been attended with so much success we are encouraged to persevere, and I have every reason to anticipate that the results of the ensuing year will be equally satisfactory with the past.

I have the honor to remain with the highest respect and consideration,

Your Lordship's
Most obedient & very
Faithful humble servᵗ
T S Raffles

His Excellency
The Marquess of Hastings
&c &c &c

Appendix III
Letter from Raffles to John Tayler from Singapore, 9 June 1819[262]
(referenced on p. 88).

Private

Singapore 9th. June 1819

My dear Sir,

You will I am sure be happy to hear that the Settlement I had the satisfaction to form in this very centrical and commanding Station has had every success, and that our Port is already crowded with shipping from all the Native Ports in the Archipelago – We only require confidence in the permanency of our tenure to rise rapidly into importance – My proceedings have met the unreserved approbation of Lord Hastings and although I have had much to contend with from the narrow views of the Penang Government there is little reason for apprehension provided we can manage the Dutch –

I have not yet seen or heard any thing from M^c.Quoid,[263] but I have heard of him and that he is doing well – the consignments to his charge having turned out better than first expected – It is said he has taken a House at Batavia but whether a permanent residence or otherwise I know not – When he took this step he could not have heard of our Establishment at this place where I think he should immediately turn his attention – I would recommend his establishing himself here forthwith & before I quit the place I will secure for him all the accommodation he will require – I am not very sanguine in any prospects of support the Dutch may hold out, & am inclined still to think English property at Batavia very insecure – As I hope however to leave this in a few days for Bencoolen and shall communicate with Batavia I shall have a better opportunity of stating my sentiments after communication with McQuoid himself[264] –

I have experienced a good deal of opposition & unfair Treatment from Colonel Bannerman, whose views will no doubt be opposed to mine – I conclude he will be anxious to secure the Succession of the Gov^t of Pinang to his Son in Law Phillips[265] who I am told has applied for it – but I hope the point is already settled in my favour – at all events I rely on the strenuous exertions of my friends to secure the Succession for me[266] – Every public Interest is best consulted by such an arrangement – and personally I certainly have stronger Claims than can be set up by the other party – unless it is to be considered as an heir loom in the Colonel's family –

I have not received more than one Letter from you since I left England – & that of a very distant date –

Lady Raffles unites in Kindest regards to Mrs Tayler & I remain

My dear Sir
Always yrs sincerely
T S Raffles

John Tayler Esqr
&c &c &c

Appendix IV
Four Letters from Raffles to the Marquess of Lansdowne[267]
(referenced on pp. 121–123).

Letter 31
Raffles to Lansdowne
15 April 1820

Bencoolen 15th. April 1820 –

My Lord,

*   I avail myself of the first opportunity which has offered, to acknowledge the receipt of your Lordship's Letter of June last giving cover to Lord Carnarvon's[268] note on the subject of Sumatran plants – and I am extremely happy that it is in my power to pay immediate attention to his wishes – I forward to him by the present opportunity some of the most splendid flowers of our forests, several of which will I believe be quite new in England – I have taken the liberty of writing to his Lordship direct, and I will only add my request that you will again assure him of the real satisfaction I shall feel if my humble exertions can in any way tend to improve his Collection or afford him gratification.*

*   We abound in the richest productions and altho' much has not been yet done in bringing them into practical use, no time has been lost and no effort spared to obtain an account of them and ascertain their real value and importance – Pending the discussions which are taking place in Europe on political questions I am devoting a considerable portion of my time to the pursuits of Natural History[,] in Zoology as well as Botany and I trust the result will prove that our labour has not been in vain – I have the pleasure to forward by the present opportunity a descriptive Catalogue of the Mammalia contained in my Collection,[269] a large portion of which was recently forwarded to Sir Joseph Banks[270] – and I trust it is needless to observe that if there is any thing in these regions which may interest your Lordship or your friends, nothing will afford me more real pleasure than to be honored with your Commands and to attend to your wishes –*

*   I feel much flattered by your Lordship's kind notice of my exertions in the interior of Sumatra – they were well intended, and at one time promised very satisfactory results but the check which I have received from the Ministry and the occupation of Padang by the Dutch[271] has thrown a damp over all the fair*

prospects which I had once indulged for the improvement and civilization of this noble Island –

Not having met with that support for the extension of our influence in Sumatra which I had calculated upon, my attention has been for some time turned in another direction and your Lordship will doubtless have heard of the important position I have been fortunate enough to establish at Singapure[,] the ancient Maritime Capital of the Malays – The rapid rise of this important Station during the year that it has been in our possession is perhaps without its parallel – When I hoisted the British flag the population scarecely amounted to 200 souls, in three months the number was not less than 3,000, and it now exceeds 10,000[,] principally Chinese – No less than 173 sail of vessels of different descriptions, principally Native, arrived & sailed in the course of the first two months, and it already has become a Commercial Port of importance – I consider myself extremely fortunate in the selection and in not having had to complain of any one of the almost invariable difficulties attending the establishment of new Settlements – I have however, as your Lordship must be aware, had other & more serious difficulties to encounter, but as I have been successful I shall not complain of them – I allude particularly to the opposition of the Dutch & more immediately to that of the Gov^t of Pinang which I am ashamed to say, to secure a local and personal interest, united all its efforts with those of the Dutch to drive me from this ground – I have however maintained it till now, and every object contemplated from what could be done in this Country has been more than attained – the establishment has more than equalled my anticipations and its effects have been more marked and sudden than I could have contemplated tho' not more so than I wished.

From the intimate knowledge which I possessed of the Dutch Character in these seas and the peculiar situation in which the Archipelago was left by the Convention,[272] it was impossible for me not to foresee nearly all that has happened unless our Ministry interfered – While in England I did my utmost to persuade the public Authorities of the necessity of some interference and the importance of its being immediate, and I thought I had succeeded in making an impression – the Instructions given to me were to watch the motions of the Dutch and other European Powers generally[273] but certainly I did not obtain any authority for attacking them – I was a little disappointed at the loose manner in which so important a question was attempted to be shuffled off, but still I thought them sufficient and did not hesitate to declare my intention to act upon them – What unaccountable weakness can have induced Ministers to disavow me in the manner they have done is yet to be explained – I can make every allowance for the peculiar circumstances under which they may have been placed with regard to the Dutch, and also for the desire of Lord Castlereagh that the question respecting the transfer of Java might not be agitated, but yet they need not have gone quite so far as to sacrifice me and truth to the Dutch and policy – It is of course my intention to demand explanation and I have already taken measures for the transmission of a formal defence of my conduct against the unmerited & unhandsome attack of my Lord Bathurst in answer to your Lordship's Speech – Until however all questions are settled with the Dutch I am not anxious to intrude any matter of a personal nature and I therefore defer forwarding these Papers until we hear what has been the final decision in Europe – It is somewhat remarkable that in this case the East India Company have pursued more consistency and character than the Government –

I have long since succeeded in convincing the highest authority in the Country that the spirit of aggrandizement evinced by the Dutch and their manifest endeavors to establish absolute supremacy in the Eastern Seas rendered it indispensable for us to adopt precautions with a view to avert the injury and degradation which awaited us –

Our views in these Seas have ever been confined to the security of our own commerce combined with the freedom of other Nations and altho' we had the means while in possession of Java of aggrandizing ourselves, we restored to the Dutch their noble colonies without having taken one step towards step towards the encrease of our power – This may have been very magnanimous, but of the policy much cannot be said, since we find the first acts of the new Dutch Authorities to be the reduction to Vassalage of the States which we had treated as independent and to impose Treaties on those States, the main object of which was to exclude our Commerce from their Ports –

My object was therefore to warn our Government that measures might be taken in time, and I am happy to add that there is now but one conviction in this Country on the subject – namely "that the Dutch Authorities in India have been actuated by a spirit of Ambition, by views of boundless aggrandizement and especially by a desire to obtain the power of monopolizing the Commerce of the Eastern Archipelago and of excluding us from those advantages which we have always enjoyed and which we only wish to share in common with the other Nations of the Earth" – these are words which have been used by high *official Authority and are of course communicated in the confidence of private intercourse, but they are so impressive of the real state of the case that I should have found it difficult to find others which would have better conveyed my own Sentiments –*

Every thing hinged upon Singapore, and that point obtained, as negative has been put to all further pretensions at exclusion on the part of the Dutch; and all we hope is, that the Ministry at home may act in the same spirit and complete in Europe what has been so successfully began in this Country.

The Dutch have been most deservedly driven out of Palembang and have hitherto failed in all attempts to establish themselves notwithstanding their last expedition consisted of upwards 3,000 men[274] – The particulars of this affair will have reached your Lordship through the Public Prints and I lately sent the Duke of Somerset a newspaper which appeared to me to contain a pretty correct narrative of these transactions – I cannot however refrain from quoting for your information the concluding Paragraph of the Sultan's appeal to me on the subject – He expresses himself as follows after detailing the particulars of the retreat of the Dutch[:] "I however place the utmost reliance on your care and regard Sir, for the people with black Skins as well as for their black skinned Sovereign, for it is to the British alone that all Nations of Blacks all over the World have to look for protection and support and all the late Commotion and unhappy consequences in Palembang are solely to be attribute to the Dutch refusing to abide by and follow up the arrangements introduced by the English, and to the People of Palembang's decided preference of them to those substituted by the Dutch –"

Your Lordship will observe that these expressions are from the old Sultan, whom I had deposed and against whom my efforts were made[275] – and it is not a little satisfactory to find that he should still have so high a respect for us – He has regained the Throne and perhaps deserves to maintain it for the noble struggle he is making for the independence of his Country – I am sorry however to say that the unfortunate Prince with whom our Treaty was made and from whom we obtained the Cession of Banca,[276] is still a close Prisoner in the Mountains of Java, removed from all communication with his family and Country – surely this is not to last for ever & something must be done to obtain his person from the Dutch – He has been so unfortunate that I imagine he cares but little for the honours of a Throne, but some handsome provision ought to be made for him & at any rate he ought to be placed under our protection – This is a point which merits Parliamentary enquiry and your Lordship would do an essential service to

the cause of humanity and the honour & character of Great Britain, by demand-
ing his safe delivery into our hands – It is now nearly two years that he has been
a Prisoner – his followers and adherents all look to me, even his Rival the present
Sultan advocates his cause, and the whole Malayan Race are anxiously awaiting
the result of the deliberations in Europe, to know who is the strongest, the English
or the Dutch, and the decision whether our boasted philanthropy and justice is
to be depended upon, or reckoned as specious as our policy –

In consequence of the Dutch having been driven out of Palembang, Banca
has become nearly independent of their authority & they have only one Station
left on the Island. At Rhio their conduct has been much of the same stamp as
at Palembang and accounts have lately been received of their having also been
driven out of that Port – At Sambas & Pontiana on Borneo, they have been
openly insulted without the power of resisting it, and as new troubles are break-
ing out at Macassar and Celebes, there seems a fair chance of their being obliged
to retreat within their undisputed Territories of Java and the Moluccas beyond
which in justice to us they ought never to have stept –

They of course attribute the whole of their misfortunes to me, perhaps very
justly – My interference at Palembang was the first check they received, but the
establishment of Singapore gave the final blow – And in order to profit by our
present advantage it is essential that we should decide upon some settled policy
for the future – Nothing can well exceed our past folly but I can hardly suppose
the experience of another Century to be wanting to prove to us where our true
interest lies – after contending with the Dutch for nearly a Century for superi-
ority in Java, we were driven out of Bantam and content to establish ourselves
at Bencoolen[,] a place possessing no one advantage political or commercial[277]
– Another Century has since elapsed and we find ourselves again driven out of
Java – but profiting by our experience, we have selected a spot, Singapore, of all
others the most advantageous both for Political & Commercial purposes – but
even this will be useless to us unless we pursue some steady and consistent line of
policy for its management.

In the enclosed Paper which is the Copy of a Memorandum I some time
since delivered to Lord Hastings,[278] *your Lordship will perceive what my ideas on*
the subject are – The Paper is of course confidential but I have reason to believe
the plan suggested is fully concurred in by the highest authority in this Country –

If our object in the Eastern Seas & in China is Commerce and Commerce
alone, I am not aware of any plan so easy of adoption or so unobjectionable as

that of making our Stations free Ports – in a political point of view it will have the effect of preventing and deterring other European Nations from settling on the neighbouring Coasts – for our Continental possessions will enable us to do that without considering it as a loss which no other Nation could do except at a dead loss, in consequence of the great distance of their power – this is particularly applicable to the French[,] Russians & Americans – We can not only afford to maintain our Eastern Stations without levying duties at them, but by doing so we improve the general Trade and consequent prosperity of our Continental possessions – No other Nation could afford to maintain such Stations without levying duties –

In a few years, if the System on which I have commenced, is followed up, the whole of the Eastern Archipelago will be clothed from Great Britain, and I see no reason why Ava[,] Siam[,] Cochin China and even a large portion of China may not follow the example – but I fear I have intruded too long on your Lordship's time already, and I will be satisfied by referring you to the Paper I have enclosed for all further particulars –

While recently in Bengal I took the liberty of enclosing to your Lordship a Plan for the establishment of a College at Singapore[279] – This Plan united with a Port free of duties and vexations, will I am convinced have far more effect in raising our Character and improving our Interests than any other that could be adopted –

Should your Lordship continue to feel an interest in the Affairs of this quarter of the World, I shall always feel myself honoured in the opportunity of communicating every information within my reach –

I request to offer my best respects to Lady Lansdowne,[280] and with every assurance of respect and esteem to remain

Your Lordship's
Faithful and very
obedient & humble S^t
T S Raffles

The Marquess of Lansdowne
&c &c &c

Letter 32
Raffles to Lansdowne
19 January 1821

Bencoolen 19ᵗʰ. January 1821

My Lord,

I have been much flattered by the interest you have kindly taken in my humble efforts to improve our political and Commercial influence in this quarter, that I am induced to hope you will spare a few moments to run over the enclosed Papers which are intended to form part of the 1ˢᵗ. Volume of our Agricultural Proceedings[281] – The Papers themselves are not written with much attention to style but they may serve to convey to you in as few words as practicable, a tolerably correct idea of the nature of our Establishments in the vicinity of Bencoolen, the System which has heretofore prevailed, and the principles on which alone any beneficial change can be calculated – I beg to draw your particular attention to the Paper entitled 1ˢᵗ. Report of the Agricultural Society as containing a just & fair narrative of the course of measures which have tended to retard the progress of this hitherto very unprofitable Settlement[282] – I am now pushing our agricultural industry in every direction and am happy to say that in one year I have quadrupled the grain produce of the Country and that if my measures are only followed up by permission to Europeans from England to colonize and settle, even this wretched Establishment will soon rival the richest portions of the West Indies – British Capital and British industry are alone wanting to the prosperity of the place[283] –

Bencoolen however, altho' my chief residence, forms at present but a very inconsiderable portion of my jurisdiction – Singapore which instead of a minor Station has turned out on experiment to be the most important in the Eastern Seas, naturally engages my chief attention – and I am happy to say our Establishment there has succeeded beyond all possibility of calculation – In point of Commercial importance it already rivals Batavia, and its whole charge scarcely exceeds £10,000 a year, ten times which amount might be collected were I to allow of the Collection of even moderate duties – but I am so satisfied that all our more Eastern Settlements should be in the strictest sense of the word free Ports that I will not admit of even the shadow or supposition of a Custom House restriction or duty – The fate of Singapore however now rests with abler heads and no doubt in better hands than mine, and we must trust to the wisdom[,] *foresight and energy of H M. Ministers to retain for us what to the Dutch is of no value but to us is invaluable indeed –*

Another portion of my domain and which has not yet attracted much attention is our Settlements on the North West Coast of Sumatra to the Northward of Padang – All questions with the Dutch being as far as concerns our interference in this Country at an end, my attention has been principally devoted during the last year to the development and improvement of our more certain and permanent, because undisputed, possessions and in this quarter the Islands which lie off Sumatra and almost in sight of it have particularly attracted my notice – One of these, Pulo Nias, in sight of Tappanooly was known to be inhabited, to have a considerable export of Slaves and to be in some degree cultivated – but this was all – neither the extent of the population, the State of Civilization or cultivation had been enquired into, and Europeans knew very little more than that such an Island and such a people existed –

Various enquiries soon induced me to think very highly of this Island and the result of two Missions enabled me at once to appreciate its importance and to take measures for securing it from the grasp of the Dutch whose Emissaries were known to be in the neighbourhood – and I have now the satisfaction to state that all the Chiefs and People have in the most formal and solemn manner entered into a Treaty acknowledging the Sovereignty of Great Britain, abolishing the Slave Trade and giving us the universal Supremacy over the Island[284] – The population is certainly not less than 230,000 and the Island throughout is one complete Sheet of the richest Cultivation imaginable – it affords a large grain export, and is in almost every respect the reverse of what we find on the opposite Coast of Sumatra – I cannot perhaps give your Lordship a better idea of the Country and People than by quoting a few Passages from an official Report of the Gentlemen who were deputed to examine the Country –

"Its superficies may be estimated at nearly 1500 square miles. The surface of the Country is for the most part uneven rising into Hills of no considerable elevation and plentifully watered with streams in every direction – The soil is of unequalled fertility, having in general a basis of lime which appears to be of coral origin – Not only the alluvial flats but the sides of the Hills up to their very summits, present a sheet of cultivation the richest than can be imagined – There is not a vestige of primaeval forest in any part which we visited, the whole has disappeared before the force of industry – The villages are always situated on the very pinnacles of the Hills, yet they are always embosomed in Cocoa Nut and

fruit Trees of the great luxuriance, while the land beneath them is devoted to Rice, Sweet Potatoes and other Articles of Supply[.]"

"We have little hesitation from the result of (these) enquiries in estimating the total population of the island at not less than 230,000 souls which compared to the surface gives 153 to the Square Mile. This may give some idea of the flourishing state of the Country and we feel confident that it will be found to fall short rather than exceed the reality[.]"

"The Nias People are highly valued for their industry[,] ingenuity and fidelity – Our whole intercourse with them has given us a most favourable impression of their Native Character and of their Capabilities of improvement – Notwithstanding the disadvantages of a secluded situation, the absence of all instruction and example, and the insecurity arising from a state of internal division, they have drawn forth by their industry the resources of their fertile Country to a greater degree than has yet been effected by any of their Neighbours on the Coast of Sumatra – The extent of their grain export would alone be sufficient evidence of their industry but the same spirit pervades their whole economy – Their Towns and Villages tho' placed on elevated situations with a view to defence, are clear and neat; the ascent is facilitated by a long stair or causeway regularly built of Stone, and shaded by a Row of fruit Trees on each side, and the principal street itself is often paved in a manner than would do credit to European skill – Their Houses are built of wood in the most substantial manner raised upon strong posts, and their interior is arranged with a neatness not devoid of elegance – Attached to every Village are two enclosed Baths built of Stone, appropriated to the different sexes; any trespass by a man on that belonging to the females subjects the offender to a heavy fine – In the manufacture of their arms[,] clothing and gold ornaments (of which they wear a great many) they display great ingenuity and considerable taste – In their persons they are a handsome athletic race; their warlike habits and perhaps the nature of their Country give them an activity & vigour of frame unusual to the Inhabitants of tropical climates – They are not addicted to any practice of intoxication or gambling – Their address is frank and open; they are keen in their Commercial dealings, fond of gain, but scrupulously exact in the fulfilment of their engagements."

"All the evils arising from the imperfection of their Civil Code have been aggravated and encreased by the odious traffic in Slaves &c."

I will only add that the estimated number of slaves annually exported from Nias has not fallen short of 1500 souls – that the Chiefs have unanimously and *unreservedly entered into engagements to abolish it in toto, and that the British Flag having now been hoisted, the Island & its Inhabitants may be considered as an integral part of the British Dominion.*

I have not time at the present moment to enter fully as I could wish on this important acquisition – but as these People appear never to have had any communication or Instruction either from Europeans[,] Hindus or Mahometans and are perhaps as original a race of beings as have at any time been found in so advanced a Stage of civilization, I hope I may bespeak the weight of your influence with the philanthropic and serious part of our Country to further the objects I have in view – perhaps there never was a more interesting field opened for the philosopher than the contemplation of the present state of these people, or for the Philanthropist and Christian Missionary for active and beneficial exertion –

*I purpose at an early period communicating many particulars respecting Neas to my esteemed friend M*r*. Wilberforce[285] with a request that he will make such fact public as may appear to be of sufficient interest.*

I have to apologize to your Lordship for this hasty and incomplete Sketch of my present objects, and throw myself on your liberality and kindness for an excuse – May I beg that you will present my best respects to Lady Lansdowne and Believe me My Lord

> *With the highest respect &*
> *Esteem,*
> *Your Lordship's*
> *very faithful and*
> *Obed humble S*t*.*
> *T S Raffles*

In consequence of the restoration of Padang to the Dutch, and my having been prohibited from extending British influence in Sumatra, the Dutch are about to occupy Menangcabau and to build a fort on the ruins of the ancient Capital – and I think it will soon appear that when once the resources of Sumatra are disclosed, it will be found a more important and valuable possession than even Java itself – The Dutch unfortunately have the most valuable and fertile Provinces and if we do not very soon change our System we may expect to lose all influence whatever – We are now confined to what may be called the back Settlements and the only population worth noticing not yet under Dutch Sway are the People of Neas, and the Battas[,] a Nation of Cannibals, but respecting whom the European World is as much in the dark as they were regarding the Natives of Neas – I of course do not include Acheen – where we have very good Agreements on Paper – but nothing further – Were the Dutch excluded from Sumatra I would undertake in three years that it should more than rival Java and afford provision for not less than 50 to 100,000 Englishmen – but I fear there is no chance of my being put to the test –

The Marquess of Lansdowne
&c &c &c

Letter 33
Raffles to Lansdowne
1 March 1822

Bencoolen 1ˢᵗ. March 1822

My Lord
    Long continued illness and a series of domestic afflictions have hitherto pre-vented my acknowledging the receipt of your Lordship's kind letter forwarding the Report of the Lords on Eastern Trade[286] –
    The spirit with which the Enquiry appears to have been entered into & the general tenor of the evidence brought forward have proved a great support to my proceedings, and I have now the advantage of advancing an object which is admitted by the Legislature to be important and essential to the Commerce of the Nation – Our interests in the Eastern Seas have hitherto suffered principally from the indifference of our Government, and their entire ignorance of their value and importance –
    I could have wished that the evidence adduced had been more specific – it would have relieved the question from that general and speculative character which has exposed it to attack by steady & plain men – and I think that even among the Records of the India House much more detailed information might have been found – It is impossible not to concur with Mʳ Charles Grant in nearly all that he says,[287] and I am most happy to find that whatever may be his opinion regarding China, he admits the advantage and importance of a free Trade and permanent British Establishment in the Archipelago –

I have much satisfaction in reporting that my Settlement of Singapore still continues to advance, steadily but yet rapidly – The certainty of its permanent retention by us is alone wanting to ensure its prosperity – From the enclosed Abstract of Tonnage[288] your Lordship will be able to judge of the extent and nature of the Trade that is carried on – hitherto it has been merely a Port for Barter and Exchange, and Merchandize has not been stored on the Island to any extent, but as Capital accumulates and Mercantile Establishments are formed, Store Houses will be built & the Trade of course encrease in proportion to the additional facilities that will be afforded –

It is my intention to go round to Singapore in the course of a few months in order to make such general arrangements as will admit of the expansion and rise of the Settlement without endangering the principle on which it is established – There is so great an inclination in our Indian Government to drive a revenue that the greatest precaution is necessary to prevent the levying of duties – and the establishment of vexatious Regulations – My health has suffered so much, and as I shall have little to do in India after the full establishment of Singapore, I look to the possibility of my returning to England in all next year – I have applied for a Successor – and I sincerely hope that the final arrangements for the future management of Singapore may be delayed till I arrive[.]

Our intercourse with Siam continues not only uninterrupted but is rapidly encreasing – We sent a Kind of Embassy there lately with the view of ascertaining the State of the Country and to pave the way for further direct communication – The gentleman deputed was a Merchant of Singapore[289] and united this object with a Commercial Speculation – he was very well received & the King has returned a very complimentary Letter to the Resident of Singapore – and as far as Commercial intercourse is concerned, it appears that while we respect their Port Regulations and do not interfere with politics we shall always be welcome Visitors – These Port Regulation are annoying & harassing to Shipping but are only what might be expected from a weak and jealous Government determined not to place their Capital or the dignity of the State within the risk of insult or injury from foreign Visitors – At the period of this visit no less than 200 large Junks sailed from the Siam River for Singapore and other parts of the Archipelago, and it would appear that the Siamese still maintain a direct intercourse with Japan[,] a considerable part of the cargo obtained by our Commercial Ambassador being composed of Japan Copper &c –

The riches of Siam are great – its agriculture is extensive and its population dense – It is to the Countries of the Archipelago to the Northward of the Equator what Java is to those which lie to the South – the principal Granary – and it furnishes both Rice and Salt to greater extent and at lower prices than Java. Ivory[,] Gold and Sugar are at present the principal Exports for the European Market – for China it furnishes many important supplies; and in return Opium[,] Piece Goods and Europe[,] Chinese & Indian manufactures are demanded – The extent to which the British manufactures can be eventually introduced can only at present be conjectural, but if we refer to the general introduction of our Cottons which has taken place in Java and elsewhere where they have been advantageously received, it may be fair to infer that as our intercourse encreases Siam may afford a Mart for at least an equal quantity to that now sold in Java and its Dependencies – The progress may be slow at first – and it will of course be gradual, but the result eventually if we avoid political quarrels and harassing interference & intermeddling may I think be considered as certain.

I do not however calculate so much from any direct Trade with Siam by British Ships, as from what must naturally result at our Station of Singapore which is rapidly becoming the grand Port of exchange for Siamese Goods – Such are the natural and obstinate jealousies and prejudices of the Siamese (in common with the Chinese & other States of the kind) that they will never be able to give all the latitude and security to our Ships frequenting their Port which our Merchants will require – the Governm^t. being bad and the public officers corrupt[,] the latter will of course encrease in their exactions and extortions until we have all the inconveniences and uncertainties which now prevail in China from similar causes and effects –

It is a remarkable fact that the produce of Siam can even now be purchased at a lower rate at Singapore than at Siam itself – In the article of Sugar there is a difference of one Dollar in seven in favour of Singapore – This arises from the article being conveyed thither in Native Vessels who export without the duties and vexations which the foreign Trader is liable to, and who eagerly flock to a free and independent Port where they may carry on their speculations without controul or annoyance –

The article which I still consider as most capable of extension is Cotton Manufactures – We now regularly import into China upwards of 20,000 Tons annually of Raw Cotton the produce of the British Territories in India – Why should we thus be encouraging the industry and manufactures of China at the expense of our own – surely our Manufacturers can make the same descriptions of Cloth from the same material, and our machinery is of little use if it does not undersell the manual labour of the Countries we trade with.

I am too weak at the present moment to go further into the subject but I hope at no distant period to have the honor of addressing your Lordship more at length – In the mean time I beg you will consider that no exertions of mine will be wanting to place within your Lordship's reach every essential information which it may be interesting to you to receive. I am already engaged in collecting the details for a practical and very ample Report on the Commerce of these Seas[290] –

Mr Crawfurd has been deputed to visit Siam[,] Cochin China &c[291] – At the former place he will find no difficulty in establishing such Commercial Relations as shall protect us against rival European interests & more we don[']t require & ought not to demand – The King has long assured me that as far as Commerce went he would always meet our wishes – but he dreads political interference – With regard to Cochin China, I fear that Country is so dismembered by internecine commotions that much advantageous commercial intercourse cannot at present be expected – a Knowledge however of the actual State of the Country, and a Survey of the numerous harbours &c will doubtless be important.

By the present opportunity we send home upwards of 100 Tons of the finer spices – Nutmegs – Mace & Cloves – the produce of Bencoolen,[292] and the Planters are anxious to contract for the supply of Great Britain in future years – this will effectually destroy the Dutch Monopoly[.]

With my best respects to Lady Lansdowne I have the honor to remain

your Lordship's
Most obliged &
Faithful humble [St]
T S Raffles

The Marquess of Lansdowne
&c &c &c

Letter 34
Raffles to Lansdowne
20 January 1823

Singapore the 20ᵗʰ. Janry 1823

My Lord,

In February last I took the liberty of forwarding to your Lordship an Abstract Statement of the Trade of Singapore during the two first years and a half of its establishment, and I have now much satisfaction in transmitting a more detailed and authentic account of this Trade during the past year 1822, from which you will perceive that the improvement has been nearly in a geometrical ratio and that the Station is rapidly rising in value and importance.

The Expences of the Settlement have in no year exceeded £10,000 – and we have already a local Revenue to nearly that amount without any Tax whatever on the Trade. Land which was the other day covered with primeval forest or in a state of Swamp has already a high value and a few lots conveniently situated for Mercantile Establishments sold lately for upwards of 50,000 Dollars –

The contrast between the rising interests of this place and the heavy and burdensome establishment of Bencoolen is peculiarly striking – The one has only been established for four years and under circumstances of every possible political disadvantage – The other has been established for upwards of a Century and has always been aided by the Company's Capital, and the disbursements of a regular establishment – The annual expences of Singapore are less than the <u>monthly</u> charges of Bencoolen, while the Capital turned in Trade is in nearly the same proportion in favor of the former –

With the view of establishing a landed interest as far as the anticolonial principles of the Court of Directors will admit, I have open'd a Register for all land bought into Cultivation and provided for the Magistracy from the body of European Residents[293] – These Regulations with a declaration of the entire freedom of the Port, will I trust furnish a solid groundwork on which successors my proceed –

It may be satisfactory to your Lordship to know that I have been able to establish a Press in the English[,] Malay and Chinese Characters and that it is already in some activity – As a first specimen which will stand in need of your indulgence I have the honor to enclose Copies of the several Regulations above alluded to.[294]

It is a most consolatory reflection that since the establishment of Singapore under the British Flag not a single case of Piracy has happened in its vicinity; notwithstanding these Straits were previously considered as more dangerous than any other part of the Eastern Seas – all descriptions of People have found better employment in the pursuits of Commerce or Agriculture, and piracy seems to be abandoned as disreputable and comparatively unprofitable.[295]

Singapore still continues under all the disadvantages of uncertainty as to its retention, and ungenerous rivalry almost amounting to hostility on the part of the Dutch who will not allow a Vessel to clear out for the Port, and subject all goods brought from thence to a duty of 16 pr Cent beyond what they would be liable to from other Ports – If under these circumstances its rise is so rapid and at the same time steady, we may be permitted to look forward and with more enlarged views whenever it is freed from these political difficulties – It is generally expected that the new Governor General[296] will bring out the decision of the home author-ities, and in this case, if it is favorable, the confidence established will be sufficient to enable us to cope with all commercial rivalry on the part of our Neighbours –

In lately examining the Accounts of the Spanish Settlement of Manilla, I was much surprised to find that the Trade of that long established possession, having a population of two millions and a half and a large European Establishment and Native Army, scarcely exceeds that already enjoyed by Singapore – I may here mention that late accounts from Manilla report the detection of a very formidable Conspiracy to overthrow the present Government – 15 officers of Rank had been arrested with the principal Magistrate of the City; and the independent Spirit of the South Americans would appear to have found its way to this quarter –

I have the honor to remain with the highest respect and esteem,
Your Lordship's
Most obliged and
Faithful humble S[t]
T. S. Raffles

The Marquess of Lansdowne
&c &c

Notes

ABBREVIATIONS USED IN THE NOTES

Add. MSS. Additional Manuscripts (British Library)

Asiatic Journal *The Asiatic Journal and Monthly Register for British India and its Dependencies* (London)

BCMS The Bute Collection at Mount Stuart (Isle of Bute, Scotland)

BKI *Bijdragen tot de Taal-, Land- en Volkenkunde* [Journal of the Humanities and Social Sciences of Southeast Asia] (KITLV Royal Netherlands Institute of Southeast Asian and Caribbean Studies, Leiden)

BL British Library

CUL Cambridge University Library

HA Hastings Papers in the Bute Collection at Mount Stuart

HC Honourable East India Company

HEIC Honourable East India Company

JMBRAS *Journal of the Malayan (Malaysian) Branch of the Royal Asiatic Society* (Singapore, Kuala Lumpur)

JSBRAS *Journal of the Straits Branch Royal Asiatic Society* (Singapore)

J.Soc. Bibphy Nat. Hist. *Journal of the Society for the Bibliography of Natural History* (London)

MSS. Eur. European Manuscripts (Asia, Pacific & Africa Collections, British Library)

NAS National Archives of Singapore

NLScotland National Library of Scotland (Edinburgh)

NLS National Library Singapore

ODNB [Old] *Dictionary of National Biography*
VBG Verhandelingen van het Bataviaasch Genootschap van Kunsten en Wetenschappen
[Transactions of the Batavian Society of Arts and Sciences] (Batavia, Jakarta)
VKI Verhandelingen van het Koninklijk Instituut voor Taal-, Land- en Volkenkunde
[Transactions of the Royal Institute for Philology, Geography and Ethnology]
(Leiden)

NOTES TO CHAPTER I

1 D.C. Boulger, *The Life of Sir Stamford Raffles* (London, 1897), p. 319. Lord
Hastings's "vacillation" is to be detected in the despatch of the Governor-General in
Council to the Secretary of the Prince of Wales Island government of 26 December
1818, which states that as reports had been received of a Dutch expedition having sailed
from Melaka to Riau, it was deemed that the only course left open to the Supreme
Government was to refer the whole matter to the authorities at home, and that "Sir
Stamford Raffles will of course on receipt of this information … relinquish the prose-
cution of the mission confided to his management, as provided by his instructions" (BL:
Bengal Secret Consultations, vol. 305). This was followed by another despatch dated
20 February 1819 which stated that "Sir Thomas Raffles was not justified in sending
Major Farquhar eastward after the Dutch protested; and, if the Post has not yet been
obtained, he is to desist from any further attempt to establish one" (BL: Bengal Secret
Consultations, vol. 307; Boulger, *Raffles*, p. 319; C.E. Wurtzburg, *Raffles of the Eastern
Isles* (London, 1954), p. 510). It was this despatch which encouraged the Prince of Wales
Island government to oppose Raffles's settlement at Singapore. Raffles himself had also
been instructed by the Supreme Government on the same day that if Farquhar's endeavours in founding a settlement had proved unsuccessful, "you will be pleased to desist
from any further attempts to form a new establishment, and will consider the mission
entrusted to you … as having terminated" (BL: Bengal Secret Consultations, vol. 307).

2 C.H. Philips, *The East India Company 1784–1834* (Manchester, 1968), p. 231;
Hastings to Secret Committee, 14 May 1819, BL: Bengal Secret Letters, vol. 18: "The
position of Singapore appears to be well selected for the protection of our commerce
in these Seas, and therefore we consider it to be a valuable post which it is desirable to
retain".

3 "Address from Singapore. *To the Most Noble Francis, Marquess of Hastings, K.G.,
G.C.B. &c. &c. &c.*", *Asiatic Journal*, vol. XVI, no. 91 (July 1823), p. 72. The Address was
signed by Raffles, who undoubtedly wrote it, and by upwards of 40 European inhabitants, the Sultan and Temenggong of Singapore, and "the chiefs of the various classes of
native inhabitants, consisting of Chinese, Siamese, Javanese, Malays, Arabs, Chooliahs,
and others now established at that interesting and rapidly improving settlement". In
a reply addressed to Raffles, Hastings wrote: "That the prosperity of Singapore may
be permanent, and that it may in a special degree attach upon you, Honourable Sir,

as well as upon each of those who joined you in conferring on me the honour which I am acknowledging, is the fervent wish of Your most obedient and humble servant, Hastings".

4 J.W. Fortescue, *History of the British Army* (London, second edition, 1910–30), vol. 6 (1921), p. 251. For a contemporary account of the military achievements of Lord Moira, see the *Military Panorama* for January 1813, reprinted in the *Java Government Gazette* (Supplement), 16 October 1813.

5 E.A. Smith, *George IV* (New Haven and London, 1999), p. 144; P.D. Nelson, *Francis Rawdon-Hastings, Marquess of Hastings: Soldier, Peer of the Realm, Governor-General of India* (Madison, Teaneck, 2005), p. 145.

6 On Hastings generally, see Nelson, *Marquess of Hastings*; Major Ross-of-Bladensburg, *The Marquess of Hastings, K.G., Rulers of India* series (Oxford, 1893); Anon, "Sketch of the History and Administration of the Marquess of Hastings", *Asiatic Journal*, vol. XVI, no. 95 (November 1823), pp. 421–30; vol. XVI, no. 96 (December 1823), pp. 525–38; vol. XVII, no. 97 (January 1824), pp. 1–16; vol. XVII, no. 98 (February 1824), pp. 117–35; H.T. Prinsep, *History of the Political and Military Transactions in India during the Administration of the Marquess of Hastings 1813–1823* (London, 1825), 2 vols.; Marquess of Hastings, *Summary of the Administration of the Indian Government, Oct. 1813, to Jan. 1823* (London, 1824, reprinted Malta, 1824, Edinburgh, 1825); Thomas Rowlandson, *The Grand Master or Adventures of Qui Hi? in Hindostan. A Hudibrastic Poem in Eight Cantos by Quiz* [William Combe] (London, 1816); Viscount Mersey, "Earl of Moira, Marquess of Hastings, 1814–1823", *The Viceroys and Governors-General of India 1757–1947* (London, 1949), pp. 41–5.

7 *The Private Journal of the Marquess of Hastings, K.G. Governor-General and Commander-in-Chief in India*, (ed.) The Marchioness of Bute (Second edition, London, 1858), vol. I, pp. 40–1.

8 John Bastin, *The Native Policies of Sir Stamford Raffles in Java and Sumatra: An Economic Interpretation* (Oxford, 1957), p. 17.

9 Ibid., pp. 18–21.

10 T.S. Raffles, "The Charges of Major General Gillespie, against The Honourable T.S. Raffles, Leutenant [*sic*] Governor of the Island of Java, with various papers and documents, in refutation of them, relating to the administration of The British Government in that Island and its Dependencies" (Batavia, 1814), hereafter cited as "The Charges of Major General Gillespie"; Boulger, *Raffles*, pp. 218–45; C.E. Wurtzburg, *Raffles*, pp. 328–47. Raffles also fell out with Hastings over his attempts to regulate the importation and registration of slaves in Java and its Dependencies since the Governor-General believed that the territories did not belong to the East India Company and that the regulations resulted in the disposal "prematurely of property that might belong to the Company" (Boulger, *Raffles*, p. 182).

11 Hastings, *Journal*, vol. I, pp. 222–4. Sir John Fortescue, author of the monumental history of the British Army, considered Gillespie to be "the bravest man who ever

wore the King's uniform" (*A Gallant Company or Deeds of Duty & Discipline from the Story of the British Army* (London, 1927), p. 106). Despite his admiration for Gillespie, Hastings considered him rash, and Lady Nugent, wife of General Sir George Nugent (1757–1849), wrote in her Journal on 14 November 1814, when news arrived at Calcutta of Gillespie's death at Kalunga: "Alas! I am afraid he sought his own destruction; for, latterly, his mind was certainly sadly disturbed, and, in my long and many conversations with him, I could not but see that natural impetuosity, and his extraordinary vanity, and love of fame, had led him into false ideas, and errors, that would embitter his future life" (F. Cundall (ed.), *Lady Nugent's Journal* (London, 1939), p. 384).

12 "The Charges of Major General Gillespie", p. 179; E. Wakeham, *The Bravest Soldier, Sir Rollo Gillespie, 1766–1814: A Historical Military Sketch* (Edinburgh, London, 1937), pp. 226–43; Wurtzburg, *Raffles*, pp. 341–2. Raffles wrote to his friend, William Brown Ramsay, at the India House on 21 November 1814: "Lord Moira had no sooner assumed the Government than he opposed himself to every thing which Lord Minto had done, and took part with my opponents – ... it is a thousand to one that Lord Moira's party carries the day for a time – disappointed of the patronage of Java, opposed to all Lord Minto's arrangements, and possessing strong prejudices, it may easily be seen, how forcible the arguments are against our œconomy &c". (BL: MSS.Eur.D.742.20).

13 Governor-General in Council to Court of Directors, 8 December 1815, BL: Bengal Political Letters Received, vol. 12. This harsh verdict by the Supreme Government was qualified by the opinions of N.B. Edmonstone and Archibald Seton, both members of the Supreme Council, and friends of Raffles, who in separate Minutes expressed their belief in his integrity and moral character (Minutes dated 18 June 1814, BL: Java Factory Records, vol. 63). The Governor-General in Council therefore informed the Court of Directors that "nothing has appeared in the course of the deliberations respecting Mr. Raffles's conduct to authorise an opinion affecting his moral character, and although he has not succeeded in administering the extensive and important duties of the Government of Java with that degree of efficiency which is indispensable to secure the advantages held out by Mr. Raffles himself from the possession of the colony, yet there does not appear to be reason to apprehend that Mr. Raffles is not competent to acquit himself with due benefit to his employers in the less complicated duties of the Residency at Bencoolen" (Boulger, *Raffles*, pp. 239–41).

14 Court of Directors to Governor-General in Council, 5 May 1815, BL: Despatches to Bengal, vol. 69.

15 Raffles to Hastings, 2 October 1815, BCMS: HA/11/1/2.

16 Hastings to Raffles, 4 December 1815 (draft), BCMS: HA/11/5/1. Raffles gave a curious rationalisation for his removal from the post of Lieutenant-Governor of Java in a letter to William Brown Ramsay dated 18 October 1815: "On the main point however, my removal, the directors are perfectly clear & final – but as it was impossible for two such high characters as Lord Moira and myself to continue at loggerheads, it was thought wise, as is the usual course in such cases, to let the weakest go to the wall – there is

nothing disreputable or disgraceful in my removal in this manner, and altho I had a right to expect very different treatment, a better knowledge of the world should have taught me the folly of depending on such an expectation" (BL: MSS.Eur.D.742.20).

17 Charles George Blagrave was appointed to the Bengal Civil Service in 1804 and arrived in India two years later. In 1810 he was Assistant to the Opium Agent at Bihar, having in January of the previous year married a Miss Jane Colvin. He arrived in Java with his wife on 1 December 1811 on his way to take up an appointment as Second Assistant to the Resident of Ambon, but as he was unable to secure a passage late in the season, he was appointed Acting Secretary to the government of Java. Raffles stated subsequently that he was "wholly incapable of performing the duties of the office", and that "neither his general talents nor his personal habits were such as to enable me to make him my confidential Secretary" ("The Charges of Major General Gillespie", p. 183). Even so, Raffles invited him and his wife to the Christmas festivities at Government House, Bogor, in 1812. Thereafter, Blagrave became involved in an unauthorised purchase of an East India Company brig, using his domestic servant as a front, and compounding the matter by not having sufficient funds to complete the transaction. The performance of his official duties was "more and more unsatisfactory", and he became the "loudest" critic of the Government's policy of selling public lands to meet the worsening economic situation in Java. In February 1813 Raffles tried to persuade him to take up his original appointment at Ambon, which he at first consented to do, but he changed his mind and refused to acknowledge Raffles's authority to remove him from his post in Java pending an appeal to the Supreme Government. Raffles next offered him a free passage to the Moluccas and agreed to continue his salary as Secretary until his arrival, but the offer was declined and Raffles consequently removed him from his post. Blagrave left Java for Calcutta two months later, full of rancour and with a determination to press charges against Raffles for his participation in the sale of lands. He secured an interview with the Governor-General (BCMS: HA/11/9/22) and was examined before the Supreme Council but without, apparently, making much impression. His charges, however, were confirmatory of those laid subsequently by Gillespie, and therefore could not be ignored. ❡ Gillespie himself, before departing from Java, had become reconciled with Raffles, the reconciliation being effected by Lord Minto's son, Captain the Hon. George Elliot, who discusses the matter in his privately printed *Memoir* (London, reprinted 1891, pp. 102–4), where he adds that in his opinion, Raffles was "unfit to govern, and had the fatal misfortune of never inspiring Europeans with respect". Raffles also wrote an account of his reconciliation with Gillespie, citing the testimony of his friend, William Robinson, that on 10 October 1813, the day of his departure from Java for Calcutta on board the ship *Troubridge* (Humphreys), Gillespie had stated that he "lamented the differences that formerly subsisted between the Lieutenant Governor and himself, … that he had a sincere friendship [regard] for Mr. Raffles, and he would defend the measures of his Administration wherever he went" ("The Charges of Major General Gillespie", pp. 179–80; Appendix PPP, p. 332). His attitude soon changed and he

was already speaking against Raffles when the ship called at Pinang, the change being attributed by Wurtzburg (*Raffles*, pp. 303, 328) to the presence of Blagrave on board the *Troubridge*, and to his poisoning Gillespie's mind against Raffles during the voyage. In fact, Blagrave had sailed for Bengal six months earlier, in May 1813, and Gillespie's fellow passenger was Blagrave's wife Jane, an undoubtedly more insinuating influence than her husband. Blagrave's letters to C.M. Ricketts, a member of the Supreme Council (note 71) are in BCMS: HA/11/9/22. There is an interesting anonymous contemporary annotation in the copy of "The Charges of Major General Gillespie" in the Rhodes House Library, Oxford: "Mr Raffles has reason to praise God that he had such an enemy to deal with as Mr Blagrave. What would have come of him had Mr John Crawfurd [Resident at Semarang, later Resident at Singapore] been consulted? Long ago he would have sunk back into that insignificance from whence he never ought to have arisen". ❡ Blagrave had been reprimanded by the Supreme Government in January 1815 for the "disrespectful terms" he used in speaking of Raffles as Lieutenant-Governor of Java since these were also held to be "disrespectful to the Government to which [he] addressed himself". The reprimand does not appear to have had an adverse effect on Blagrave's career in the service of the East India Company since he was appointed Collector of Tirhut in 1814, and Collector of Rangpur in 1815. After two years' leave in Europe in 1821, he was appointed Collector of Etawah, Upper Provinces, in 1824, and during 1835–6 he held various appointments, including those of Collector of the Jungle Mahals and Hijili and Salt Agent and Superintendent of the Salt Chokies at Bhulua, Jessore and Chittagong. He died at Chittagong on 16 June 1836. Sixteen of his wife's Indian drawings are now in the British Library (M. Archer, *British Drawings in the India Office Library* (London, 1969). vol. I, pp. 129–31.

18 In a despatch to Bengal dated 13 February 1817, the Court of Directors stated that after "a scrupulous examination of all the documents", the charges of Gillespie and Blagrave levelled against Raffles, insofar as they impeached his moral character, "have been disproved, to an extent which is seldom practicable in a case of defence", and although Raffles's purchase of land was "very indiscreet", this did not "at all derogate from those principles of integrity, by which we believe his public conduct to have been uniformly governed", *Extract Public Letter from the Honourable Court of Directors to the Supreme Government in Bengal. Dated the 13ᵗʰ February 1817* (privately printed by Raffles, pp. 1–[4]). In an appeal to the Directors of the East India Company on 27 January 1816, Raffles had defended his land revenue and other reforms in Java as being in conformity with the views of Lord Minto (Boulger, *Raffles*, pp. 206–7).

19 John Bastin, *Letters and Books of Sir Stamford Raffles and Lady Raffles: The Tang Holdings Collection of Autograph Letters and Books of Sir Stamford Raffles and Lady Raffles* (Singapore, 2009), p. 203, n. 81; John Bastin, *Sir Stamford Raffles's* The History of Java: A Bibliographical Essay (Eastbourne, 2004).

20 Bastin, *Letters and Books of Sir Stamford Raffles*, pp. 230–1, n. 29.

21 Ibid., pp. 231–2; p. 203, n. 75, p. 237, n. 30, n. 32.

22 Note 37.

23 Note 267. Four letters of Raffles to Lord Lansdowne dated between April 1820 and January 1823 are in the possession of the National Library Singapore and are printed in Appendix IV. On Lord Lansdowne, see note 267.

24 Bastin, *Letters and Books of Sir Stamford Raffles*, pp. 232–3, 239–40, n. 47.

25 Ibid., p. 212, n. 175; pp. 215–16, n. 212; A.T. Embree, *Charles Grant and British Rule in India* (London, 1962). On Grant's favourable opinion of Raffles and Singapore, see note 287.

26 Bastin, *Letters and Books of Sir Stamford Raffles*, p. 204, n. 94.

27 Raffles was elected a Fellow of the Royal Society on 20 March 1817, his principal supporters being the orientalist, William Marsden, and the surgeon, Sir Everard Home (*The Record of The Royal Society of London* (London, Edinburgh, 1940, p. 449). He appears to have attended the meetings of the Royal Society on a least eight occasions during the first half of 1817 when he dined at the Royal Society Club, and at other times after his return to England in 1824 (Sir Archibald Geike, *Annals of the Royal Society Club* (London, 1917), pp. 253, 284, 287, 290; T.E. Allibone, *The Royal Society and its Dining Clubs* (Pergamon Press, Oxford, 1976), pp. 149, 150, 164.

28 E. Smith, *The Life of Sir Joseph Banks, President of the Royal Society, with some Notices of his Friends and Contemporaries* (London, 1911); H.C. Cameron, *Sir Joseph Banks* (Sydney, reprinted 1966); H.B. Carter, *Sir Joseph Banks 1743–1820* (London, reprinted 1991); J. Gascoigne, *Joseph Banks and the English Enlightenment: Useful Knowledge and Polite Culture* (Cambridge, 1994); N. Chambers (ed.), *The Letters of Sir Joseph Banks: A Selection, 1768–1820* (London, 2000). The contents of Raffles's four letters to Banks dated 18 September 1814, 14 August 1818, 4 March 1819 and 22 March 1820 are summarised in W.R. Dawson (ed.), *The Banks Letters: A Calendar of the manuscript correspondence of Sir Joseph Banks preserved in the British Museum, the British Museum (Natural History) and other collections in Great Britain* (London, 1958), p. 692. In his letter to Banks dated 4 March 1819, Raffles refers to his founding of Singapore. A holograph letter of Raffles to Banks written from Java on 3 December 1815 is in the Tang Holdings Collection, Singapore (Bastin, *Letters and Books of Sir Stamford Raffles*, p. 423).

29 See references in John Bastin, *The Natural History Researches of Dr Thomas Horsfield (1773–1859), First American Naturalist of Indonesia* (Singapore, 1990, reprinted Eastbourne, 2005); John Bastin, "Dr Joseph Arnold and the Discovery of *Rafflesia Arnoldi* in West Sumatra in 1818", *J. Soc. Biblphy Nat. Hist.*, vol. 6, pt. 5 (1973), pp. 305–72; John Bastin, "Sir Stamford Raffles and the Study of Natural History in Penang, Singapore and Indonesia", *JMBRAS*, vol. LXIII, pt. 2 (1990), pp. 1–25, and in the works listed in note 28 above. Banks expressed his high opinion of Raffles in a letter to Dr. Thomas Horsfield in 1817: "We are all here delighted with the acquaintance of Governor Raffles; he is certainly among the best informed of men, and possesses a larger stock of useful talent than any other individual of my acquaintance" (Lady Raffles, *Memoir of the Life and Public Services of Sir Thomas Stamford Raffles …* (London, 1830), p. 449).

30 Sir Miles Nightingall (1768–1829) replaced Gillespie as Commander of the Forces in Java in October 1813. He was the natural son of Charles, 1st Marquess and 2nd Earl Cornwallis (1738–1805), and had gained an impressive military reputation in India under Wellesley. He had been strongly recommended to Raffles by the Governor-General Lord Minto, who described him as "a man of honour, and a gentleman in the highest degree". He and his wife, Lady Florentia Nightingall, became close friends of Raffles, and it was as "a friend" that Nightingall wrote a private and confidential letter to Hastings dated 4 October 1815 expressing his strong belief in Raffles's probity and his support for his administration in Java: "I solemnly declare on the word of a soldier that I have uniformly found Mr. Raffles ... a most honorable, upright public servant, Indefatigable in promoting the Welfare & Prosperity of this fine Colony, as well as attentive to the Interests of the Company" (BCMS: HA/11/9/2). Hastings replied on 4 December 1815: "Of the zeal & intentions of that Gentleman I am disposed to entertain a full belief: But it would be wrong in me to conceal my opinion that his conduct of the Company's interests has been singularly injudicious. The grievous expense incurred in the furtherance of objects the benefits of which (as there was no chance of our ultimately retaining the Island) we could never recoup, was a fundamental error; and, even had nothing else excited the dissatisfaction of the Court of Directors, was sure to entail that order for his removal which we have received. That the Island promises to pay for its maintenance is a very inadequate compensation for the sums which it has hitherto cost" (BCMS: HA/11/9/3). ⦅ Another of Raffles's influential supporters was John Fendall (1761–1818), who succeeded him as Lieutenant-Governor of Java and its Dependencies on 12 March 1816. He adopted a friendly attitude towards Raffles, continuing the principles of his administration and employing his staff (*The Journal of Thomas Otho Travers 1813–1820*, (ed.) John Bastin, *Memoirs of the Raffles Museum*, no. 4, 1957 (Singapore, 1960), pp. 79–81, hereafter cited as Travers, *Journal*). When he returned to Calcutta on 3 September 1817 Fendall became Chief Judge in the Sudar Diwani and he was subsequently appointed as third member of the Supreme Council where his knowledge of Java and his support of Raffles had an important bearing on Lord Hastings's views. ⦅ An additional possible factor in accounting for Hastings's more favourable attitude towards Raffles after they became acquainted in Calcutta in 1818 was that they were both Freemasons. Raffles had been initiated into the Craft and passed on to the Second Degree at a ceremony in Java in October 1811 at the Lodge "Virtutis et Artis Amici", which had been established by the Worshipful Master, Nicolaus Engelhard (1761–1831), a former Governor of Java, on his coffee estate Pondok-Gedeh, near Bogor. Among the other Masonic brethren present on the occasion was the Governor-General Lord Minto, the Commander of the Forces in Java, Colonel Robert Rollo Gillespie, and the newly appointed Dutch member of Council, Herman Warner Muntinghe (1773–1827), who was initiated along with Raffles. Nearly two years later, on 5 July 1813, at an emergency meeting of the Lodge "De Vriendschap" at Surabaya, Raffles took the Third Degree in Freemasonry to become Worshipful Brother Raffles, and shortly before departing from

Java in March 1816 he received Perfection in the Eighteenth Degree in the Rose Croix Chapter "La Vertueuse" at Jakarta (H. Banner, *These Men were Masons* (London, 1934), pp. 117–36). His Masonic activities continued at Bengkulu in the Lodge "The Rising Sun", details of which are recorded in Travers, *Journal, passim*. Hastings himself had been appointed Grand Master of the Scottish Freemasons on becoming Commander-in-Chief in Scotland in 1803, and after his nomination as Governor-General he was made Acting Grand Master of India by the Duke of Sussex. He was presented with a welcome address as Past Acting Grand Master of England by the Freemasons of the Madras Lodge during his brief stay there in September 1813, and on 27 December 1813 a ball and supper was given for him and the Countess of Loudoun by the Freemasons of Calcutta. Within five weeks of his arrival he had constituted at Calcutta a new Lodge, "The Moira, Freedom and Fidelity", and re-established the Provincial Grand Lodge of Bengal. He was active thereafter in promoting Freemasonry in Poona and other places in India (R.F. Gould, *The History of Freemasonry*, London 1910, vol. VI, pp. 329–31).

   31 Raffles to Hastings, 16 April 1818, BCMS: HA/II/I/3.

   32 Hastings to Raffles, 6 July 1818 (draft), BCMS: HA/II/5/2; Lady Raffles, *Memoir*, p. 368.

CHAPTER II

   33 Raffles had been presented to George Canning (1770–1827) at the Prince Regent's levee on 3 February 1817, and he shortly afterwards sent him a copy of his paper, "Our Interests in the Eastern Archipelago" (note 34). Canning strongly opposed Raffles's policies in Sumatra, and wrote critically of him in a private letter to Hastings from the India Board on 30 January 1819 (see pp. 105–6 above). But after he became convinced of the importance of Singapore as a British commercial centre in South-East Asia, he worked hard to secure its retention during the Anglo-Dutch negotiations which led to the Treaty of London in 1824. Raffles wrote to him expressing his approval of the terms of the Treaty, which left Singapore under British control, and on 11 October 1824 Canning replied that he was "greatly pleased and gratified" by his response, as there "could not be a more competent judgment than yours on such a subject, or one which I should have been more desirous of having in favour of our mode of dealing with it – I cannot deny that your extreme activity in stirring difficult questions and the freedom with which you committed your Government without their knowledge or authority to measures which might have brought a War upon them, unprepared, did at one time oblige me to speak my mind to you in Instructions of no very mild reprehension – But I was not the less anxious to retain those fruits of your Policy which appeared to me really worth preserving – And I have long forgotten every particular of your conduct in the Eastern Seas except the Zeal and ability by which it was distinguished" (BL: MSS. Eur.D.742.3).

34 T.S. Raffles, "Our Interests in the Eastern Archipelago", enclos. in Raffles to Nicholas Vansittart, 23 October 1817, BL: Add Ms 31237 f.241; Boulger, *Raffles*, pp. 268–73.

35 Boulger, *Raffles*, p. 272.

36 Raffles to Secret Committee, 14 April 1818, BL: Sumatra Factory Records, vol. 47; Lady Raffles, *Memoir*, pp. 305–6.

37 Raffles to Charlotte, Duchess of Somerset, 15 April 1818, BL: MSS.Eur.D.742.24. Raffles's friendship with Charlotte Seymour, Duchess of Somerset (born 6 April 1772), was said to have been that which "he values & clings to above every other". This may have had something to do with the fact that she was much the same age as his first wife, Olivia Mariamne, and there was also the obvious attraction of her social standing. She appears to have been a warm and kind-hearted woman who attracted many of the intelligent men of her day (Lady Guendolen Ramsden (ed.), *Correspondence of Two Brothers* (London, 1906), pp. 12–13). The poet Samuel Rogers was particularly attached to her, and Byron, on the eve of his departure from England in 1816, wrote in a farewell letter: "Your Grace is one of the few whom I would not willingly see for ye *last* time". She was also a particular friend of Sir Joseph Banks, President of the Royal Society, whose letters to her contain a warmth of feeling not generally found in his other correspondence (Chambers, *The Letters of Sir Joseph Banks*, Letters 118, 121, 122, 124). She was fond of society, and liked to be surrounded by intelligent men and women with whom she engaged in "bright and clever conversation". She was always in delicate health and her suffering increased as she grew older so that she was obliged to receive her friends while reclining on a sofa in the drawing room. She seems to have had a happy relationship with her husband, Edward Adolphus Seymour, 11th Duke of Somerset (1775–1855), whom she married on 24 June 1800. Elizabeth Heber in a letter to the Revd. Reginald Heber dated 5 July 1800 describes the occasion of the Duke's proposal of marriage: "Her father [Archibald, 9th Duke of Hamilton and 6th Duke of Brandon (1740–1819)] when shewing the house took the young Duke into his daughter's apartments where they found the young Lady surrounded with books, on further inspection, the Duke was so much pleased with the collection in which she had shewn so much taste and judgement, that an offer of marriage immediately ensued and was accepted. The daughters of Duke Hamilton were all well educated under the eye of their excellent Mother [Lady Harriet Stewart, daughter of the 6th Earl of Galloway]" (R.H. Cholmondeley (ed.), *The Heber Letters* (London, 1950), p. 119). ❧ Wurtzburg (*Raffles*, p. 417) connects Raffles's election as a Fellow of the Royal Society on 20 March 1817 (note 27) to his friendship with the Duke of Somerset, who was an active Fellow of the Royal Society, and thus to his friendship with the Duchess and her father, the Duke of Hamilton. It was certainly about this time that Raffles became acquainted with the Duchess as his first letter to her is to be dated about May 1817 when his book, *The History of Java*, was published. In this letter Raffles thanks her for the gift of a pen, which he received on his return from dining with the Court of Directors of the East India Company: "I value this peculiar mark of your Grace's kindness and flattering attention far beyond all the dignities or riches which those Princes of

the East could confer – … You have I fear put the pen into very unfit hands; it is true I have written a Book, but then your Grace has not read it – and it is probable that when you have, you will regret that you have been instrumental in my writing more" (BL: MSS. Eur.D.742.24). This letter began a correspondence which continued for the rest of his life, and the fact that she carefully preserved his letters is a measure of the affection and esteem she felt for him, writing to him in 1825: "What a pity such a Character [as you] was not sent out [as] Governor General of India! How much good w^d. you have done, not only to India but to England" (BL: MSS.Eur.D.742.27). The most revealing indication of his feelings for her is afforded by a postscript to a letter he wrote to her from Fort Marlborough on 15 April 1818: "I have just closed all my dispatches and as you are my *Alpha* and *Omega* – the first and last in my thoughts – I cannot resist adding one line to say farewell – and god bless you – Forget me not – and as I love you and yours so do you continue to love me and mine – farewell TSR" (BL: MSS.Eur.D.742.24). She subscribed her letters to him: "My D^r. Sir Stamford y^{rs}. With much regard", "with affectionate regard", "with much regard", "with kind regards", "yours truly", "I remain My Dr Sir Stamford yrs Sincerely & faithfully", and she refers to him in one of her letters as "an esteemed friend". She died less than a year after him, on 10 June 1827, aged 55. Copies of the books he sent to her seem to have been dispersed over the years. His inscribed copy of *Substance of a Minute … on the Establishment of a Land Rental on the Island of Java* (London, 1814) was listed in Maggs Catalogue 413 (1921), item 901, and a similarly inscribed copy of the second volume of *Malayan Miscellanies* (Sumatran Mission Press, 1822), is now in the National Library of Malaysia. He sent her a copy of the first (and only) volume of the *Proceedings of the Agricultural Society, Established in Sumatra* (Baptist Mission Press, Bencoolen, 1820), with a covering letter dated 20 May 1821 in which he wrote, "perhaps on our account, you may read [it] with some little interest".

38 Raffles to Secret Committee, 3 July 1818, BL: Sumatra Factory Records, vol. 47.

39 M.L. van Deventer, *Het Nederlandsch Gezag over Java en Onderhoorigheden sedert 1811* (The Hague, 1891), vol. I, pp. 257–9; Raffles to Secret Committee, 3 July 1818, BL: Sumatra Factory Records, vol. 47.

40 Raffles to Marsden, 7 April 1818, Lady Raffles, *Memoir*, pp. 293–4. The Chart of "Caloombyan Harbour" by Lieutenants W.H. Hull and W. H. Johnston was published in London by James Horsburgh, Hydrographer to the East India Company, on 2 August 1819, and is reproduced in Lady Raffles, *Memoir*, facing p. 311. On Raffles's attempts to establish a British settlement in Semangka Bay, see P.H. van der Kemp, "Raffles' Bezetting van de Lampongs in 1818", *BKI*, vol. 50 (1899), pp. 1–58.

41 Raffles to Hon. George Dowdeswell, Vice-President in Council, Bengal, 6 July 1818, with enclosures, BL: Sumatra Factory Records, vol. 47.

42 Raffles to Salmond, 20 June 1818, BL: Sumatra Factory Records, vol. 47. The military contingent was under the command of Lieutenant Thomas Haslam (1790–1832) of the 20th Bengal Native Infantry with overall authority vested in Captain Francis Salmond, who was instructed to afford the Sultan "that protection to the extent of

your means, and to require that the Dutch withdraw all pretensions and in no way further interfere with the affairs of Palembang". See P.H. van der Kemp, "Palembang en Banka in 1816–1820", *BKI*, vol. 51 (1900), pp. 384–95. The "Diary" kept by Salmond during his journey from Bengkulu to Palembang is printed in *Malayan Miscellanies* (Sumatra Mission Press, Fort Marlborough, 1822), vol. II, no. 3, pp. 12. Salmond had served as Master Attendant at Fort Marlborough since 1810 and was judged by Raffles to possess "great activity, zeal and firmness". On learning of Salmond's death on 23 November 1823, he wrote: "I have just received information that my dear and valued friend Salmond is no more … Salmond was as dear and intimate with us as our own family. I have just opened his will, and find he has nominated me as his sole executor in the following words:– 'I appoint my *only* friend Sir Stamford Raffles to be my executor, and I pray to God he will take charge of my estate and children'" (Lady Raffles, *Memoir*, p. 563). As executor, Raffles sold Salmond's land at Panurunan for 1,350 Madras Rupees to his brother-in-law, John Watson Hull (1792–1842) (note 258). Salmond was the brother of Colonel James Salmond, Secretary in charge of military correspondence in the Examiner's Office at India House, London. Some interesting remarks on the Salmond family are contained in Averil Mackenzie-Grieve, *Time and Chance: An Autobiography* (London, 1970), pp. 51–3.

43 Raffles's "Protest" was enclosed in a letter to Van der Capellen dated 12 August 1818 (BL: Sumatra Factory Records, vol. 47). It was subsequently printed in *The Annual Register* and in many newspapers in the United Kingdom, including *The Times* (notes 45, 46).

44 Raffles to Charlotte, Duchess of Somerset, 13 August 1818, BL: MSS.Eur.D.742.24

45 "Protest of Sir Thomas Stamford Raffles, lieutenant-governor of Fort Marlborough, against the aggressions of the Dutch in the Malayan Archipelago", *The Annual Register, or a View of the History, Politics, and Literature, For the Year 1819* (London, 1820), pp. 216–32.

46 Notably in *The Times*, 14 August 1818, *The Globe* (London), 13, 14, 16, 21, 25 January 1819, *The Edinburgh Evening Courant*, 16, 18, 25 January, 20 February 1819, &c.

47 Raffles to Secret Committee, 12 August 1818, BL: Sumatra Factory Records, vol. 47.

48 Secret Committee to Hastings, 30 October 1818, BL: Despatches to Bengal, vol. 79.

49 Bastin, *Sir Stamford Raffles in Java and Sumatra*, pp. 87–9.

50 Court to Bengal, 5 April 1816, BL: Despatches to Bengal, vol. 72; BL: Bengal Public Consultations, 18 March 1814; Van der Kemp, *BKI*, 51 (1900), pp. 665–6.

51 H. Visser, "Iets over het Landschap de Pasemah Oeloe Manna en zijne tijdelijke onderwerping door Sir Thomas Stamford Raffles". *TBG*, vol. XXVIII (1883), p. 317.

52 "Extract proceedings of the Lieutenant Governor of Bencoolen", 23 May 1818, BL: Bengal Public Consultations, 31 December 1819.

53 Lady Raffles, *Memoir*, p. 318.

54 Treaty, dated 23 May 1818, BL: Sumatra Factory Records, vol. 47; Visser, *TBG*, vol. XXVIII, pp. 324–6.

55 Bengal to Court, 31 December 1818, BL: Bengal Letters Received, vol. 80; Court to Bengal, 28 June 1820, BL: Despatches to Bengal, vol. 84.

56 P.H. van der Kemp, "Sumatra's Westkust naar aanleiding van het Londensch Tractaat van 13 Augustus 1814", *BKI*, vol. 49 (1898), pp. 205–306.

57 Ibid., pp. 205–22; 252–9; Raffles to Court, 6 July 1818, BL: Sumatra Factory Records, vol. 47; Lady Raffles, *Memoir*, p. 387.

58 Bastin, *The Natural History Researches of Dr Thomas Horsfield*, pp. 65–6.

59 Lady Raffles, *Memoir*, pp. 340–66, 387–8.

60 Treaties with the rulers of the Padang Highlands and Minangkabau, 20, 24 July 1818, BL: Sumatra Factory Records, 47; Lady Raffles, *Memoir*, p. 388. In pursuing these measures to counter Dutch influence in Sumatra, Raffles assumed some degree of political authority, which he believed had been given to him following discussions with the Chairman and Deputy Chairman of the East India Company in London in 1817. See pp. 101–106 above.

61 Lady Raffles, *Memoir*, pp. 363, 480: "I would, in fact, re-establish the ancient authority of Menangkabu, and be the great Mogul of the Island".

62 Raffles to Secret Committee, 5 August 1818, BL: Sumatra Factory Records, vol. 47.

CHAPTER III

63 Raffles to Marsden, 16 October 1818, Lady Raffles, *Memoir*, p. 369. In a letter to Sir Robert Harry Inglis dated Singapore 12 June 1819, ibid., p. 401, he states: "It may be satisfactory to Sir Hugh [Inglis] to know that Lord Hastings has made the *amende honorable*; expressed in the handsomest terms his regret that he should ever have viewed my proceedings in Java in another light, and his approbation and applause of the general principles which regulated my Government, which he is pleased to say were as creditable to me as honourable to my country". On Hastings's proposal for a division between British and Dutch territorial interests in the Malay Archipelago, see his Minute recorded for the Supreme Government on 2 January 1819 (BL: Bengal Secret Consultations, vol. 307).

64 Raffles to Marsden, 14 November 1818, Lady Raffles, *Memoir*, p. 371. See also Raffles to Marsden, 31 January 1819: "You are already apprised how much I have been disappointed in the necessity of foregoing all the advantages which might have resulted from my visit to Pageruyong; it did not suit the politics of Bengal that they should be followed up" (Lady Raffles, *Memoir*, p. 376).

65 Raffles to Charlotte, Duchess of Somerset, 15 November 1818, BL: MSS. Eur.D.742.24; Raffles to Adam, 16 November 1818, BL: Bengal Secret Consultations, vol. 305.

66 Ross-of-Bladensburg, *The Marquess of Hastings*, p. 185; Hastings to Secret Committee, 17 July 1819: "the views of the Dutch are to all appearance boundless" (BL: Bengal Secret Letters, vol. 18). See also Hastings to Secret Committee, 25 November 1818, 14 January 1819, BL: Bengal Secret Letters, vol. 18; and the Supreme Government to the Commissioners-General, Batavia, 26 June 1819: "The spirit of aggrandizement, evinced in the proceedings of the Commissioners-General of His Netherlandish Majesty and their manifest endeavours to establish the absolute supremacy of the Netherlands in the Eastern [S]eas, made it necessary for us to adopt precautions with a view to avert the injury and depredation, which could not fail to ensue from a listless submission to the unbounded pretensions displayed by your nation" (P.H. Van der Kemp, "De Singapoorsche Papieroorlog", *BKI*, vol. 49 (1898), p. 484). For an account of Barakpur and its Menagerie, where Raffles and Lady Raffles were guests of Hastings, see The Marquis Curzon of Kedleston, *British Government in India: The Story of the Viceroys and Government Houses* (London, 1925), vol. II, pp. 1–46. Hastings made many improvements to the gardens and house, more than doubling its size. It was during her visit to Barakpur that Lady Raffles was given the opportunity of riding on one of the numerous elephants kept in captivity.

67 Adam, Chief Secretary to Government, to Raffles, 28 November 1818, BL: Java Factory Records, vol. 71; Wurtzburg, *Raffles*, p. 461. Hastings declared in a Minute to the Supreme Council dated 2 January 1819: "The indisputable authority of the Straits of Malacca and Sincapore is a necessary counterpoise at all times to the authority of the Dutch in the other line of communication [Straits of Sunda]" (BL: Bengal Secret Consultations, vol. 307).

68 Raffles to Charlotte, Duchess of Somerset, 15 November 1818, BL: MSS.Eur. D.742.24.

69 Raffles to Marsden, 14 November 1818, Lady Raffles, *Memoir*, p. 371.

70 John Adam was born on 4 May 1779, the eldest son of William Adam, Lord Chief Commissioner of the Jury Court for Civil Causes in Scotland, and Eleanor Elphinstone, second daughter of Charles, 10th Lord Elphinstone, and a cousin of the Hon. Mountstuart Elphinstone, later Governor of Bombay. He was educated at Charterhouse and Edinburgh University and was appointed a Writer on the Bengal establishment of the East India Company in 1794. He arrived at Calcutta in February 1796 and was drawn into the Bengal Secretariat during the administration of Marquess Wellesley. He was appointed Secretary in the Military Department by Lord Minto in 1809, and in the following year he met Raffles in Calcutta. This was when the Chinese scholar Thomas Manning (1772–1840) took up residence with Adam and Raffles became Manning's friend, the two of them, with John Leyden, and the missionary Dr. Joshua Marshman, often dining together and spending long hours at Leyden's house discussing philological and theological subjects (*Asiatic Journal*, vol. XXXIII n.s. (1840), p. 183; Marshman, *Life and Times of Carey, Marshman, and Ward* (London, 1859), vol. I, pp. 437–8). In 1812 Adam became Secretary to the Government in the Secret, Foreign

and Political Departments and acted as such during the administration of the Marquess of Hastings, as well as being his Private Secretary. In this influential position he sided against Raffles when Major-General Robert Rollo Gillespie preferred charges of mal-administration against him in 1813–14 (notes 10, 17, 18). In 1817 Adam was nominated as a provisional member of the Supreme Council and he succeeded to this position on the departure of C.M. Ricketts for England on 9 January 1819 (note 71). Subsequently, as senior member of the Supreme Council, he exercised the powers of Governor-General for seven months on Hastings's departure on 13 January 1823, during which time he opposed the principles of freedom of the press espoused by James Silk Buckingham (1786–1855) as editor of the *Calcutta Journal*, and he took firm measures against the Hyderabad firm of Palmer & Co., which had become embroiled in a scandal involv-ing loans to the Nizam of Hyderabad. On 16 April 1825 he sailed from Calcutta for Liverpool on the *Albion* (Swainson) but died off Madagascar on 4 June. A full-length portrait of him by Sir Thomas Lawrence after sketches by George Chinnery was com-missioned for the Town Hall in Calcutta, but it was later placed in Government House, Calcutta, and subsequently moved to New Delhi. The portrait is interesting in that it depicts Adam without the spectacles he habitually wore and which are clearly shown in Chinnery's sketches (P. Conner, *George Chinnery, 1774–1852: Artist of India and the China Coast* (Woodbridge, Suffolk, 1993), pp. 119–20; R. Hutcheon, *Chinnery: The Man and the Legend* (Hong Kong, 1974), p. 33). See Anon., "The Honourable John Adam", *Asiatic Journal*, vol. XX, no. 119 (November 1825), pp. 485–504; Anon., [J.S. Buckingham?], "The 'Honourable' John Adam, and the Asiatic Journal", *The Oriental Herald, and Journal of General Literature*, vol. VIII (January to March, 1826), pp. 30–41; *ODNB*, vol. I, p. 87.

71 Raffles to Charlotte, Duchess of Somerset, 25 November 1818, BL: MSS.Eur. D.742.24. Charles Milner Ricketts was born on 21 April 1776, the son of George Poyntz Ricketts and Sophia (*née* Watts). He was appointed a Writer on the Bengal establish-ment of the East India Company in 1792 and in the same year he held the appointments of Assistant to the Secretary to Government and Resident at Rangpur. Thereafter he served as Opium Agent at Bihar (1798) and in other posts until 1811, when he was appointed Secretary to the Supreme Government in the Public Department. He became Principal Private Secretary to Lord Hastings in 1813, and again in 1817, and was appointed Chief Secretary to Government in 1815. In December 1817 he became a member of the Supreme Council and President of the Board of Trade. Through his close personal friendship with Hastings, who admired his "great talent", knowledge and energy, he exercised considerable influence on the Governor-General, which was reinforced by his political connections in England, notably with his cousin, Robert Banks Jenkinson, 2nd Earl of Liverpool (1770–1828), Prime Minister between 1812 and 1827. Ricketts and Raffles had long known each other, but it was only during the latter's visit to Calcutta in 1818 that they commenced what Raffles termed "an intimacy". It was at this time that Ricketts added his support for the project of establishing a British set-tlement at the southern entrance of the Melaka Straits, as Raffles explained in a letter

to Charlotte, Duchess of Somerset, on 26 November 1818: "In our arrangements for the Eastern Islands, Mr Ricketts one of the members of the Supreme Council and principal advisor of Lord Hastings has been induced to take the lead – he embarks for England in January and I have taken the liberty to give him a letter of introduction to your Grace" (BL: MSS.Eur.D.742.24). Raffles does not appear to have set much store by Ricketts's political influence in England, writing to the Duchess of Somerset on 17 December 1819, "the influence of those in authority has been too powerful for his consistency that I am in consequence not to place much confidence in his exertions". However, Raffles's own ambition of becoming Governor of Prince of Wales Island in 1819 rested, as he explained to the Governor-General on 29 September, "mainly on the influence of M^r. Ricketts and the favourable opinion of your Lordship". On Ricketts's return to England, Lord Liverpool secured for him the seat of Dartmouth in the House of Commons. Ricketts was a Fellow of the Geological Society of London and he was accordingly given a number of geological specimens collected by Dr. Thomas Horsfield during Raffles's journey to Minangkabau in 1818. He was responsible for introducing Raffles to the two French naturalists, Pierre Diard and Alfred Duvaucel (note 162), and he arranged for them to accompany him to Sumatra (Raffles to Hastings, 17 June 1819, BCMS: HA/II/1/15). He died on 7 September 1867, aged 91, having been twice married.

72 W. Farquhar, "Memorandum relating to the Settlement of Malacca", October 1816, BCMS: HA/II/12.

73 The Malay and Dutch texts of Farquhar's treaty with Riau, 19 August 1818, are printed in E. Netscher, "De Nederlanders in Djohor en Siak 1602 tot 1865. Historische Beschrijving", *VBG*, vol. XXXV (1870), pp. 252–4. The English version is recorded in BL: Bengal Secret Consultations, vol. 305, and W.G. Maxwell and W.S. Gibson, *Treaties and Engagements affecting the Malay States and Borneo* (London, 1924), pp. 115–16. Farquhar's report of his proceedings in drawing up the treaty of 2 September 1818 is in Van der Kemp, *BKI*, vol. 49 (1898), pp. 444–6.

74 Note 76.

75 Hastings to Secret Committee, 25 November 1818, BL: Secret Letters from Bengal (second series), vol. 1. Hastings also addressed a letter to the Chairman of the East India Company, James Pattison, on the following day: "The real extent of our dissatisfaction with Sir Stamford ... does not forbid our availing ourselves of his activity and intelligence. He was led away by a zeal which though not altogether discreet, was laudable under his conviction that time could not be spared for a reference to this Government. To withstand the injurious measures prosecuted by the Dutch appeared to him indispensable and he would have been right had the means existed of opposing their encroachment with effect. Possessing as they did a naval superiority ... it thence behoved us to counteract the insidious designs of our neighbours by a patient policy" (Private Letters of Hastings to Chairman, 1818–19, 26 November 1818, cited Philips, *East India Company*, pp. 230–1). Canning at the India Board saw Hastings's letter and warned

him that his ideas on the subject contrasted with those of the government. In a despatch dated 22 May 1819, the Secret Committee also expressed opposition to employing Raffles on any mission that would bring him into contact with the Dutch, and to "the extension in any degree to the Eastern islands of that system of subsidiary alliance which has prevailed, perhaps too widely, in India" (Boulger, *Raffles*, pp. 326–7).

76 Adam, Chief Secretary to Supreme Government, to Raffles, 28 November 1818, BL: Java Factory Records, vol. 71; Boulger, *Raffles*, pp. 298–301; Wurtzburg, *Raffles*, pp. 461–4.

77 Supreme Government to Farquhar, 28 November 1818, NAS: Singapore: Letters to Bencoolen, 1819–20, L10, fol. 14; Bengal Secret Consultations, vol. 305; *The Courier*, 19 May 1830; Cowan, *JMBRAS*, vol. XXIII, pt. 2 (1950), pp. 85–7; Wurtzburg, *Raffles*, p. 465. Farquhar appears to have been informed of Raffles's mission to the Eastward before he left Melaka, so one would suppose that when he arrived at Pinang he would have expected to accompany him on the mission. However, in *The Courier*, 19 May 1830, Farquhar states explicitly that when he arrived at Pinang he was "on [his] way to Europe", a statement confirmed in his "Memorial" of 1824: "Your Memorialist had obtained permission to be absent on a visit to Europe for three years, and on his return to Penang after the surrender of Malacca at the close of the year 1818 … he was making his arrangements for availing himself of this permission, when Sir S. Raffles arrived at Penang as Political Agent to the Governor-General" (Boulger, *Raffles*, p. 354). Lady Raffles, *Memoir*, pp. 376–7 confirms the fact that on Raffles's arrival at Pinang he found that Farquhar "had already engaged his passage to England, in a vessel which was to sail in a few days" but that he was "prevailed upon to alter his arrangements" after being given charge of the new settlement.

78 Wurtzburg, *Raffles*, pp. 458, 467. John Palmer was born in 1767, the son of Major (later Lieutenant-General) William Palmer, confidential secretary of Warren Hastings. He was head of the largest Agency House in Calcutta, Palmer & Co., which had extensive connections not only in India but also with many parts of South-East Asia, including Pinang and Java. Palmer showed considerable interest in these places and visited Borneo, Java, Bengkulu and, later, Singapore. He became involved with the plantation economy of Java during the 1820s and entered into negotiations with the Dutch authorities to advance loans sufficient to underwrite the colonial government's debts. After 1825 Palmer & Co. over-speculated in credit and trade and was seriously affected by the commercial crisis in England during 1825–6, which led to its bankruptcy in 1830, six years before Palmer's death. His manuscript letter-books are in the Bodleian Library, Oxford, and afford evidence of the large number of his correspondents, who included Raffles and Farquhar.

79 The Treaty concluded by Vice-Admiral J.C. Wolterbeek with Raja Jaafar in Riau on 27 November 1818 was signed on his flagship ZM *Tromp*, Netscher, *VBG*, vol. XXXV, pp. 254–7. An English version of the Treaty is in Bengal Secret Consultations, vol. 308.

80 Boulger, *Raffles*, pp. 301–2; Chief Secretary Government of Fort William to Raffles, 5 December 1818, BL: Java Factory Records, vol. 71; Wurtzburg, *Raffles*, pp. 465–6.

81 Raffles to Charlotte, Duchess of Somerset, 26 November 1818, BL: MSS.Eur. D.742.24.

CHAPTER IV

82 Raffles to Charlotte, Duchess of Somerset, 10 December 1818, BL: MSS.Eur. D.742.24.

83 Note 79; BCMS: HA/11/9/76d.

84 Government of Fort William to Prince of Wales Island, 28 November 1818, BL: Java Factory Records, vol. 71. John Alexander Bannerman was described at this time by Captain J.G.F. Crawford of the Bombay Marine survey ship *Investigator* as "a plain, old, little man, ruddy and hale" who, despite his age, at first sight "might be taken for a man of 45". He was, in fact, in his 60th year, having been born on 5 June 1759, the second son of the Revd. David Bannerman (1712–1810) and Janet (*née* Turing). He was appointed a Cadet on the Madras military establishment of the East India Company and sailed for India on 16 January 1777. He was gazetted Ensign in the Madras Native Infantry on 9 April 1778, Lieutenant on 8 January 1782, Captain on 6 August 1794, Major on 29 September 1798, and Lieutenant-Colonel on 17 June 1800, having taken part in the British capture of Sri Lanka from the Dutch four years earlier, and having also served in the Mysore War during 1799 (*East India Military Calendar* (London, 1826), vol. III, pp. 296–8). He returned to England in 1800 and retired from the army three years later. In January 1807 he entered Parliament for Bletchingly, but failed to gain re-election later that year. He was elected a Director of the East India Company in April 1808 and served for eight years before being appointed Governor of Prince of Wales Island following the death of William Petrie on 27 October 1816 (note 196). He arrived at Pinang on 24 November 1817 and assumed the government on landing. His Commission as Governor is printed in the *Prince of Wales Island Gazette*, 29 November 1817, and his letter to the Governor-General Lord Hastings on taking up his appointment is in the Bute Collection at Mount Stuart (HA/11/9/65). ⌑ It was this "plain, old, little man" with 42 years of service in the East India Company that Raffles encountered when he arrived at Pinang on 31 December 1818 with orders to establish a competing British settlement further south at the entrance of the Melaka Straits. Bannerman at first appeared to be supportive of Raffles's mission, but, according to William Jack, he was "a weak man, with violence of temper sufficient to commit any folly or absurdity" (Burkill, *JSBRAS*, no. 73 (1916), p. 158), and under the influence of his son-in-law, W.E. Phillips (note 192), he mounted strong opposition to Raffles's plans, employing every device in his armoury, including a refusal to send military reinforcements to Singapore, and making an extraordinary appeal to Farquhar to abandon his post as Resident and Commandant of Singapore in order

to avoid conflict with the Dutch (Minute by Bannerman, 14 March 1819; Bannerman to Farquhar, 16 March 1819; Farquhar to Bannerman, 3 April 1819, BL: Bengal Secret Consultations, vol. 308; Boulger, *Raffles*, pp. 317–18). For these actions, Bannerman was severely reprimanded by the Supreme Government in a despatch dated 8 April 1819 (Boulger, *Raffles*, pp. 324–5), prompting him to write to Raffles on 8 May: "I lose no time in acquainting you that I have just received dispatches from the Supreme Government relative to your occupation of Singapore, and in obedience to the order conveyed … I have now to offer you any aid in Troops, Transports or Stores you may require for your establishment at Singapore" (BL: Bengal Secret Consultations, vol. 309). He attempted to justify his actions in a letter to Hastings dated 18 May 1819: "I have received a lesson which shall teach me how I again presume to offer opinions as long as I live … I am sorry, my Lord, to have trespassed on your time but I have a whole life of character to defend and in this vindication I hope I have not borne harder than what is necessary on Sir S. Raffles and others. I have taken particular care to have here no personal controversy or cause of personal dispute with that gentleman" (Wurtzburg, *Raffles*, p. 517). He died less than three months later on the evening of 8 August 1819 from stomach cancer, and was succeeded by Phillips, despite Raffles's attempts to be appointed. ⁜ An obituary notice in the *Madras Courier* stated that Bannerman's mind "was endowed with every exalted sentiment, his heart filled with every amiable affection by which human nature is capable of being ennobled or adorned" (*Asiatic Journal*, vol. IX, no. 52 (March 1820), p. 312), and an inscription on a commemorative marble tablet in St. George's Church, Pinang, is equally effusive in praising his "Spotless Integrity and Unshaken Firmness of his Public Character, and of the Great Utility of his Public Life" (Harfield, *Christian Cemeteries of Penang & Perak*, pp. 49–50; J. and C. Bastin, "Some Old Penang Tombstones", *JMBRAS*, vol. XXXVII, pt. I, (1964), p. 127). Bannerman had eight children by Anne (*née* West) whom he married at Palamcotta, Madras, on 8 September 1789. He brought three of his daughters with him to Pinang, the eldest of whom married W.H. Phillips in 1818 (note 192). A contemporary portrait of Bannerman is reproduced in Arnold Wright, *Twentieth Century Impressions of British Malaya* (London, 1908), p. 23.

85 Bannerman to Raffles, 31 December 1818, enclos. in Bannerman to Hastings, 1 January 1819, BCMS: HA/11/9/76a,76b; BL: Bengal Secret Consultations, vol. 307; P.H. van der Kemp, "De Commissiën van den Schout-bij-Nacht C.J. Wolterbeek naar Malakka en Riouw in Juli-December 1818 en Februari-April 1820", *BKI*, vol. 51 (1900), pp. 1–100. Evidence of Bannerman's initial co-operation with Raffles is also afforded by the testimony of Captain J.G.F. Crawford of the Bombay Marine in his Diary (Wurtzburg, *Raffles*, p. 471). For Bannerman's subsequent opposition to Raffles's policy, see Boulger, *Raffles*, pp. 317–19, 321–3.

86 Bannerman to Hastings, 1 January 1819, BCMS: HA/11/9/76a. See also Cowan, *JMBRAS*, vol. XXIII, 2 (1950), pp. 87–8; Marks, *VKI*, vol. XXVII (1959), p. 33.

87 Raffles to Bannerman, 1 January 1819, BL: Bengal Secret Consultations, vol. 307. It is interesting that the Prince of Wales Island government suggested in an

earlier despatch to the Supreme Government dated 28 November 1818, which reflected Farquhar's views, the possible acquisition of the Karimun Islands if the Dutch established themselves at Riau, though "the expence of forming a Settlement on an uninhabited island would be enormous" (BL: Bengal Secret Consultations, vol. 305). Cowan (*JMBRAS*, vol. XXIII, pt. 2 (1950), pp. 80–2) gives a date of 19 September for this despatch. *Cf.* Marks, *VKI*, vol. XXVII (1959), p. 26.

88 Bannerman to Adam, 8 January 1819; Raffles to Bannerman, 4 January 1819, BL: Bengal Secret Consultations, vol. 307. In a private letter to Hastings dated 1 January 1819, Bannerman complained that Raffles regarded his mission to Aceh (note 103) as of "subordinate importance" (BCMS: HA/11/9/76a).

89 Bannerman to Raffles, 15 February 1819, BL: Bengal Secret Consultations, vol. 308; Wurtzburg, *Raffles*, p. 473; BCMS: HA/11/9/79.

90 Bannerman to Adam, 8 January 1819, BL: Bengal Secret Consultations, vol. 307. In a subsequent letter to Adam dated 16 February 1819, Bannerman set out clearly his difficulties in dealing with Raffles: "If under the conviction (which I feel) that he is violating his instructions I decline to afford him assistance, my conduct will be branded as proceeding from petty jealousy & private pique. – If on the other hand I afford him every support, I shall participate in the responsibility of all the mischief which I know will ensue, or I shall hereafter be condemned by the Supreme Gov^t. for aiding him in his quixotic schemes" (BCMS: HA/11/9/80).

91 Raffles to Marquess of Hastings, 8 January 1819, BCMS: HA/11/1/4.

92 Raffles had already briefly raised the subject of Russian influence in the Malay Archipelago in his paper, "Our Interests in the Eastern Archipelago", which he submitted to George Canning, President of the India Board of Control in 1817 (Boulger, *Raffles*, p. 272), and also in a despatch to the Secret Committee dated 5 August 1818 in which he reported that in 1815 Sultan Jauhar al-Alam Syah of Aceh (note 103) had written to the Emperor of Russia agreeing to a Russian settlement in his country on condition of receiving assistance in the maintenance of his authority. Raffles claimed that the Sultan's letter had been sent on a Russian ship but he was unaware if a reply had been received. He also reported rumours that a Dutch mission from Batavia was about to set out for Aceh, and that the Dutch might have been the medium of communication between Russia and Aceh (BL: Sumatra Factory Records, vol. 47; Lee Kam Hing, *The Sultanate of Aceh: Relations with the British 1760–1824* (Kuala Lumpur, 1995), pp. 275, 309, n. 6). But the view he expressed in his letter of 8 January 1819 to Hastings rests on what he claims was recent intelligence from Batavia and Melaka which suggested that the Dutch had the support of Russia in their plans, and he repeats these rumours in a letter to the Supreme Government of the same date to justify the urgency of acquiring a station commanding the entrance of the Straits of Melaka (BL: Bengal Secret Consultations, vol. 307). It might be thought that Raffles was obsessive in his fears of Russian intervention, but the Governor of Prince of Wales, Colonel Bannerman, also wrote of a possible Russian threat to British interests due to the presence of Russian ships in the region (Lee, *Aceh*,

p. 263). The rumours concerning Russian activities at this time stemmed from the publication in English in 1813 and 1814 of the accounts first published in German and Russian respectively by Admiral Adam Johann von Krusenstern (1770–1846) and Captain Urey Lisiansky (1773–1837) of their voyage round the world in 1803–6 in the ships *Nadeshda* and *Neva* by order of Tsar Alexander I. Raffles's reference in his letter to Hastings of the Sandwich Islands obviously draws on these accounts, especially that of Lisiansky's *A Voyage Round the World in the Years 1803, 4, 5 & 6* (London, 1814), which devotes the whole of Chapter VII, pp. 115–37 to an "Account of the Sandwich Islands". This, however, in no way explains the statement made by Raffles in an undated letter addressed to "My dear Sir" (probably a newspaper editor) which he wrote in Calcutta late in 1818 on the threat to the "safety of our Indian Empire". The threat he considered came not only from the alarming increase in Dutch naval power in Asia, but also from Russia, which "is said to have it in contemplation to open a direct communication with Batavia, and an Agent is now in Bengal securing [?] connections to support a Russian Estab^l. in the Eastern Islands". The letter (in a private collection) ends with the surprising statement that Raffles had obtained this information on that day directly from the man himself. Who this Russian agent was can only be a matter of conjecture, but the views he expressed in conversation with Raffles were sufficient to add to his already exaggerated fears of a Russian threat to British power in the region.

93 Raffles to Adam, 16 January 1819, BL: Bengal Secret Consultations, vol. 307.

94 In 1818 Captain John Monckton Coombs was authorised by the Prince of Wales Island government to undertake a political mission to Aceh (Lee Kam Hing, *The Sultanate of Aceh*, pp. 258–69), and in the following year he was appointed as joint agent with Raffles to settle a difficult dynastic dispute in the sultanate (note 103). Coombs was on the Madras military establishment, having been appointed a Cadet in 1800, and subsequently Lieutenant in the 1st Regiment of Madras Native Infantry. He briefly commanded the honorary escort attached to the Rajah of Mysore, and in 1802 he served as Acting Adjutant of his corps. In 1806 he was promoted Captain and in the following year he became Deputy Judge Advocate to the Mysore division of the army. He was subsequently appointed Assistant Quarter-Master-General and afterwards officiated as Judge Advocate at several courts-martial. In 1812 he was appointed aide-de-camp and private secretary to Governor William Petrie (note 196), and shortly after his arrival at Pinang he was appointed Town-Major, a position he held under the three following governors. In August 1825, after his promotion to Lieutenant-Colonel, he returned to Europe on sick-leave, after receiving a public tribute for his services from the Governor in Council of the Prince of Wales Island (*East India Military Calendar*, vol. III, pp. 34–9).

95 Raffles to Marsden, "Nearchus, off the Sandheads, Dec. 12, 1818": "My attention is principally turned to Johore, and you must not be surprised if my next letter to you is dated from the site of the ancient city of Singapura" (Lady Raffles, *Memoir*, p. 374).

96 Raffles to Adam, 16 January 1819, BL: Bengal Secret Consultations, vol. 307.

97 Captain Daniel Ross (1780–1840) and Captain John Garritt Fisher Crawford (died 1843), hydrographers of the Bombay Marine, were instructed in 1818 to extend their survey of the China Seas to the southern region of the Melaka Straits where they were engaged by Raffles, against their wishes, to survey the Karimun Islands and Singapore (Raffles to Bannerman, 4 January 1819, BL: Bengal Secret Consultations, vol. 307). Ross had first been ordered to survey the southern coast of China in 1806 and from his base at Macau he had conducted surveys of the Paracels, with part of the coast of Cochin China and Palawan. Later, after his survey of Singapore, he conducted surveys of the coast of Tenasserim, the Mergui Archipelago and Rangoon. At the conclusion of the surveys of the China Seas in 1820, during which his health was affected, he was presented with £1,500 by the Court of Directors of the East India Company in recognition of his fourteen years' service (Van der Kemp, *BKI*, vol. 49 (1898), p. 460). His charts were published by the East India Company and those of the Melaka Straits were incorporated into the charts of Captain James Horsburgh, including the South China Sea, with Taiwan, Borneo, the Malay Peninsula, and Singapore, which was published in London in 1846 in two sheets, each measuring 26⅝ × 39⅝ inches. Ross's original chart of Singapore was printed in the *Calcutta Journal* on 1 May 1819 (note 127). He was the first to introduce scientific methods into marine surveys and was accordingly designated "The Father of the Indian Surveys". In 1823 he succeeded to the post of Marine Surveyor-General at Calcutta, but ten years later he resigned his appointment and returned to Bombay, where he was appointed Master Attendant and also President of the Bombay Geographical Society. (C.R. Low, *History of the Indian Navy (1613–1863)* (London, 1877), vol. I, pp. 394–6, 402 and *passim*; L.S. Dawson, *Memoirs of Hydrography* (Eastbourne, c. 1885), pt. I, pp. 43–4; Wurtzburg, *Raffles*, pp. 469–70). ❡ Captain Crawford of the Bombay Marine survey ship *Investigator* was junior to Ross but later rose to the rank of Captain Superintendent in the Indian Navy (Low, *Indian Navy*, vol. II, pp. 10–11). The "Diary" he kept during the 1818–19 survey of the south-eastern China Sea and the Straits of Melaka contains the most important eye-witness account of the founding of Singapore. It was formerly in the possession of Mr. C.R. Wylie of Kirribilli, Adelaide, and the sections on Singapore were edited by Flinders Barr and published in the *Straits Times* in five instalments on 4, 11, 18, 25 October and 1 November 1937. The "Diary" seems to have disappeared, but long extracts from it were made by C.E. Wurtzburg for his biography of Raffles and these are now in the Cambridge University Library. Another important survival of the surveys made by Ross and Crawford is an album of drawings made by Lieutenant John Michael Houghton on board the *Discovery* of China coastal scenes and a single topographical view of Singapore made at the time of Raffles's founding of the settlement. The album ("Views of the China Seas and Macao taken during Capt. D. Ross' Surveys by M. Houghton 1815–19") was listed as item 21 in the 2010 Catalogue of the London bookseller, Bernard J. Shapero, for £stg.100,000. Other coastal profiles of Singapore possibly by Houghton are reproduced in *JMBRAS*, vol. 83, pt. 1 (2010), pp. 1–7.

CHAPTER V

98 Raffles to Farquhar, 16 January 1819, BL: Bengal Secret Consultations, vol. 307.

99 Lieutenant Francis Crossley (1786–1846) of the Bengal European Regiment (to which he had been appointed Ensign on 4 January 1807) was on sick-leave from his Regiment when he was engaged by Raffles as his Acting Secretary on the mission to Singapore. At the ceremony of the signing of the Treaty by Sultan Hussain Muhammad and Temenggong Abdul Rahman on 6 February 1819, he was given the task of reading out aloud in English to those assembled the various clauses of the Treaty. On the same day, he was appointed by Raffles to take charge of the Pay Department, Stores and Commissariat at Singapore, but he soon fell out with Farquhar over building rights in the island, which is perhaps not surprising given William Jack's description of him as a "hard head", "who to good abilities joins a bluntness more than usual even among Englishmen" (Burkill, *JSBRAS*, no. 73 (1916), p. 187). Raffles expressed "the greatest confidence" in his "discernment & judgement", and he wrote favourably of him in paragraph 38 of his despatch to the Supreme Government dated 13 February 1819 (above). But he was not confirmed in his post at Singapore (Raffles to Holt Mackenzie, 15 January 1823, BL: Sumatra Factory Records, vol. 49), so he proceeded on furlough to England where, according to Lady Raffles, in a letter to her sister-in-law, Mary Ann Flint, in October 1824, he had married prior to returning to India – "his wife I am told is no beauty but I have no doubt [he] has made a good choice" (BL: MSS.Eur.D.742.15). He was on furlough in China and England in 1833.

100 Samuel Garling was born on 11 October 1793 in Middlesex, the son of John Frederick Garling (1750–1835) and Caroline (*née* Burr). He was appointed a Writer on the Fort Marlborough establishment in 1809 and arrived at Bengkulu on 11 November of the following year. In February 1811 he became Second Assistant to the Resident at Seluma and Manna, and on 7 November 1814 Assistant in charge of the Out-Residency of Krui, before being promoted ten days later to the position of Resident. He was appointed Accountant to the Fort Marlborough government in January 1818 and served in the secretariat at Bengkulu under Raffles, who gave him the additional post of Malay Translator, which he soon resigned. After being in charge of stores at Singapore early in 1819 he was employed on a mission to Pahang (Van der Kemp, *BKI*, vol. 49 (1898), p. 479), contrary to the views of the Supreme Government (ibid., pp. 498–9), but in September he was ordered by Raffles to return to Bengkulu (NAS: L10, fol. 79), at which time a deficiency was found in the stores he managed (NAS: L10, fols. 89–90). In 1822 he was appointed temporary Secretary to the Fort Marlborough government and he acted as Resident between 19 February and 18 July 1823 during Raffles's absence in Singapore. He later served as Resident Councillor at Melaka and Pinang between 1826 and 1849, and acted briefly as Governor. His important collection of Malay manuscripts was destroyed in a fire on a ship anchored in Pinang harbour, the loss being compared at the time with Raffles's similar losses in the ship *Fame* in 1824. Garling retired to England after 46

years' service and died at Tunbridge Wells, Kent, on 6 December 1857. His elder brother Frederick Garling (1779–1819) also served on the East India Company's establishment at Fort Marlborough, becoming Resident at Seluma and a participant in Salmond's mission to Palembang in 1818 (note 42).

101 Francis James Bernard was appointed provisionally by Raffles as Master Attendant and Marine Storekeeper in February 1819. He was born in London in about 1796, the son of Charles Bernard, Comptroller of Taxes for the City of London. In 1810 he volunteered to join the Bengal Pilot Service but was discharged in March 1815. He married Farquhar's eldest daughter, Esther (1796–1838), at Calcutta on 26 June 1818, and was given command of Farquhar's privately owned brig *Ganges*, which played an important part in the events connected with the founding of Singapore. His eldest child, Agnes Maria, was born in Singapore on 25 July 1819, the first recorded birth in the settlement. He was superseded as Master Attendant at Singapore by Raffles's brother-in-law, William Flint, R.N. (1781–1828) (note 214), on 24 April 1820, but in the same year he was placed in charge of the police department, initially without regular pay, but later on a fixed monthly salary of 150 Spanish dollars (Gibson-Hill, *JMBRAS*, vol. XXXIII, pt. 1 (1960), pp. 5–16). In 1824 he helped to establish Singapore's first newspaper, *The Singapore Chronicle* (Gibson-Hill, *JMBRAS*, vol. XXVI, pt. 1 (1953), pp. 175–99), but soon relinquished his interest in the paper. In 1827 Bernard deserted Esther and engaged in trading activities in Java and eastern Indonesia, where in 1840 he met the future Rajah of Sarawak, James Brooke, who described him as "a gentleman of intelligence", an opinion not shared by Raffles, who regarded him as a "low character". Bernard appears to have died at Batavia on 19 December 1843.

102 Henry Ralfe (1791–1869) was Lieutenant in the Bengal Regiment of Artillery and not the gunnery officer of the *Nearchus* as stated by Wurtzburg, *Raffles*, p. 483. He was appointed by Raffles as Assistant Engineer at Singapore in charge of the ordnance and military stores on 7 February 1819 (NAS: L10, fol. 2) on a monthly salary of 200 Spanish dollars., and in that capacity he had the greatest difficulty in providing for the supply of tents and other equipment due to the "very limited supply of stores with which we were furnished from Prince of Wales Island on our first coming here" (NAS: L10, fols. 419–20). As the officer commanding the artillery he was responsible for raising the first defence works on the island as well as the battery on the knoll (later known as Scandal Point) covering the beach between the mouths of the Bras Basah and Singapore rivers. He first became acquainted with Raffles in Java where he was Lieutenant-Fireworker with a Detachment of Bengal Artillery stationed at Weltevreden. In 1812 he accompanied the punitive expedition against Palembang under Colonel Robert Rollo Gillespie, and after its capture he was appointed Commandant of artillery and Commissary of ordnance on the island of Bangka. In January 1813 he returned to Java and was appointed to command the artillery at Banten in west Java. In March 1815 he proceeded to Europe because of ill health and returned to Bengal in 1818, being appointed in November of that year to command a detachment of artillery

at Bengkulu. He remained in his post at Singapore until November 1821 when he was allowed to return to Bengal on account of ill health, and a few months later he proceeded to England. He was particularly solicitous to the needs of Captain Thomas Otho Travers and his family when the latter was waiting in Singapore to replace Farquhar as Resident and Commandant, being described by Travers at the time as "our kind and worthy friend Ralfe" (*Journal*, p. 150). He was described in similar terms by Lady Raffles when he was staying at Cheltenham in October 1824, as "warm hearted as ever", having by then, as she informed her sister-in-law, Mary Ann Flint, become "quite cured of his passion for Mrs. T[ravers]" (BL: MSS.Eur.D.742.15). He served at Prince of Wales Island between 1826–8 as Military Secretary and aide-de-camp to the Governor and returned to England on furlough in 1828. H.F. Pearson, *People of Early Singapore* (London, 1955), pp. 27–33 contains a somewhat imaginative account of him.

103 The long-standing conflict between Sultan Jauhar al-Alam Syah and elements of the Panglima sagis (chiefs), *orang kaya* and *ulubalang* for control of the sultanate of Aceh, which resulted in the dethronement of the established ruler in 1814, and the brief succession of Syed Hussein, the leading Asian merchant in Pinang, and then of his son, Syed Abdullah, as Sultan Syarif Saif al-Alam Syah, is examined in Lee Kam Hing, *The Sultanate of Aceh: Relations with the British 1760–1824* (Kuala Lumpur, 1995). The divided but largely supportive opinion in government and commercial circles in Pinang in favour of Sultan Saif al-Alam Syah came into conflict with Raffles's long-standing friendship with Sultan Jauhar al-Alam Syah and his firm belief in the desirability of supporting legitimate Asian rulers. His appointment as senior agent to Captain John Monckton Coombs (note 94) in the mission to Aceh further alienated opinion in Pinang, and especially offended the Governor, Colonel John Alexander Bannerman (note 84), who considered that Coombs by his experience of Acehnese affairs should have had seniority. The Treaty concluded by Raffles and Coombs on 22 April 1819 recognised the legitimacy of Sultan Jauhar al-Alam Syah as ruler of Aceh and the removal of Saif al-Alam and his family to Pinang with the compensatory payment of a pension or annuity. The rights of free trade to the ports of Aceh, the regularisation of duties at those ports, and the possible appointment of a British accredited agent to Aceh, were also provided for in the Treaty.

104 Burkill, *JSBRAS*, no. 73 (1916), pp. 156–7. On Jack, see note 169.

105 Raffles to Bannerman, 18 January 1819, MSA: HA/11/1/6; BL: Bengal Secret Consultations, vol. 307.

106 "Diary of Capt. J.G.F. Crawford", *Straits Times*, 11 October, 1937; Wurtzburg, *Raffles*, p. 483; Van der Kemp, *BKI*, vol. 49 (1898), p. 407; Wurtzburg, *Raffles*, p. 483.

107 Crawford, "Diary", *Straits Times*, 11 October 1937; Wurtzburg, *Raffles*, p. 483.

108 "The Memorial of William Farquhar …", Boulger, *Raffles*, p. 354.

109 H.T. H[aughton], "Landing of Raffles in Singapore. By An Eye-Witness", *JSBRAS*, no. 10 (1882), pp. 285–6; Wurtzburg, *Raffles*, p. 484.

110 Enclosure in Prince of Wales Island to Supreme Government, February 1819, BL: Bengal Secret Consultations, vol. 308.

111 Maxwell and Gibson, *Treaties and Engagements*, pp. 116–17. Raffles was unaware at the time that Temenggong Abdul Rahman, although not a signatory to the Dutch Treaty with Riau of 27 November 1818 (note 79), had given his consent to it.

112 Note 116.

113 Crawford, "Diary", *Straits Times*, 11 October 1937; Haughton, *JSBRAS*, no. 10 (1882), p. 286.

114 The Portuguese captured Johor Lama on 15 August 1587. See I.A. Macgregor, "Johore Lama in the Sixteenth Century", *JMBRAS*, vol. XXVIII, pt. 2 (1955), pp. 103–15.

115 Raffles to Marsden, 31 January 1819, Lady Raffles, *Memoir*, p. 376.

116 Farquhar to Raffles, 2 February 1819, BL: Bengal Secret Consultations, vol. 308. An account of Farquhar's reception at Riau is recorded in Crawford's "Diary", *Straits Times*, 11 October 1937, 18 October 1937, and in Raja Ali Haji ibn Ahmad, *The Precious Gift (Tuhfat al-Nafis)*, (transl.) Virginia Matheson and Barbara Watson Andaya (Kuala Lumpur, 1982), pp. 226–7.

117 BL: Bengal Secret Consultations, vol. 308; Maxwell and Gibson, *Treaties and Engagements*, pp. 117–19; Braddell, *Journal of the Indian Archipelago*, vol. VII (1853), pp. 331–2.

118 See C.H. Wake, "Raffles and the Rajas: The Founding of Singapore in Malayan and British Colonial History", *JMBRAS*, vol. XLVIII, pt. 1, pp. 47–73, and Kwa Chong Guan, "Why did Tengku Hussein sign the 1819 Treaty with Stamford Raffles?", *Malays/Muslims in Singapore: Selected Readings in History 1819–1965*, (ed.) Khoo Kay Kim *et al.* (Singapore, 2006), pp. 1–35.

119 The correspondence is printed in R. Braddell, *Journal of the Indian Archipelago*, vol. IX (1855), pp. 444–6; *Notes and Queries*, (ed.) W.E. Maxwell, Straits Branch Royal Asiatic Society (Singapore, 1887), pp. 104–13; C.B. Buckley, *An Anecdotal history of Old Times in Singapore* (Singapore, 1902), vol. I, pp. 50–1; Kwa Chong Guan, *Malays/Muslims in Singapore*, pp. 11–17. The letter of Temenggong Abdul Rahman to Adriaan Koek, senior member of the Dutch Council at Melaka, dated 16 February 1819 (in which he states that he and Tengku Hussain were "powerless to say anything" against the British occupation of Singapore and that "we in no way separate ourselves from the Dutch") was written to afford a measure of protection against any future difficulties with the Dutch, who naturally attempted to exploit it in the "Paper War" with the British. Farquhar, when he learned of the correspondence, obtained from Temenggong Abdul Rahman a "signed statement" in which he admitted that although such a letter had been written to Koek, "my motive for so writing arose solely from the apprehension of bringing on me the vengeance of the Dutch at some future period – But I here call God and his Prophet to witness that the English established themselves at Singapore with my free will and consent; and that from the arrival of the Honourable Sir Stamford Raffles no troops or effects were landed, or anything executed but with the free accord of myself and of the

Sultan of Johor". This statement was also signed by the Sultan (Farquhar to Raffles, 1 March 1819, BL: Bengal Secret Consultations, vol. 308; Boulger, *Raffles*, p. 315; Buckley, *An Anecdotal history of Old Times in Singapore*, vol. I, p. 52).

120 Raffles to Farquhar, 6 February 1819, NAS: Singapore: Letters to Bencoolen, 1819–20, L10, fols. 2–10; BL: Bengal Secret Consultations, vol. 308; Braddell, *Journal of the Indian Archipelago*, vol. VII (1853), pp. 325–31; Buckley, *Anecdotal History of Old Times in Singapore*, vol. I, pp. 41–4; Wurtzburg, *Raffles*, pp. 495–500.

121 Raffles to Young, 12 January 1819, BCMS: HA/11/1/5, Appendix I. Young was as rabid a hater of the Dutch as Raffles, as he confirmed in a letter to Hastings dated 15 February 1819: "I hate the Dutch very cordially – particularly the Colonial Dutchman & most particularly the Oriental Colonial Dutchman" (BCMS: HA/11/9/23). He added, for good measure, that he "despised the little Scotch 'Invasion' now called a Government at P.W. Island", but, with remarkable prescience, he considered Raffles's "transactions as likely to turn out of equal political importance in the Eyes of England & of Europe".

122 Raffles to Young, 12 February 1819, BCMS: HA/11/1/7.

CHAPTER VI

123 Raffles to Adam, 13 February 1819, BL: Bengal Secret Consultations, vol. 308.

124 Maxwell and Gibson, *Treaties and Engagements*, pp. 116–17.

125 Farquhar to Raffles, 2 February 1819, BL: Bengal Secret Consultations, vol. 308.

126 Maxwell and Gibson, *Treaties and Engagements*, pp. 117–19.

127 Captain Ross's Survey of the Harbour of Singapore is presumably the same or similar to the "Plan of Singapore Harbour February 1819" printed in the *Calcutta Journal* on 1 May 1819, and reproduced in Bastin, *Letters and Books of Sir Stamford Raffles*, p. 254, or the variant "Plan" reproduced in Langdon and Kwa Chong Guan, *JMBRAS*, vol. 83, pt. 1 (2010), p. 3. Ross's report on the Singapore Harbour dated 7 February 1819 is in NAS: L10, fols. 19–21. It is interesting that the Master Attendant, F.J. Bernard (note 101), in forwarding a copy of the report to Farquhar on 16 February 1819, noted certain points with regard to depths of water to be drawn by the ships and the necessity of erecting cautionary buoys (NAS: L10, fol. 19). The *Calcutta Journal* of 19 March 1819 contains a report on Raffles's founding of Singapore, which, with a mis-dated reference to 4 February 1819, was subsequently published in *The Times* in London on 7 September 1819 (Van der Kemp, *BKI*, vol. 49 (1898), pp. 471–2).

128 This Sketch "on a larger Scale" is not enclosed in the despatch in the British Library.

129 Note 102.

130 Note 99.

131 Note 127.

132 Raffles to Hastings, 15 February 1819, BCMS: HA/11/1/8.

CHAPTER VII

133 This "Sketch of the Harbour of Singapore" is not recorded in the Bute Collection at Mount Stuart.

134 The Anglo-Dutch negotiations, which led to the Treaty of London in 1824 and the recognition of Singapore as a British possession, are detailed in Marks, *VKI*, vol. XXVII (1959); P.H. van der Kemp, "De Geschiedenis van het Londensch Tractaat van 17 Maart 1824", *BKI*, vol. 56 (1904), pp. 1–244.

135 Note 85.

136 Raffles had taken the precaution of ordering the troops returning to India from service at Bengkulu to be available "for the purpose of garrisoning any post occupied by us in the states of Rhio, Lingen and Johore". He therefore suggested that they should return to Calcutta via the Straits of Sunda instead of by the northerly route (note 171). The order, which was issued by Raffles while off the Sandheads (Lady Raffles, *Memoir*, p. 374), and therefore technically within the jurisdiction of the Supreme Government, resulted in his being severely reprimanded. See Van der Kemp, *BKI*, vol. 49 (1898), pp. 406, 454–6; Boulger, *Raffles*, pp. 305–6.

137 The design of the Blockhouse based on Hastings's extensive military experience is not extant. What was eventually erected in Singapore was the work of Lieutenant Henry Ralfe of the Bengal Regiment of Artillery (note 102).

138 Note 99.

139 This seems to be a fair appraisal of Farquhar's character, which accounts for his waywardness in the administration of Singapore and his future conflict with Raffles.

140 Sultan Jauhar al-Alam Syah (note 103).

141 Raffles to Adam, 16 February 1819, BCMS: HA/II/I/9.

142 The future political control of Singapore became the essential issue of contention between Raffles and the Pinang authorities with Bannerman maintaining in his despatches to Bengal that the new settlement of Singapore should be placed under the authority of Prince of Wales Island government.

143 David Skene Napier was the son of Macvey Napier (1776–1847), librarian to the Writers of the Signet in Edinburgh, editor of the *Edinburgh Review*, and the first Professor of Conveyancing in the University of Edinburgh, in which capacity he arranged for the conferment by the University of the Honorary degree of LL.D. on Raffles. David Napier arrived at Singapore in 1819 from Calcutta, where he had been introduced to Raffles by John Adam (note 70). In the following year Farquhar provisionally appointed him to take charge of the police, but Raffles refused to confirm the appointment (NAS: L10, fols. 318, 326). He had apparently been promised an appointment on the Fort Marlborough establishment by Raffles, but instead he set up the mercantile firm Napier & Scott in 1820 with Charles Scott (of Scott's Hill). He and his wife Anna were the most intimate of Raffles and Lady Raffles's friends during their stay in Singapore between October 1822 and June 1823. Anna Napier died on 3 November

1826, leaving her husband inconsolable, though he married soon afterwards. The firm of Napier & Scott was dissolved in 1829, and Napier formed a new company, Napier & Co., with his elder brother, William Napier ("Puffing Billy"), the erstwhile friend of Rajah James Brooke. He died on 17 December 1836 in Peebleshire, Scotland.

144 Raffles to Young, 16 February 1819, BCMS: HA/II/I/10.

145 BL: Bengal Secret Consultations, vol. 308; Van der Kemp, *BKI*, vol. 49 (1898), pp. 456–7. Jan Samuel Timmerman Thijssen (1782–1823) was appointed with Vice-Admiral J.C. Wolterbeek to resume control of Melaka from the British Resident and Commandant, Major William Farquhar, in 1818, and he assumed the duties of Governor on 21 September of that year. He was the second husband of Gesina, eldest daughter of the former Governor, Abraham Couperus, who surrendered Melaka to the British in 1795. Timmerman Thijssen returned to Java before the British conquest of the island in 1811, and during the British period he was the most outspoken Anglophile among the Dutch citizens, praising in a speech at Batavia on 24 August 1814 the decision by the Governor-General Lord Minto to appoint an interim British administration under Raffles as "the most fortunate moment which Java had ever known" (*Java Government Gazette*, 27 August 1814). He went even further in lauding Lord Minto himself: "His Sovereign has conferred on him the dignity of an Earl, but the Almighty has recorded his name in the Annals of Philanthropy, and at a future period we may expect to behold our Noble Benefactor in the Mansions of Heaven, decorated with the emblems of sincerity and virtue" (ibid., 23 August 1814). ❦ Timmerman Thijssen and his wife entertained Raffles and his first wife, Olivia Mariamne, at their magnificent house at Kampong Melayu, near Meester Cornelis, which had originally belonged to Governor-General Willem Arnold Alting, and they named their daughter after her, Olivia Ambrosina Gesina Hendrina Timmerman Thijssen, with both Raffles and his wife acting as the child's godparents at her christening on 15 September 1813. In October of the previous year Timmerman Thijssen renamed his ship *Pekin* the *Governor Raffles*, and at a sumptuous entertainment on the occasion he expressed the wish that "the ship *Governor Raffles* might prove worthy in her future career of the honorable appellation she was that moment receiving" (ibid., 24 October 1812). He served as a Member of the Bench of Magistrates at Batavia during most of the British period while also engaged in commercial activities in the firm of Timmerman Thijssen & Westermann, which acted as agent of the Calcutta house of Palmer & Company (note 78). It was presumably because of this independent role, and because of his family connections, that he escaped censure by the Dutch Commissioners-General for being too close to the British administration, and he was accordingly appointed Governor of Melaka. Raffles's letter to him of 17 February 1819 informing him of the British occupation of Singapore was therefore received from a former friend, but one who was now an enemy of his nation. He had already heard of the British settlement at Singapore before the receipt of Raffles's letter and had informed Vice-Admiral Wolterbeek of the development in a letter dated 3 February 1819 (Van der Kemp, *BKI*, vol. 49 (1898), p. 458). He derived some comfort

from the fact that Colonel John Alexander Bannerman, the Governor of Prince of Wales Island (note 84), was also opposed to Raffles's new settlement, but his hopes of exploiting the situation foundered on the firm stand taken by Lord Hastings and the Supreme Government in Bengal. ❡ Munsyi Abdullah in his *Hikayat* gives a critical account of Timmerman Thijssen's administration of Melaka and states that "the Governor died with an evil reputation" (Hill, *JMBRAS*, vol. XXVIII, pt. 3 (1955), pp. 136, 298 n. 4), his death occurring at Melaka on 14 January 1823. John Anderson, during his mission to the east coast of Sumatra in 1823, found that the Malays at Siak also believed that Timmerman Thijssen's death was a "just punishment" for his unauthorised removal of the Johor regalia from Riau in 1822, and that he "was seized with a sort of stupor or delirium, the moment the regalia came into his possession" (*Mission to the East Coast of Sumatra in M.DCCC.XXIII* (London, 1826), p. 170). (See also D. Kraal, *JMBRAS*, vol. 83, pt. 1 (2010), pp. 9–26.) Interestingly, the Secret Committee of the East India Company regarded the seizure of the regalia as evincing an unnecessary degree of hostility by the Netherlands authorities when the matter was reported to London by the Supreme Government on 9 May 1823 (BL: Correspondence of the Board with the Secret Committee, 24 December 1823; BL: Bengal Secret Letters, vol. 20). For Timmerman Thijssen generally, see F. de Haan, "Personalia der Periode van het Engelsch Bestuur over Java 1811–1816", *BKI*, vol. 92 (1935), pp. 652–3); D. Meyer Timmerman Thijssen, *Twee gouverneurs en een equipagemeester: In en om Malakka 1778–1823* (Bilthoven, 1991); Brian Harrison, "Holding the Fort: Melaka under Two Flags 1795–1845", MBRAS Monograph no. 14 (1985).

146 Raffles to Charlotte, Duchess of Somerset, 22 February 1819, BL: MSS.Eur. D.742.24.

147 Raffles to Hastings, 28 February 1819, BCMS: HA/II/I/11. Farquhar had himself addressed two letters directly to the Supreme Government on 1 March 1819 and 8 April 1819 reporting on the progress of Singapore (Van der Kemp, *BKI*, vol. 49 (1898), p. 472). In the present letter to Hastings, Raffles tries to explain the embarrassing fact that the Dutch Treaty with Riau, concluded on 27 November 1818 (note 79), had been made with the knowledge of Temenggong Abdul Rahman.

148 Raffles to Dowdeswell, 5 May 1819, BCMS: HA/II/I/12.

149 Raffles's idea that the Equator should constitute the division between the British and Dutch spheres of influence in South-East Asia was shared by Hastings and others at the time. It was formally adopted as a principle in the Treaty of London of 1824 (note 134).

150 Raffles's reconciliation with the Prince of Wales Island authorities did not last long because of the continued disagreement about the legitimacy of Singapore as a British settlement and particularly about its future administration (note 142). On Raffles's mission to Aceh, see P.H. van der Kemp, "Raffles' Atjeh-Overeenkomst van 1819", *BKI*, vol. 51 (1900), pp. 159–240; Bastin, *Essays on Indonesian and Malayan History*, pp. 171–3.

151 Raffles to Hastings, 19 May 1819, BCMS: HA/11/1/13.

152 Bannerman wrote to Farquhar on 16 March 1819 stating that although it was not the province of the Prince of Wales government to furnish him with instructions, yet the documents he now enclosed from the Supreme Government (see note 1 above) "may serve to guide your judgement, how far you will be justified in shedding blood in the maintenance of your post", and that the HCS *Nearchus* and the brig *Ganges* would afford him with ample means for removing his party from Singapore, especially as "you must not expect any reinforcements from this Government till a reply is received from the Supreme Government" (BL: Bengal Secret Consultations, vol. 308; Boulger, *Raffles*, p. 318). On the following day, Bannerman wrote an extraordinary letter to the Governor of Melaka, Jan Samuel Timmerman Thijssen (note 145), on hearing rumours that a Dutch force was to be sent to seize the British post at Singapore, calling on him to maintain "the friendly relations subsisting between our respective countries" and asking him to recommend to the Netherlands government in Java the adoption of a policy of "moderation and goodwill" (BL: Bengal Secret Consultations, vol. 308; Boulger, *Raffles*, p. 316).

153 Note 162.

154 The Bishop of Calcutta was Dr. Thomas Fanshaw Middleton (1769–1822), who, within a few months of his arrival at Calcutta on 28 November 1815, began a long visitation of his diocese in southern and western India, during which period he visited Goa and Sri Lanka, and, later, Pinang, though the visit is not recorded in Bishop Eyre Chatterton's *A History of the Church of England in India since the Early Days of the East India Company* (London, 1924), pp. 123–9. He died at Calcutta in July 1822, his Episcopate lasting just seven years, during which time he established the Bishop's Mission College at Calcutta to educate members of the local clergy. He was succeeded by Bishop Reginald Heber (1783–1826), whose wife became friendly with Lady Raffles in England when as widows they were publishing with John Murray the biographies of their husbands.

CHAPTER VIII

155 Raffles to Farquhar, 25 June 1819, NAS: Singapore: Letters to Bencoolen, 1819–20, L 10, fols. 71–5; Braddell, *Journal of the Indian Archipelago*, vol. VII (1853), pp. 333–5; Buckley, *Anecdotal History of Singapore*, vol. I, pp. 56–8; Wurtzburg, *Raffles*, pp. 522–3.

156 Buckley, *Anecdotal History of Singapore*, vol. I, pp. 58–9; Maxwell and Gibson, *Treaties and Engagements*, pp. 120–1.

157 Raffles to Hastings, 8 June 1819, BCMS: HA/11/1/14.

158 John Tayler of the East India Agency House of Edmund Boehm & John Tayler, Bishopsgate Church-yard, and later New Bond Street and Broad Street, London. He appears to have joined the firm of Edmund Boehm of Bishopsgate Church-yard in about 1806 and was a friend of Raffles during the time he was a clerk at the India House,

London. He was his agent when he was in Pinang and Java, and was active on his behalf in 1814 when Major-General Robert Rollo Gillespie preferred charges against his administration in Java (notes 10, 13, 18). In a letter to the 2nd Earl of Minto (1782–1859) dated 27 August 1814, he referred to Raffles as his "very intimate Friend", and in another letter to Minto of 4 September 1814 he assured him that "from a long friendship I possess the Highest Confidence in His Honor & integrity" (NLScotland: Minto Papers Box 84/2). He was one of the sureties for the Bond and Covenant of £10,000 dated 10 October 1817 which Raffles signed when he was appointed Lieutenant-Governor of Fort Marlborough. Two years later the firm of Boehm & Tayler went bankrupt, as Raffles informed Colonel John Peter Addenbrooke (c.1753–1821) in a letter from Bengkulu dated 22 July 1820: "My Agents Messrs Boehm & Tayler have failed! but I am happy to say I have not suffered seriously" (John Murray Archives, NLScotland). Tayler died on 7 January 1820 at Twickenham, shortly after the collapse of his firm. A letter written to him by Raffles from Singapore on 9 June 1819 is printed in Appendix III.

159 Raffles states in a letter to Sir Robert Harry Inglis dated Singapore 12 June 1819: "I have just received letters from Lord Hastings, conveying his entire approval of my proceedings, and an assurance that he is too well aware of the importance of the position, and of the necessity of opposing the encroachments of the Dutch, not [to] be deeply interested in the success of the establishment", Lady Raffles, *Memoir*, p. 398.

160 Raffles to John Tayler, 9 June 1819, NLS: RRARE 959.5703 RAF.

161 Raffles to Charlotte, Duchess of Somerset, 11 June 1819, BL: MSS.Eur.D.742.24.

162 Pierre Diard (1795–1863), a pupil of the comparative anatomist, Baron Georges Cuvier (note 168), arrived at Calcutta in 1817, and was joined in May of the following year by Cuvier's step-son, Alfred Duvaucel (1793–1824). During the seven months prior to their meeting with Raffles they had been collecting in the region north of Calcutta and had despatched to the Museum d'Histoire Naturelle in Paris a number of important natural history subjects, including a description of the Malayan Tapir (*Tapirus indicus* Desmarest), based on a drawing of the animal sent from Melaka to the Asiatic Society, Calcutta, in 1816 by Major Farquhar, and on a living specimen sent from Bengkulu to the Barakpur Menagerie by the Acting Resident of Fort Marlborough, George John Siddons (*fl.* 1787–1838) in the same year. (See Lady Raffles, *Memoir*, pp. 373–4.) The two French naturalists accompanied Raffles to Pinang, Aceh, Singapore and Bengkulu, but later fell out with him for the reasons detailed in their correspondence printed in Lady Raffles, *Memoir*, pp. 702–23. Raffles dispossessed them of their large collections and shipped them to England, together with an accompanying "Descriptive Catalogue", which was published in the *Transactions of the Linnean Society of London*, vol. XIII (1821–3), pp. 239–74, 277–340. This established Raffles's reputation as a zoologist, which was further enhanced when he founded the Zoological Society of London in 1826, but the "Descriptive Catalogue" was mainly the work of his Secretary, Dr. William Jack (note 169).

163 Note 162.

164 Raffles to Hastings, 17 June 1819, BCMS: HA/11/1/15.

165 Raffles's engagement of the two French naturalists (note 162), dated 7 March 1819, is printed in Lady Raffles, *Memoir*, pp. 372–3.

166 The researches of the pioneering American naturalist, Dr. Thomas Horsfield (1773–1859), in Java were patronised by Raffles after the two men met at Surakarta in December 1811 shortly after the British conquest of the island. He later accompanied Raffles and Lady Raffles on their journey to central Sumatra, when Raffles concluded his treaties with the Minangkabau rulers (note 60). For an account of Horsfield's scientific activities in Java and Sumatra, see John Bastin, *The Natural History Researches of Dr Thomas Horsfield (1773–1859) First American Naturalist of Indonesia* (Oxford University Press, Singapore, 1990, reprinted Eastbourne, 2005).

167 See Ray Desmond, *The India Museum 1801–1879* (London, 1982), pp. 32–47.

168 Baron Georges Léopold Chrétien Frédéric Dagobert Cuvier (1769–1832), Professor of Natural History at the Collège de France, and later Chancellor of the University of Paris. He proposed the natural system of animal classification and established the sciences of palaeontology and comparative anatomy. Raffles knew of his work, and his international standing would have encouraged him to engage his step-son, Alfred Duvaucel, and his colleague, Pierre Diard, to undertake natural history research in west Sumatra (note 162).

169 William Jack was the most gifted of the naturalists associated with Raffles in Indonesia and, according to the American botanist, E.D. Merrill, "unquestionably one of the most able botanists ever to become associated with the tremendously rich and the then very little known flora of the Malay Peninsula and Archipelago". Jack was only 23 years of age when he first met Raffles in Calcutta and agreed to accompany him to Bengkulu as his secretary and personal physician, and he died less than four years later. Yet Merrill has affirmed that "no botanist who has concentrated on a study of the flora of the region has accomplished so much of lasting value in such a limited time". He was born on 29 January 1795 at King's College, Aberdeen, where his father, William Jack Sr. (1768–1854) was Regent. He was educated at the Grammar School in Aberdeen and later at King's College, where he graduated M.A. in 1811 at the age of 16. After passing the examination as Fellow of the Royal College of Surgeons in London in January 1812, he secured an appointment as Assistant Surgeon on the Bengal Medical Establishment of the East India Company and sailed for India on his eighteenth birthday. He was attached to the Regiment of Artillery at Dum Dum, and he served during the Nepal War in 1814–16. Raffles met him late in 1818 at the house of Nathaniel Wallich (1785–1854) at the Botanic Garden in Calcutta, and he engaged him to accompany him during his mission to the Eastward. He died at Bengkulu of pulmonary tuberculosis on 15 September 1822. See W.J. Hooker, "Description of Malayan Plants. By William Jack. With a brief Memoir of the Author, and Extracts from his Correspondence", *Companion to the Botanical Magazine*, vol. I (1835), pp. 121–47; Bastin, *JMBRAS*, vol. LXIII, pt. 2 (1990), pp. 1–25.

170 Raffles to Hastings, 17 June 1819, BCMS: HA/11/1/16. See note 136.

171 Captain Nicholas Manley of the 20th Regiment of Bengal Native Infantry was born at Cullompton, Devon, on 3 March 1784, the son of the Revd. Henry Chorley Manley. He was appointed Cadet in the military service of the East India Company in 1798, and gazetted Ensign on 19 December 1799, Lieutenant on 29 May 1800 and Captain on 12 April 1814. After serving in the Nepal War (1814–16) he was posted to Fort Marlborough, where he was Commandant of the Local Corps. When the three Companies of the 1st Battalion 20th Regiment of Bengal Native Infantry were relieved of duty and ordered to return to Bengal early in 1819, he followed Raffles's instructions to direct the troop transports *Cornwallis*, *James Scott*, and *Marchioness Wellesley* via the Straits of Sunda to the entrance of the Melaka Straits in the expectation that they might be needed to garrison a new settlement there, and subsequently Raffles's more explicit instructions of 3 March 1819 "to proceed without delay to the Port of Singapore where a British Station has been established, & where you will be pleased to consider yourself under the general orders of the Resident Major Farquhar" (NAS: L 10, fol. 93). The troops formed part of the garrison at Singapore during the period when the Prince of Wales Island government refused military support for the infant settlement (NAS: L 10, fols. 25–28, 33, 35), but they were ordered to proceed to Calcutta in June 1819 after reinforcements had arrived (NAS: L 10, fols. 62–3). Manley raised an additional company of the Fort Marlborough Local Corps in Calcutta in January 1821, and he was promoted Major on 26 August 1822. He died at Pinang on 23 May of the following year. (Harfield, *Christian Cemeteries of Penang & Perak*, p. 154). He was held in such esteem that when news of his death reached India a General Order was issued to the commanding officer at the cantonment at Barakpur for the Battalion to go into mourning. As indicated in his letter to Hastings, Raffles had a high opinion of him, as did his friend, Captain Thomas Otho Travers, who shared a bungalow with him at Barakpur on his first appointment in India, when Manley was Adjutant to the Regiment. Travers later succeeded him as Commandant of the troops at Fort Marlborough (Travers, *Journal*, pp. 118–19).

172 Raffles's official despatch to the Supreme Government of the same date, which reports in greater detail the rapid progress of Singapore (BL: Sumatra Factory Records, vol. 47), is printed in Van der Kemp, *BKI*, vol. 49 (1898), pp. 473–80.

173 Raffles to Hastings, 22 June 1819, BCMS: HA/11/1/17. Raffles's remarks on Borneo in his letter to Hastings can only be understood with reference to his official despatch to the Supreme Government of 22 June 1819 (note 172). It is interesting to note that the Directors of the East India Company, in a despatch to the Supreme Government of 8 August 1820, suggested that in the event of Singapore being abandoned, "you will not fail to communicate to us your opinion, whether there be any other spot, either on Borneo or more to the eastward at which it might be expedient to form a British establishment, by way either of naval station or of depôt" (Van der Kemp, *BKI*, vol. 49 (1898), p. 527).

174 This sketch of the defences of Singapore is not in the Bute Collection at Mount Stuart.

175 Raffles's proposals for the extension of British influence in Borneo at this time reflect his earlier attempts to form connections with the rulers of western Borneo when he was Lieutenant-Governor of Java. See John Bastin, "Raffles and British Policy in the Indian Archipelago, 1811–1816", *JMBRAS*, vol. XXVII, pt. 1 (1954), pp. 93–9; Graham Irwin, "Nineteenth-Century Borneo A Study in Diplomatic Rivalry", *VKI*, vol. XV (1955), pp. 12–34.

176 BCMS: HA/II/1/17. For a summary of Farquhar's negotiations with the Netherlands Commissioners at Melaka, see Van der Kemp, *BKI*, vol. 51 (1900), pp. 4–20; Marks, *VKI*, vol. XXVII (1959), pp. 22–5.

177 Raffles to Hastings, 20 August 1819, BCMS: HA/II/1/18.

178 On the retrocession of Padang to the Netherlands, see P.H. van der Kemp, "Sumatra's Westkust naar aanleiding van het Londensch Tractaat van 13 Augustus 1814", *BKI*, vol. 49 (1898), pp. 205–22, 238–69.

179 Note 60. The Board of Control under Canning wrote to the Court of Directors on 25 March 1819 with respect to Raffles's treaty arrangements with Minangkabau: "the conclusion without any instruction or authority whatever, by a Gentleman in charge of a subordinate commercial Factory, of a Treaty by which the British Government is bound in new engagements with a Native Prince of Sumatra, appears to the Board to afford a fresh proof of the inconvenience that cannot fail to result from the continuance at Bencoolen of a person, however individually respectable, who has in so many instances overstepped the limits of his duty" (BL: Letters from the Board to the Court, vol. 5; Wurtzburg, *Raffles*, p. 477).

180 On the settlement formed by Raffles at Semangka Bay in 1818, see pp. 15–17 above.

CHAPTER IX

181 Notes 45, 46.

182 Marks, *VKI*, vol. XXVII (1959), p. 29.

183 Letter dated 21 January 1819, BL: Letters from the Board to the Court, vol. 5, and letter dated 23 January 1819, BL: Letters from the Court to the Board, vol. 6.

184 *Asiatic Journal*, vol. VII, no. 39 (March 1819), pp. 325.

185 Lady Raffles, *Memoir*, p. 455.

186 BL: Sumatra Factory Records, vol. 41; Lady Raffles, *Memoir*, pp. 303–4; Boulger, *Raffles*, p. 267.

187 Raffles to Adam, 16 November 1818, BL: Bengal Secret Consultations, vol. 305; Wurtzburg, *Raffles*, pp. 456–7. Sir Robert Townsend Farquhar (1776–1830), son of Sir Walter Farquhar, Physician in Ordinary to the Prince of Wales, served as Assistant Resident of Banda, and Resident of Ambon between 1799 and 1802. He was Lieutenant-Governor of Prince of Wales Island during 1804–5, and following the capture of Mauritius by the British in 1810, he was appointed Governor and Commander-in-Chief

of the island. He served as a Member of Parliament for Newton and afterwards for Hythe between 1825 and 1830. See W.G. Miller, "Robert Farquhar in the Malay World", *JMBRAS*, vol. LI, pt. 2 (1978), pp. 123–38.

188 BL: MSS.Eur.D.742.20.

189 BL: MSS.Eur.D.742.20.

190 BCMS: HA/11/9/25. In a despatch to Raffles dated 7 January 1819, the Secretary of the East India Company, Joseph Dart, with the approval of the Board of Control, and after discussions by the Secret Committee, stated: "When the Court ... signified to you their desire to receive early and constant information of the proceedings of the Dutch and other European Nations, and that you had their authority in the event of any intelligence appearing to be of a nature to require secrecy, to address your Letters to the Secret Committee, it was not the Court's intention (nor was it indeed within their competence) to take the correspondence upon those subjects out of the ordinary course, or to interfere with the relation in which the Residency of Bencoolen is placed ... towards the Supreme Government ... The Court never ... intended that you should entertain a correspondence with the Secret Committee distinct from that which ... you maintain with the Supreme Government ... it certainly never occurred to those by whom the Instructions were drawn that any subordinate officer in the service of the Company (by whatever designation distinguished) could suppose himself to be authorized to maintain a direct correspondence with the Court of Directors, and to look for direct instructions from them on his local concerns passing by the Supreme Government of India ... In consequence of the general tenor of your Letters, I am commanded to convey to you the desire of the Court that you carefully abstain from any communication with the Dutch authorities, or with any of the Native States, which may, in any way, pledge the British Government, without distinct authority to that effect from ... Fort William" (BL: Sumatra Factory Records, vol. 41).

191 It is interesting to note that on the day Canning wrote this letter to Hastings, Raffles was concluding his preliminary Agreement with Temenggong Abdul Rahman for the establishment of a trading factory on the island of Singapore. On Canning and his part in the retention of Singapore, see note 33.

CHAPTER X

192 William Edward Phillips (1769–1850) went to India as a Cadet and in 1791, under the auspices and patronage of Lord Cornwallis, he joined H.M.'s 74th Regiment, rising to the rank of Captain. He was appointed Fort Adjutant of Bangalore and Assistant in the Military Auditor-General's office at Fort William before being invalided out of the army. In 1800 he was appointed by Marquess Wellesley as Secretary to the Lieutenant-Governor of Prince of Wales Island, Sir George Leith, and he served in the same capacity under Leith's successor, Sir Robert Townsend Farquhar (note 187), on whose departure he was left in charge of the government for some 18 months.

With the establishment of the Presidency government of Prince of Wales Island in 1805 Phillips was appointed Collector of Customs and Land Revenue on a salary of $6,000 per annum, the same as that paid to Raffles as Assistant Secretary. While continuing to act as Collector of Customs and Land Revenue, and also as Magistrate, he gained a temporary seat in the Council in 1806 and this was regularised in April of the following year, after the death of Governor Phillip Dundas. On grounds of seniority Phillips became third member of the Prince of Wales Island Council when Charles Andrew Bruce became Governor in March 1810, and although Raffles was appointed Lieutenant-Governor of Java and its Dependencies in the following year, Phillips continued to have seniority in service over him, acting as Governor of Prince of Wales Island on five occasions before being given the substantive post on 4 June 1820, following a direct personal appeal to Hastings in a letter dated 10 August 1819 (BCMS: HA/11/9/84a). Phillips enclosed in this letter to Hastings a copy of a "Memorial" he had addressed to the Court of Directors of the East India Company on 24 March 1819 as "a timely appeal" because Raffles, "during his late Residence at this Settlement, has avowed his expectation of succeeding to the Government of this Residency" (BCMS: HA/11/9/84c). ℭ The long-standing enmity between Phillips and Raffles went back to the beginning of the Presidency government in 1805, and is attested by Raffles in a letter to John Leyden (1775–1811) of 15 December 1810 in which he states that Phillips had "a most rancorous hatred" of him (BL: Raffles-Minto Collection, vol. 3, fol. 177v). And, indeed, Phillips in his "Memorial" to the Court of Directors stated that "in the event of Sir Stamford Raffles obtaining the appointment he desires, your Honble Court will permit me to retire to my Native Land". As a member of Council and son-in-law of the Governor, John Alexander Bannerman (note 84), Phillips was able to wield considerable influence in opposing Raffles's plans to establish a British settlement at Singapore. Dr. William Jack complained to Nathaniel Wallich in Bengal in January 1819 that Phillips was "an artful designing character, utterly devoid of principle, who is the prime mover of all mischief, without appearing as a principal, and who does not care to what extremities he urges the other while he himself remains secure from the consequences" (Burkill, *JSBRAS*, no. 73 (1916), p. 158). This, of course, reflected the opinion of Raffles, who at a welcoming dinner given for him and Lady Raffles at Pinang by Bannerman on 31 December 1818, remarked that although Phillips was "a worthy good fellow", he did not possess capacities sufficient to set the Thames on fire (Wurtzburg, *Raffles*, p. 471). Considering that this was said in front of Phillips's father-in-law, it can hardly be rated as the most sensitive of remarks, Phillips having married Bannerman's eldest daughter, Janet, in a double wedding ceremony on 30 July 1818, when his niece Jane, daughter of the Revd. James Patrick Bannerman, was also married to Lieutenant Henry Burney of the 20th Regiment of Bengal Native Infantry, Military Secretary and Acting Town Major of Pinang. The insensitivity of Raffles's remark was compounded by the fact that Phillips's sister-in-law, Mrs. Henry Burney, was also present at the dinner. ℭ Phillips occupied the post of Governor of Prince of Wales Island until 30 August 1824, when he retired to England with his wife, who bore him a total of 10 children, two of whom died at Pinang. Phillips was presented with a gold cup and a farewell address by the European inhabitants of Pinang (*Asiatic Journal*, vol. XX, no. 115 (July 1825), pp. 93–5), and he received a similar address from the Sultan of Kedah, to which he replied (ibid., vol. XIX, no. 113 (May 1825), p. 708). Before Phillips's tenure of the post of Governor, no one holding the appointment from the time of the Presidency Government in 1805 had lived to return to his native land. Phillips proved a notable exception, as he lived for 24 years in retirement in England until 1850, when he died in London at the age of 80. It must be said that the criticism of Phillips by Raffles and his supporters does less than justice to him. Ridley considered him "an able man" with a good understanding of the land revenue system of Pinang, and he ascribed to him the origin of the Ayer Hitam gardens in Pinang (*JSBRAS*, no. 25 (1894), pp. 165–6). His building of Suffolk House was perhaps his most notable achievement in Pinang. A collection of family papers relating to Phillips and Bannerman (note 84) was placed on permanent loan at the Royal Commonwealth Society in 1983, and these papers were later deposited in the Cambridge University Library, where also will be found in the C.E. Wurtzburg Collection of Raffles Miscellaneous Papers, vol. 5, a two-page typescript relating to Phillips taken from the family Bible. I have not had access to these materials for this note.

193 Travers, *Journal*, p. 135. See also Raffles to Sir Robert Harry Inglis, 12 June 1819: "… it was conceived that whenever Colonel Bannerman might vacate Penang, my succession to that government would be the means of uniting all our interests" (Lady Raffles, *Memoir*, p. 396). On Raffles's expectations of succeeding to the post of Governor of Prince of Wales Island, see his letter to John Tayler dated 9 June 1819 in Appendix III.

194 Raffles to Hastings, 29 September 1818, BCMS: HA/II/I/19.

195 John James Erskine, formerly a Mate of an East Indiaman, was appointed Marine Assistant and Store Keeper in the Presidency Government of Prince of Wales Island in 1805. He was granted a commission of 2 per cent on all goods handled, with the guarantee that his income would never be less than Sp.$6,000 a year, which was the same as Raffles's salary. While still retaining the position of Warehouse Keeper he later became a member of the Pinang Council. On his retirement in March 1822 he was presented with a farewell Address by the Chinese inhabitants of the island (*Asiatic Journal*, vol. XVI, no. 92 (August 1823), pp. 201–2), by whom he was known as the "Second King of Penang". Mt. Erskine was named after him. In 1809 he built one of the new bungalows on North Beach (Northam) Road adjoining Raffles's house, "Runnymede". He supported Raffles against Bannerman and Phillips in the deliberations of the Prince of Wales Island government in 1819, and he was regarded by Raffles as a friend, which is therefore curious that Raffles should refer to him in such a way in his letter to Hastings. Raffles nominated him as an Honorary Member of the Agricultural Society of Sumatra when it was established at Bengkulu in 1820 (note 261).

196 William Petrie, Governor of Prince of Wales Island, was born in 1747 and died at Pinang on 27 October 1816, aged 68 years. Before succeeding Archibald Seton

as Governor, he had been a member of the Council of Fort St. George for more than 18 years and had twice served as Governor. He wrote a pamphlet, *A Statement of Facts delivered to the right Honourable Lord Minto … on his Late Arrival at Madras* (London, 1810), containing an account of the mutiny of military officers at Madras in the previous year. On his departure from Madras in September 1812 to take up his appointment at Pinang, he was presented with a farewell Address by the "native inhabitants" (*Java Government Gazette*, 19 December 1812). Raffles wrote to him from Java outlining his policy for the suppression of piracy in the Malay Archipelago and proposing the stationing of British agents at the principal ports (Lady Raffles, *Memoir*, p. 227), but Petrie characterised his ideas as "chimerical and impracticable" in a Minute dated 23 July 1814 in which he also expressed his conviction that Raffles's "repeated attempts to interfere with the Malay States to the Eastward of the Straits of Malacca … will prove very prejudicial to our Eastern trade" (Wurtzburg, *Raffles*, p. 321). His monument in the old Protestant Cemetery in Pinang records the fact that he had been in the service of the East India Company for more than 51 years, and it was in recognition of this fact that the Directors of the Company granted a pension to his widow, who did not live long to enjoy it as she died at her house in Baker Street, London, on 20 March 1819. She was not, in fact, legally his widow, but seemingly a Eurasian woman named Mrs. Warren, the daughter of an officer in the French army at Pondicherry. She bore him five children, and in a poignant letter to Lord Hastings from Pinang on 2 October 1815 (BCMS: HA/II/9/51), a year before his death, Petrie pleaded with him to place under his protection "an amiable Lady, who from motives of the purest and most disinterested affection and attachment followed me to this unhappy Island". Hastings appears to have exerted himself in the matter and supported her claim for a pension. Petrie was a Fellow of the Royal Society and had corresponded from Madras in May 1787 with Sir Joseph Banks on the subject of Indian snakes (Dawson, ed., *The Banks Letters*, p. 668).

197 On Raffles's reforms in west Sumatra, see Bastin, *Raffles in Java and Sumatra*, pp. 72–134.

198 John Lyon Phipps died at Pinang on 22 July 1819, aged 30 years, leaving a widow and infant child "to bewail their early loss". Her name was Marianne Bailey and Phipps had married her two years earlier. He had been appointed to the Prince of Wales Island government in 1804 and had served as Assistant in the office of Paymaster before becoming Accountant and Auditor. He was one of the witnesses to the marriage of Raffles's sister, Leonora, to Dr. Billlington Loftie.

199 Travers, *Journal*, p. 135.

200 Raffles to the Marquess of Hastings, 5 October 1819, BCMS: HA/II/1/20.

201 Lady Raffles, *Memoir*, pp. 412–15.

202 Thomas Colclough Watson, the son of Colonel Jonas Watson, aide-de-camp to the Duke of Kent, and Harriett (*née* Colclough), was born on 20 June 1787, probably in Canada. He was posted to the Bengal European Regiment in 1804 and served in the Second Maratha War (1803–6). He was Honorary aide-de-camp to Raffles in Java and

recorded an account of their visit to the central districts of the island in 1814 (*Asiatic Journal*, vol. I, 1816), pp. 124–9, 233–5). He remained in Java after the end of British rule and on 25 November 1818 arrived with his wife at Bengkulu only to find that Raffles was in Calcutta. As Watson was in possession of testimonials from the Duke of Kent he immediately proceeded to Bengal but found that his letters of recommendation were of no use in obtaining preferment from Lord Hastings. He returned to Bengkulu on 30 July 1819 and two months later accompanied Raffles in the brig *Favourite* to Calcutta where this time he was fortunate in obtaining charge of the Local Corps raised for service at Fort Marlborough. He arrived with his troops at Bengkulu in March 1820, but his relationship with Raffles soured and in June 1822 he was struck off the strength of the Fort Marlborough garrison for disrespect and sent to Bengal under arrest. No proceedings were instituted against him, and he resigned his command of the Fort Marlborough Local Corps on 23 December 1822. Raffles wrote to Thomas McQuoid (note 263) from Bengkulu on 8 January 1824 complaining that Watson and his other former aide-de-camp in Java, Captain Cathcart Methven of the 20th Regiment of Bengal Native Infantry (*JMBRAS*, vol. 54, pt. 2 (1981), p. 64, n. 203), were "stirring all the powers of their evil spirits to injure my reputation" (CUL: Add Ms 7386). Watson commanded the Cawnpore Infantry Levy until in May 1824 he transferred to the newly-raised 2nd Bengal European Regiment. He was appointed a Commissioner for the transfer of the British west Sumatran settlements to the Netherlands in accordance with the terms of the Treaty of London, but he arrived too late to take part in the proceedings. He was posted Major on 21 June 1826 and Lieutenant-Colonel on 3 November 1831. Two years previously, between 24 and 28 March 1829, he paid a visit to Captain Thomas Otho Travers at Leemount, near Cork in Ireland, Travers noting in his MS Journal that although Watson possessed "the very best of hearts" and was an "honorable" and "high principled man", his head was "not abounding in sound judgment", which led him "to get into scrapes and difficulties". After his return to India, Watson died at Dhaka on 30 April 1834 of cholera. A miniature portrait of him by Chinnery is reproduced in Conner, *Chinnery*, Plate 17, p. 98.

203 [William Jack], "Substance of a Report on the Condition of Society among the Native Population of Bencoolen and its immediate subordinates on the West Coast of Sumatra, October 1819", *Proceedings of the Agricultural Society, Established in Sumatra, 1820* (Baptist Mission Press, Bencoolen, 1821), vol. I, no. II, pp. 1–52.

204 Hooker, *Companion to the Botanical Magazine*, vol. I (1835), pp. 132–3.

205 T.S. Raffles, *On the Advantage of Affording the Means of Education to the Inhabitants of the Further East* (Baptist Mission Press, Serampur, 1819), reproduced in facsimile in John Bastin, *The First Printing of Sir Stamford Raffles's Minute on the Establishment of a Malay College at Singapore* (Eastbourne, 1999).

206 T.S. Raffles, *On the Administration of the Eastern Islands* (London, 1824), reprinted in Lady Raffles, *Memoir*, Appendix, pp. 3–38.

207 Raffles to the Marquess of Hastings, 25 November 1819, BCMS: HA/II/I/21.

208 Phillips had already pre-empted this suggestion by Raffles in his "Memorial" to the Directors of the East India Company of 24 March 1819 in which he stated that "in the event of Sir Stamford Raffles obtaining the appointment he desires, your Honble Court will permit me to retire to my Native Land" (BCMS: HA/11/9/84c). See note 192.

209 Hastings to Raffles, 27 November 1819, Lady Raffles, *Memoir*, p. 420.

CHAPTER XI

210 Raffles to Charlotte, Duchess of Somerset, 27 December 1819, BL: MSS.Eur. D.742.24.

211 Raffles to Charlotte, Duchess of Somerset, "At Sea in the Bay of Bengal", 9 November 1819, BL: MSS.Eur.D.742.24.

212 Raffles to Charlotte, Duchess of Somerset, 27 December 1819, BL: MSS.Eur. D.742.24.

213 Lady Raffles, *Memoir*, p. 422.

214 Captain William Lawrence Flint, R.N., described by Raffles as "as good, and honest a fellow as ever lived", was born on 17 October 1781, the younger son of William Flint of Clackmannan in Scotland and Anne (*née* Mill). He entered the Royal Navy as a volunteer and was commissioned in April 1802. He was promoted Commander seven years later, on 1 March 1809, and reached post rank on 1 March 1811. His first command in September 1807 was in the Bay of Bengal in the sloop HMS *Rattlesnake* (16 guns), and he continued to sail in her until November 1809, though he was superseded in command by a superior officer on 7 July 1808. From February 1810 to March 1811 he commanded the hospital ship HMS *Wilhelmina* (32 guns) anchored in Pinang Roads until he was appointed to the command of the transport HMS *Teignmouth* prior to the British invasion of Java. While the ship was at Melaka he married on 2 May 1811 Raffles's sister, Mary Ann, widow of Quintin Dick Thompson, who died at Pinang in June 1809. He was appointed Prize Agent for the East India Company by the Governor-General Lord Minto after the landing of the British forces in Java, but the order was not recognised by the naval commander, Rear-Admiral Sir Robert Stopford (1768–1847). He was given several appointments by Raffles, including that of Superintendent of Forests in the island, but in October 1813 he sailed with his wife and child on the *Lord Eldon* for London to contest the loss of his appointment as Prize Agent. In this endeavour he was unsuccessful, and he returned to Java without his wife on 31 July 1815 on the *Isabella* (Scott) with Captain Thomas Otho Travers, who had gone to London with Raffles's answers to the Gillespie charges. Flint continued in his post as Superintendent of Teak Forests and for a time served as Resident of Rembang. In July 1817 he proceeded to Calcutta to pursue his claim for compensation as Prize Agent but again to no avail. He then sailed for London where on 14 June 1819 his claim was formally rejected by the Directors of the East India Company (Gibson-Hill, *JMBRAS*, vol. XXXIII, pt. 1 (1960), pp. 16–21; De Haan, *BKI*, vol. 92 (1935), pp. 544–7). He and his wife, with their

child, William Charles Raffles Flint, sailed in the private ship *Rochester* (D. Sutton) for Calcutta, where they arrived late in December 1819 to be greeted by Raffles, who took them back to Fort Marlborough in the *Indiana* (James Pearl). Leaving his wife and child at Bengkulu, Flint went first to Java to settle matters connected with his Serondol lands (De Haan, *BKI*, vol. 92 (1935), p. 546) and then to Singapore, where he arrived on 23 April 1820, apparently on board the schooner *Enterprize* (Richard Harris). He assumed the duties of Master Attendant and Storekeeper on the following day, dislodging Bernard in the process (Farquhar to Bernard, 24 April 1820, NAS: L 10, fol. 346). He soon fell out with Bernard's father-in-law, Major William Farquhar, the Resident and Commandant, which inevitably involved Raffles, who wrote to his sister from Bengkulu on 29 July 1822: "As you love & respect your Brother – for God's sake restrain Flint from committing himself with Farquhar – he has done so already & so seriously that I hardly know how to act – don't think of *yourselves* but of *me*" (BL: MSS.Eur.D.742.17). During Raffles and Lady Raffles's stay in Singapore in 1822–23 the Flints lived with them for a time in the bungalow Raffles built on the Hill. Flint and his wife remained in Singapore after Raffles's departure in June 1823, and in September 1828, in an attempt to recover his health, he took passage in the East Indiaman *William Fairlie* (T. Blair) for Macau, but he died on board on 3 October when the ship was off the coast of China. As he did not leave a Will, his wife was left virtually destitute, the sale of his little property in Singapore being taken up by Lady Raffles with A.L. Johnson and Alexander Guthrie on behalf of her sister-in-law (Gibson-Hill, *JMBRAS*, vol. XXXIII, pt. 1 (1960), pp. 31–2; Bastin, *Letters and Books of Sir Stamford Raffles*, pp. 402–3).

215 Robert Redman Hull was born at Belvidere, co. Down, on 12 September 1789. He was gazetted Cadet in the military service of the East India Company in 1804 and Ensign on 8 April 1806, two days after his arrival in India. He was promoted Lieutenant on 16 July 1807 and Brevet Captain on 1 January 1819. His health was affected by his service in the Third Maratha War (1817–19), and he was issued with a Sick Certificate, which enabled him to join Raffles and his sister on the voyage to Bengkulu on board the *Indiana* (James Pearl). Travers describes him in his *Journal*, p. 141 as "a very fine young man, and well deserving the high character given of him". He died at Bengkulu on 21 October 1820 after a severe illness of five days. Raffles reported his death to Hastings in a private letter dated 23 October 1820 (Appendix II). His Memorial at Bengkulu is illustrated in Alan Harfield, *Bencoolen: A History of the Honourable East India Company's Garrison on the West Coast of Sumatra (1685–1825)* (Barton-on-Sea, 1995), p. 483.

216 Raffles to Charlotte, Duchess of Somerset, "Off Sumatra", 12 February 1820, BL: MSS.Eur.D.742.24.

217 Travers, *Journal*, p. 140.

218 Raffles to Charlotte, Duchess of Somerset, 2 June 1820, BL: MSS.Eur.D.742.24. See note 261.

219 Raffles to Charlotte, Duchess of Somerset, 9 October 1820, BL: MSS.Eur. D.742.24.

220 Raffles to Charlotte, Duchess of Somerset, 18 April 1820, BL: MSS.Eur.D.742.24.

221 *The Times* (London), 2 February 1819. On Lord Lansdowne, see note 267.

222 Raffles to Lansdowne, 15 April 1820, NLS: RRARE 959.5703 RAF. All four let-ters of Raffles to Lord Lansdowne in the National Library Singapore are printed in Appendix IX.

223 Raffles to Lansdowne, 19 January 1821, NLS: RRARE 959.8022 RAF.

224 Raffles to Lansdowne, 1 March 1822, NLS: RRARE 959.5703 RAF. When Raffles finally left Bengkulu on the *Alexander* to assume direct responsibility for the admin-istration of Singapore in September 1822, he explained the reasons in a despatch to the Supreme Government dated 12 September 1822: "My presence at Singapore has for some time past been urgently required for the purpose of arranging and adjusting sev-eral questions which have arisen respecting the appropriation of ground and matters of Police, on which the Reports which I have received from the Resident have not enabled me to form a satisfactory judgement at a distance; and with reference to the state of my health and the necessity which may exist on that account, for relinquishing my public trusts after the close of the ensuing year, I feel a very natural desire to place the concerns of Singapore in such a train as may enable me to transfer the charge of the station with credit to myself and with every possible advantage to the public Interest" (BL: Sumatra Factory Records, vol. 49).

CHAPTER XII

225 Raffles to Holt Mackenzie, 24 March 1820, BL: Sumatra Factory Records, vol. 50; Raffles to Marquess of Hastings, 25 March 1820, BCMS: HA/II/I/22. Farquhar's wish to resign his post was subsequently withdrawn: "as the same urgent call no longer exists for my proceeding to Europe on furlough, I desire to postpone departure till [the] season of 1821–22" (Boulger, *Raffles*, p. 328).

226 Raffles to Hastings, 25 March 1820, BCMS: HA/II/I/22.

227 Note 101.

228 Note 225.

229 Raffles to Travers, 24 March 1820, NAS: Singapore: Letters to Bencoolen, 1819–20, L 10, fols. 303–12. Raffles's instructions to Travers were specific with regard to the reduced costs of the Singapore establishment and to the continuation of the princi-ples of free trade: "You will be particularly careful that no obstructions or restrictions exist in the way of the most perfect freedom of Trade[,] the convenience & facilities of the Port for shipping and Native Prows are points of the first importance and your constant attention is to be directed to them".

230 Travers, *Journal*, pp. 141 *et seq.*

231 Raffles to Farquhar, 20 March 1820, NAS: Singapore: Letters to Bencoolen, 1819–20, L 10, fols. 316–17.

232 Farquhar to Travers, 13 April 1820, NAS: Singapore: Letters to Bencoolen, 1819–20, L10, fols. 323.

233 Travers to Farquhar, 14 April 1820, NAS: Singapore: Letters to Bencoolen, 1819–20, L10, fols. 321–2.

234 Farquhar to Travers, 15 April 1820, NAS: Singapore: Letters to Bencoolen, 1819–20, L10, fol. 327.

235 Farquhar to Travers, 18 August 1820, NAS: Singapore: Letters to Bencoolen, 1819–20, L4, fols. 31–2.

236 Farquhar to Travers, 4 September 1820, NAS: Singapore: Letters to Bencoolen, 1819–20, L4, fols. 41–2.

237 NAS: Singapore: Letters to Bencoolen, 1819–20, L4, fols. 42–43, 43–4, 45, 47–52, 52–55, 56, 59–65, 66–7, 67–8, 68–71, 71–72, 101–2

238 Travers, *Journal*, p. 150. Captain Crawford, commander of the Bombay Marine survey ship *Investigator*, noted in his Diary on 12 December 1818 that Farquhar's family was varied and thoroughly "native" (*Straits Times*, 4 October 1937). See John Bastin, *William Farquhar: First Resident and Commandant of Singapore* (Eastbourne, 2005), pp. 45–8.

239 Raffles to Marquess of Hastings, 12 August 1820, BCMS: HA/11/1/23. Captain William Gordon Mackenzie was born in Edinburgh on 9 May 1785, the son of the Scottish novelist and essayist, Henry Mackenzie (1745–1831), and a brother of Holt Mackenzie, Secretary to the Supreme Government in Bengal. He arrived in India in 1802, having been appointed a Cadet in the military service of the East India Company the previous year. He took part in the British capture of the Cape of Good Hope from the Dutch in 1806 and four years later in the capture of Ambon, where he served as Third Assistant to the Resident between 1812 and 1816. He was appointed Second Assistant to the Resident of Fort Marlborough in October 1817, and in the same year he was promoted Captain. His provisional appointment as Resident of Singapore on 15 August 1820 (NAS: L4, fols. 75–7) was made by Raffles in the belief that he would be succeeding Captain Travers, but when Mackenzie learned in Singapore that Travers had been unable to dislodge Farquhar he returned to his old post at Bengkulu (NAS: L4, fols. 74–5, 77–8). He left for Calcutta early in 1823 because of ill health, but Raffles, who was expecting his early return to Bengkulu, wrote to the Supreme Government on 1 November 1823 stating that because of his own declining health, he intended "on the return of Captain W.G. Mackenzie first assistant at this Residency (now in Bengal on sick certificate) to proceed to the Cape of Good Hope, whence should no essential change take place for the better I shall eventually proceed to Europe" (NAS: L2: Raffles: Letters to London, 1822–26, fol. 60). This was followed by a letter dated 31 January 1824 in which he stated that as there had been no improvement in his health, and as he was feeling "perfectly unequal longer to carry on my public duties in the East", he had appointed John Prince, Resident at Tapanuli, to take provisional charge of Fort Marlborough pending the return of Mackenzie from Bengal (NAS: L2, fols. 61–3). Following the cession of the

British west Sumatran possessions to the Netherlands in 1825, in accordance with the terms of the Treaty of London of the previous year, Mackenzie served for a brief period as Resident of Melaka. He retired in 1840 and died on 20 July 1842.

240 Farquhar to Raffles, 16 April 1820, NAS: Singapore, Letters to Bencoolen, 1819–20, L10, fols. 329–32.

241 Raffles to Farquhar, 16 August 1820, NAS: Singapore, Letters to Bencoolen, 1820–21, L4, fols. 83–5.

CHAPTER XIII

242 Appendix II.

243 Note 215.

244 *Proceedings of the Agricultural Society, Established in Sumatra, 1820* (Baptist Mission Press, Bencoolen, 1821), vol. I (all printed). See note 261.

245 Resolution of the Supreme Government, 29 March 1823, Boulger, *Raffles*, p. 334.

246 Raffles to Charlotte, Duchess of Somerset, 26 November 1818, BL: MSS.Eur. D.742.24. Raffles was not alone in his criticism of Lord Hastings. After the period of Lord Cornwallis, who always took off his coat at dinner and allowed his guests to follow his example (Johnson, *Indian Field* Sports, pp. 220–1), and the relaxed and less formal manners adopted by Lord Minto during his time as Governor-General, the return by Lord Hastings to the elaborate ceremony adopted by Marquess Wellesley drew criticism from many in Calcutta, including General William Palmer, Military Secretary to Warren Hastings: "A Formality and stately Etiquette is introduced at the Government House not at all suited to the Habits and Manners of this Community. Whether Custom will reconcile it is doubtful; at present it rather disgusts. The Society is accumstom'd to an intercourse with its Governor of dignified affability on his part, and of respectful freedom on theirs, and will not, I apprehend, readily adopt the relations of Sovereign and Subjects. A Household Establishment is formed resembling that of Royalty – probably modelled on that of the Castle of Dublin. Be that as it may, the Transition is too abrupt to please". Sir Charles D'Oyly (1781–1845), the amateur artist of Anglo-Indian life, also complained: "I am sorry both Lord Moira and Lady Loudoun are so enveloped in formality and grandeur, for there is no approach to anything like intimacy … We have lately been accustomed to so little state that the present system assumes a character … of confinement and restriction wholly foreign from our idea of comfort" (Curzon, *British Government in India*, vol. I, pp. 213–14). Hastings justified his policy in a letter to Warren Hastings: "All appearances of Government had been strangely let down: and the consequences had a worse effect upon the minds of our own people than on the conceptions of the natives. Slight toward Government had become much the fashion and entailed many practical embarrassments" (ibid., vol. I, p. 214).

247 Raffles to Charlotte, Duchess of Somerset, 6 November 1823, BL: MSS.Eur. D.742.24. On Lord Amherst, see note 296.

248 The ship *Fame* was destroyed by fire off the coast of west Sumatra on the night of 2 February 1824.

249 Raffles to Marquess of Hastings, 9 October 1824, BCMS: HA/11/1/26.

250 Hastings to Raffles, 5 December 1824, BL: MSS.Eur.D.742.3.

251 Nelson, *Marquess of Hastings*, pp. 179 *et seq.*; Ross-of-Bladensburg, *Marquess of Hastings*, pp. 194–9; Douglas Kinnaird, *Remarks on the Volume of Hydrabad Papers, printed for the use of the East India Proprietors* (London, 1825).

252 Nelson, *Marquess of Hastings*, pp. 189–93.

253 *The Journal of Sir Walter Scott 1825–32 From the Original Manuscript at Abbotsford* (Edinburgh, 1891), p. 327. Boulger, *Raffles*, p. 221 perhaps characterises him better as "a man impregnated with the hereditary prejudices of his class, as well as those of his military profession".

APPENDIX

254 Note 103. Jeremiah Martin Johnson, Lieutenant-Colonel in the 15th Bengal Native Infantry, and Raffles's "very particular friend", being formerly "one of my right hands in Java", and presently "quite a Member of my family and … well acquainted with all my views and prospects" (BL: MSS.Eur.D.742.24). He had served as Deputy Paymaster General on the staff of Lieut.-General Sir Samuel Auchmuty (1756–1822) during the invasion of Java, and in 1813 was appointed Resident at Surakarta. He displayed an active interest in the early history of Java and discovered the temple ruins of Suku, 26 miles east of Surakarta, which are illustrated in Raffles's *History of Java* (London, 1817), vol. II, pp. 45 *et seq.* He took a large collection of Javanese antiquities with him when he left India for England on furlough in November 1818, having met Raffles in Calcutta that month. He did not set out for India again until 1822, when he visited Singapore. He returned to England in 1826 at the age of 58, "broken down woefully". He retired to St. Honore, but he was in London in April 1830 when Captain Thomas Otho Travers described him in his MS. Journal as "suffering poor fellow most severely". He died on 10 January 1833. There is a miniature portrait of him in the Victoria & Albert Museum, London.

255 Note 70.

256 Note 215.

257 Chanda in Nagpore, which was captured by the British on 20 April 1818.

258 Lieutenant John Watson Hull, a younger brother of Robert Redman Hull (note 215) and Lady Raffles, was born at Belvidere, co. Down, on 25 July 1792. He was appointed a Cadet on the Bengal military establishment of the East India Company in 1813, Ensign on 16 December 1814 (5 June 1815), when he was posted to the 1st Battalion of the 10th Regiment of Bengal Native Infantry, and Lieutenant on 30 October 1817. He served in the Third Maratha War (1817–19) and on 20 March 1819 he was ordered to proceed to Benares to join the 2nd Battalion of his Regiment. He did not immediately receive the staff appointment made vacant by the death of his brother, but he was eventually

appointed to Fort Marlborough on 11 September 1822, when Raffles and Lady Raffles were absent in Singapore. On 4 August 1823 Lady Raffles informed her sister-in-law, Mary Ann Flint, that on their return to Bengkulu in the previous month they had found him "quite well", with "every thing in such a delightful order owing to his exertions that Tom has had no annoyance, & there is nothing to do but prepare for England" (BL: MSS. Eur.D.742.15). On 20 December 1823 Raffles informed Peter Auber that he had entrusted Hull with the superintendence of the convicts at Bengkulu and that he felt "great pleasure and satisfaction in the general improvement of this class of people" (Lady Raffles, *Memoir*, p. 565). Raffles also placed him in charge of the Bengkulu spice plantations, and on 1 January 1824 he purchased on his own account part of the property at Panurunan belonging to the recently deceased Francis Salmond (note 42). Raffles intended to leave Hull at Bengkulu for a year or two after his own departure, because, as he explained in a letter to his sister, Mary Ann Flint, in January 1824, the additional time would enable him to "get enough money to buy a Wife in England whenever he goes" (BL: MSS. Eur.D.742.17). Hull appears to have had other ideas as he left Bengkulu later in 1824 after being transferred in May of that year to the 14th Regiment of Bengal Native Infantry. He was promoted Captain on 28 February 1827 and retired from the army on 13 April 1831, having earlier been appointed as one of three executors of Raffles's Will. On his return to England he married on 15 October 1835 Martha, daughter of John Younghusband, a linen merchant of Ballydrain in northern Ireland. Hull died at his house, Mount Ida, Dromore, co. Down, on 10 November 1842, his wife surviving him by nearly 35 years until her death in 31 January 1877.

259 Note 71.

260 Note 70.

261 Note 244. The Agricultural Society of Sumatra was established on 31 March 1820 at a meeting of the "principal Gentleman" of Bengkulu for the promotion and encouragement of agriculture in the British settlement. Raffles was appointed President and William Jack (note 169) Secretary. See Bastin, *Letters and Books of Sir Stamford Raffles*, p. 208, n. 125.

262 On John Tayler, see note 158.

263 Thomas McQuoid, one of Raffles's most intimate friends, was born in Ireland on 26 January 1779. After a brief period in Macau and Canton, he arrived at Pinang in November 1806, a year after the establishment of the Presidency Government. He served first as Police Magistrate and during 1808-9 as Sheriff in the Court of Judicature of Prince of Wales Island. He next proceeded to Ambon and then to Java, where in June 1812 he was appointed by Raffles as Malay Translator to the government on a monthly salary of Sp.$300. In the following month he was appointed Superintendent of the Coffee Culture and Landdrost (Resident) of Buitenzorg (Bogor) on a salary of Sp.$500, and in November 1812 he was made Chairman of the Commission for the sale of lands in the Priangan and Krawang. In the subsequent sales he purchased a landed estate in Krawang, inviting the charge of Colonel Gillespie that the purchase was in

"violation of the regulations of the island and the principles of policy by the union in the person of Mr. McQuoid of the office of Landdrost and Resident of several Regencies", a charge which Wurtzburg in his defence of Raffles found difficult to refute (*Raffles*, pp. 328–34; De Haan, *BKI*, vol. 92 (1935), pp. 605–8). McQuoid returned to England in 1817 and later that year married Elizabeth Frances Kirwan of an Anglo-Irish family from co. Galway, returning with her to Bengkulu on 25 November 1818 in the ship *Providence* (Travers, *Journal*, pp. 108 *et seq.*). At Batavia he became a partner in the firm of Skelton & Co., with J. Davidson and D.A. Fraser, and on the death of Philip Skelton in 1821 he founded the firm of McQuoid, Davidson & Co., to which Raffles entrusted some of his funds. As indicated in his letter to Tayler, Raffles hoped that McQuoid would establish himself at Singapore, and he accordingly allocated him a plot of land adjoining that of Captain Flint (note 214), but McQuoid remained at Batavia where he was able to provide hospitality for Lady Raffles when the ship *Hero of Malown* called there on 25 June 1823 and Raffles was prohibited by the Dutch authorities from landing (Lady Raffles, *Memoir*, pp. 551–4). McQuoid returned to England with his wife and two children in July 1825, news of the collapse of his firm following soon afterwards. He had been asked by Raffles to consign his funds to his London agents Fairlie, Bonham & Co., but McQuoid was unable to do so before the firm became insolvent, resulting, as Raffles told Travers, in a personal loss of £18,000. McQuoid's fortunes changed in 1828 when he was appointed Sheriff of New South Wales through the influence of Viscount Goderich (1782–1859), and he later acquired land in Australia, which he named Wanniassa after his estate in Java. But he was involved in numerous disputes and unerringly fell again on bad times, resulting in the taking of his own life in Sydney in October 1841. There is a substantial holding of materials on McQuoid's Australian career in the Mitchell Library, Sydney, including a silhouette of him (Portraits MS Room: A617), and there are nine holograph letters of Raffles to him in the Cambridge University Library (CUL: Add Ms 7386). An interesting paper by McQuoid, "Notes of Dutch History in the Archipelago, Extracted from the Records at Batavia under the Administration of Sir Stamford Raffles", is printed in *Journal of the Indian Archipelago*, vol. I, no. 2, n.s. (1856), pp. 141–93.

264 Raffles sailed directly from Singapore on 28 June 1819, arriving at Bengkulu 31 July 1819.

265 Note 192.

266 On Raffles's attempts to become Governor of Prince of Wales Island, see pp. 101–117.

267 Henry Petty-Fitzmaurice (1780–1863), 3rd Marquess of Lansdowne, was introduced to Raffles in 1817 by Charlotte, Duchess of Somerset, and he invited him to his country seat, Bowood House in Wiltshire, on 11 September of that year. Lansdowne had studied at Edinburgh University under Dugald Stewart, with contemporaries such as Brougham, Cockburn, Jeffrey, Horner, Sydney Smith and, probably, Raffles's friend John Leyden, who, like Lansdowne, was an active member of the Speculative Society.

Certainly, he later owned a copy of Leyden's *The Malay Annals* (London, 1817), edited by Raffles. Lansdowne proceeded from Edinburgh to Trinity College, Cambridge, where he graduated in 1801, and after a tour of the continent he entered Parliament as the member for Calne, delivering his maiden speech in 1804 on the Bank Restriction Act. He declined office under Pitt and allied himself with Fox and the Whigs, becoming Chancellor of the Exchequer in the Ministry of All the Talents in 1806 at the age of 25. He increased the property tax and introduced other financial measures to meet the cost of the war with Napoleon before resigning in 1807 on the Catholic Question. Two years later he succeeded to the title and entered the House of Lords, where he strongly supported the abolition of the slave trade and the liberation movements in South America. He also advocated the removal of the political disabilities of the Jews and similar relief for Catholics. He was President of the Council in the Whig administration of Lord Grey in 1830, and retained that office after Grey's resignation in 1834, later regaining it in Lord John Russell's ministry of 1846. He was regarded as the third most powerful speaker in the Lords, and his political career continued until 1861, although much affected by debilitating attacks of gout. He had a genuine love of tolerance and moderation, and was rightly described as "a very moderate whig". ⁋ Lansdowne renewed his relationship with Raffles after the latter's return to England in 1824, and wrote to him shortly after his arrival congratulating him on his escape from "fire and flood" in the ship *Fame*, and inviting him to Bowood. The Irish poet, Thomas Moore, a mutual friend of Lansdowne and Raffles, describes in his *Journal* a dinner at Bowood House on 29 October 1824, when Raffles gave an interesting account of the loss of the *Fame*, and next morning showed Moore "maps of his new settlement at Singapore", ascribing the opposition [of the Pinang government] to his "introduction of the principles of free trade so close to them" (Dowden (ed.), vol. 2, p. 772). Lansdowne declared himself a (qualified) free-trader in 1820, and he warned Raffles in a letter dated 11 April 1824 of rumours that the Government intended to introduce duties on the trade of Singapore and the other British settlements in the Straits (BL: MSS.Eur.D.742.3). He derived "much pleasure" from reading Raffles's *Statement of Services* (London, 1824), and he strongly supported his efforts to establish the Zoological Society of London, serving as Raffles's successor as President between 1827 and 1831. He was also a founder member of the Royal Asiatic Society. He wrote to Lady Raffles in 1830, after receiving a copy of the *Memoir* of her husband, "There have existed few men the record of whose lives & services could prove at once so interesting to their friends & so instructive to the publick, at a moment when they are called upon to consider the greatest questions of Eastern government & policy, when principles, the first elements as well as the practical application of which may be collected from Sir Thomas's views & actions" (BL: MSS.Eur.D.742.10)

268 Henry George, 2nd Earl of Carnarvon (1772–1833).

269 Raffles, T.S. [= W. Jack]. "Descriptive Catalogue of a Zoological Collection, made on account of the Honourable East India Company, in the Island of Sumatra and its Vicinity, under the Direction of Sir Thomas Stamford Raffles, Lieutenant-Governor

of Fort Marlborough; with additional Notices illustrative of the Natural History of those Countries", *Transactions of the Linnean Society of London*, vol. XIII (1821–3), pp. 239–74, 277–340. See note 162.

270 Note 28.

271 Note 178.

272 Van der Kemp, *BKI*, vol. 49 (1898), pp. 205–306; P.H. van der Kemp, "De Sluiting van het Londensch Tractaat van 13 Augustus 1814", *BKI*, vol. 47 (1897), pp. 239–339.

273 See pp. 93–7.

274 See P.H. van der Kemp, "Palembang en Banka in 1816–1820", *BKI*, vol. 51 (1900), pp. xii, 331–764.

275 Sultan Badr'uddin was removed as ruler by Raffles because of the part he played in the massacre of 63 members of the Dutch trading factory at Palembang in the previous year. See John Bastin, "Palembang in 1811 and 1812", *BKI*, vol. 109 (1953), pp. 300–20; vol. 110 (1954), pp. 64–88, reprinted in *Essays on Indonesian and Malayan History* (Singapore, 1961), pp. 53–91.

276 The cession of Banka was agreed by Article 1 of the Agreement between Colonel Robert Rollo Gillespie on behalf of the East India Company and the newly installed Sultan Ahmad Najmuddin of Palembang on 17 May 1812.

277 A reference to the dynastic conflict between Sultan Abulfath Abdulfatah and his son, Sultan Abunasr Abdulkahar, for control of the Banten sultanate in 1681–2, which resulted in the success of the latter aided by the Dutch East India Company, and the consequent expulsion of the English East India Company's factors from participation in the lucrative pepper trade of west Java and their establishment of an alternative trading settlement at Bengkulu (John Bastin, *The British in West Sumatra (1685–1825)* (Kuala Lumpur, 1965), pp. xi–xvi). It is interesting that Raffles knew of this incident, which fed his resentment and hostility towards the Dutch, especially when compounded by the even more notorious incident of the Ambon "massacre" of 1623. There is a reference to this subject in a brief statement in the *Calcutta Journal* of 5 February 1819, which was almost certainly written by him: "The [D]utch are at their old work again in the Indian Archipelago. They have closed all the eastern ports, obliged all the native vessels to carry [D]utch flags and [D]utch papers. They are taking possession of all the ports in Borneo, Sumatra etc. so as to form the same system of arbitrary exclusion which they exercised eve[n] before the last century, the barbarities of which, particularly those practised at Amboyna, can never been forgotten. It was here that in 1624 they first tortured and then murdered the English, thereby engrossing the whole trade of the island, and also that of Banda. The same hostility and determination to destroy all British trade in that quarter is now open and avowed. They do all in their power to lower and degrade the British name, to interrupt the operations of British merchants, residing at Batavia, and in short to harass and oppress them, wherever they present themselves" (Van der Kemp, *BKI*, vol. 51 (1900), pp. 37–8).

278 Note 206.

279 Note 205.

280 Lady Louisa Emma Fox-Strangeways, fifth daughter of Henry Thomas, 2ⁿᵈ Earl of Ilchester. She married Lord Lansdowne (note 267) on 30 March 1808 and had two sons by him. Raffles probably first met her when he stayed at Bowood on 11 September 1817. The poet Thomas Moore, who was a regular guest at Bowood, makes numerous comments on her in his *Journal* (ed. Dowden), *passim*. She died on 3 April 1851.

281 *Proceedings of the Agricultural Society, Established in Sumatra, 1820* (Baptist Mission Press, Bencoolen, 1821).

282 "Address by the President, the Hon. Sir T. Stamford Raffles, on the Institution of the [Agricultural] Society. 1820", ibid., pp. [i]–xii.

283 On Raffles's proposals for European colonisation of the Malay Archipelago, see John Bastin, "Sir Stamford Raffles's and John Crawfurd's Ideas of Colonizing the Malay Archipelago", *JMBRAS*, vol. XXVI, pt. 1 (1953), pp. 81–5.

284 Raffles obtained permission from the Supreme Government to send an official to the island of Nias "for the purpose of collecting information regarding the present state & resources of that Island", but due to his indisposition, Captain Francis Salmond (note 42) was sent in his place. The island had a large population of around 200,000, and attracted Raffles's interest because of its capability of providing additional supplies of rice for the population of the Bengkulu districts, but it was the "ravages" of the slave trade which in his view necessitated "the interference of some superior authority to prevent the ruin of the Country", especially considering the frequent appeals made to the Resident of Natal, and "the peculiar connection which had always subsisted between Pulo Neas and the Districts of the Coast, in furnishing labour & provisions". Therefore, "as the best and only means of providing for tranquillity and security of the Country, and, at the same time, of obtaining the fullest information of its real circumstances and resources", he appointed the Resident at Tapanuli, John Prince, and his secretary, Dr. William Jack (note 169) in September 1820 to visit and report on the island (Raffles to Supreme Government, 25 January 1821, BL: Sumatra Factory Records, vol. 48). (An extract from their report dated 31 December 1820 is included in Raffles's letter to Lord Lansdowne.) The treaties concluded by Prince and Jack with the rulers of Nias in December 1820 allowing for the stationing of a small British force in the island (BL: MSS.Eur.F.32: Raffles Collection, VII, 9; MSS.Eur.E.108: Raffles Collection, IX, 15) were condemned and annulled by the Supreme Government in a despatch dated 15 June 1821, which ordered Raffles to withdraw the establishment and to dissolve the entire British connection with Nias (BL: Bengal Public Consultations, vol. 29). See P.H. van der Kemp, "Raffles' betrekking met Nias in 1820–1821", *BKI*, vol. 52 (1901), pp. 584–603.

285 For an account of Raffles's relations with William Wilberforce, see Bastin, *Letters and Books of Sir Stamford Raffles*, pp. 232–3, 239–40 n. 47.

286 *Report [Relative to the Trade with the East Indies and China,] from The Select Committee of the House of Lords, appointed to inquire into the means of extending and*

securing the Foreign Trade of the Country, and to report to the House; together with the Minutes of Evidence taken in Sessions 1820 and 1821, before the said Committee:- 11 April 1821. Ordered, by The House of Commons, to be Printed 7 May 1821. Brought from The Lords 7 May 1821, pp. 420.

287 On Charles Grant, see note 25. Asked before the House of Lords Committee under the chairmanship of Lord Lansdowne if he had any opinion "as to the value of Sincapore as a mart for commerce in the East Indian islands", Grant replied: "Yes, I have turned my thoughts to that subject, which I think a very interesting one, in the relative situation of the British and Netherlands powers, in the eastern seas. I consider the position of Sincapore, and the occupancy of that place to be very important to the British interest; and I heartily wish it may be found consistent with the rights of the two nations that Great Britain may keep possession of it. I think it is remarkably well situated to be a commercial emporium in those seas; I have no doubt that it would very soon rise to great magnitude and importance; and if I may be permitted to allude to the conduct of any individuals on this subject, I must say that I think the whole proceedings of Sir Stamford Raffles have been marked with great intelligence and great zeal for the interests of his country". Asked further, almost certainly by Lord Lansdowne, if he was acquainted with "the increase of wealth, population, and trade, which has taken place at Sincapore, during the short period that has elapsed since the recent establishment there by Sir Stamford Raffles", Grant replied: "I have not in my recollection what Sir Stamford Raffles has stated upon that subject; but I remember well being struck with how much had been done in a very short time, both as to the resort of people as settlers, and of shipping for trade. It should be remembered, that it was quite an unoccupied spot when he took possession of it" (*Report*, pp. 194–5). ❧ This evidence by such an important spokesman for the East India Company must have had an enormous influence in uniting opinion in commercial and political circles in London in favour of retaining Singapore. Already in June 1820 Canning had asked the Secret Committee if the Company would "be prepared to undertake the administration of Singapore, if it is to be retained", to which the Secret Committee replied on 12 July 1820 that "upon full consideration it appears to us that an Establishment at Sincapore … is likely to prove of considerable advantage", and that "entertaining this opinion, we have no doubt that the East India Company will be prepared to undertake the Government of that settlement" (BL: Correspondence between the Secret Committee and the Board). Grant's laudatory reference to Raffles in the House of Lords *Report* would have pleased him, as would the citation in the Appendix (p. 383) of a portion of his letter to Lord Lansdowne of 15 April 1820 referring to Singapore and to the establishment of free ports. This section of the holograph letter in the possession of the National Library Singapore has been marked in ink by Lansdowne for the printer. Another Appendix to the *Report* (pp. 411–17) contains Raffles's letter to the Secret Committee of the Court of Directors dated 11 February 1814 relating to trade with Japan.

288 Apparently the same "Abstract" he sent to the Secretary of the East India Company three weeks earlier on 6 February 1822: "From this statement the Court will perceive that during the said period [January 1819 to 31 August 1821] no less than 2,889 vessels have entered at the Port, of which 383 were owned and commanded by Europeans, and 2,506 by Natives, and that their united tonnage has amounted to Tons 161,038" (BL: Sumatra Factory Records, vol. 49). This compilation was made from the monthly lists of arrival of ships, tonnage &c. for 1821 sent by Farquhar to Raffles and recorded in NAS: Singapore: Letters to Bencoolen June [=February] 1821 – Dec. 1821, L5.

289 The so-called "Embassy" to Thailand in 1821 was nothing more than a small unofficial trading venture headed by the Singapore merchant, John Morgan. He had studied law in Scotland, but after several voyages as a crew member of an East Indiaman he had settled at Batavia, where he started a retail business and, with his brother Alexander Morgan, subsequently became a partner in the local firm of Paton, Morgan & Co. (Campbell, *Java*, vol. I, p. 623). The brothers moved their operations to Singapore shortly after its foundation, and John Morgan obtained a grant of land on which to build a bungalow between High Street and the Singapore River, where in an adjoining godown he conducted his business. His relations with Farquhar were at first amicable, and as he had close trading connections with Thailand, he persuaded him to send a letter with a pair of mirrors and a sporting gun to Rama II (r. 1809–24), the subject being discussed in O. Frankfurter, "The Unofficial Mission of John Morgan, merchant, to Siam in 1821", *Journal of the Siam Society*, vol. XI, pt. 1 (1914), pp. 1–7. Morgan fell out with Farquhar after charging him in May 1822 of having acted as a commercial agent of the Singapore merchant, Claude Queiros, the matter dragging on into 1823 when Raffles became involved in the affair (Bastin, *JMBRAS*, vol. 54, pt. 2 (1981), 58, n. 164). Morgan was a strong supporter of Raffles's measures in Singapore, and his brother was one of those who framed the *Address of the Merchants of Singapore, on the occasion of the departure of the Honourable Sir T.S. Raffles in 1823* (Sumatran Mission Press, 1823). In July 1824, during John Crawfurd's period as Resident, Morgan was caught shipping 10,000 firearms and 20 cannons to Thailand along with cotton, woollen and other trading goods and he was for a time imprisoned. He appears to have left the settlement some three years later. During his time in Singapore he learned Malay from Munsyi Abdullah (*JMBRAS*, vol. XXVIII, pt. 3 (1955), p. 150), who was allowed to use his house to give instruction to other Singapore merchants (ibid., p. 175).

290 This report by Raffles on the commerce of the Eastern Seas was apparently lost in the fire on the ship *Fame* on 2 February 1824.

291 On John Crawfurd (1783–1868), see Bastin, *JMBRAS*, vol. 54, pt. 2 (1981), pp. 58–9 n. 166. For an account of his mission to Thailand, see his *Journal of an Embassy from the Governor-General of India to the Courts of Siam and Cochin China; Exhibiting a View of the Actual State of Those Kingdoms* (London, 1828).

292 On spice cultivation at Bengkulu, see Bastin, *The British in West Sumatra*, pp. xxxi–xl, 144 *et seq.*

293 Regulation III of 20 January 1823 provided "for the Establishment of a Provisional Magistracy and the Enforcement of a due and efficient Police at Singapore, with certain Provisions for the Administration of Justice in Cases of Emergency" (Lady Raffles, *Memoir*, Appendix, pp. 42–5). Regulation II "for the Port of Singapore", which was revised on 29 August 1823, stipulated that the "port of Singapore is a free port, and the trade thereof is open to ships and vessels of every nation free of duty, equally and alike to all" (ibid., Appendix, pp. 41–2).

294 Printing commenced in Singapore sometime after the arrival of the Revd. C. H. Thomsen of the London Missionary Society on 19 May 1822. He settled at Campong Gelam, where he built a house on land granted by Farquhar to his colleague, the Revd. William Milne (1785–1822). It was not until 17 January 1823 that Thomsen made formal application "to use a printing Press with which I may be able more effectively to pursue my labours as a Christian Missionary among the Malays" (NAS: Raffles: Letters from Singapore, 1823, no. 12, L12), permission being granted by Raffles six days later: "With regard to the establishment of a printing press in aid of your Labours the Lieutenant Governor gives his full sanction to the measure, and will be happy to assist the undertaking by the patronage and support of Government as far as circumstances admit" (NAS: Raffles: Letters to Singapore, 1823, no. 34, L17). Although it is possible that some printing occurred on the Mission Press in 1822 before the granting of formal permission by government, as suggested by C.K. Byrd (*Early Printing in the Straits Settlements 1806–1858* (Singapore, 1970), p. 14), the fact that Raffles wrote on the subject to Nathaniel Wallich on 5 January 1823 and to other correspondents in the same month (Bastin, *JMBRAS*, vol. 54, pt. 2 (1981), p. 17; Lady Raffles, *Memoir*, pp. 533, 536), including Lord Lansdowne, it would seem that "a small portable press, with Roman and Malay types" had newly arrived at this time. Thomsen himself wrote to the Directors of the London Missionary Society in February 1823: "We are now printing in English & Malay & have a small Type-Foundery & are doing bookbinding. Government has been pleased to honour our little Press … with printing of all public Documents both in English & Malay" (Byrd, *Early Printing in the Straits Settlements*, p. 13). ❧ Abdullah bin Abdul Kadir, who worked at the press, relates in his *Hikayat* how he cut types for the printing of Raffles's regulations (*JMBRAS*, vol. 28, pt. 3 (1955), pp. 165–6), the first of which would appear to have been the Proclamation of 1 January 1823, which stated that in future "all orders of Government … having a general application, will be printed for public information, and that translations thereof in the Malay language will be affixed in convenient stations, to be selected for the purpose". Also of the same date was "A Regulation for the Registry of Land at Singapore". In his account, Abdullah suggests (ibid., p. 166) that the regulations, which on Raffles's orders had to be printed urgently, included one relating to the prohibition of gambling, but this was only dealt with in Regulation No. IV of 1 May 1823. Raffles's regulations were printed in Singapore between 1 January and 6 June 1823, and were subsequently printed privately by him in 1824 on his return to England by Cox & Baylis, Great Queen Street, Lincoln's-Inn Fields, London, under

the title, *Singapore Local Laws and Institutions. 1823*, the text being reprinted in the Appendix to Lady Raffles, *Memoir*, in 1830 (Appendix, pp. 39–73). For a general discussion on early printing in Pinang, Melaka and Singapore, see L. O'Sullivan, "The London Missionary Society: A Written Record of Missionaries and Printing Presses in the Straits Settlements, 1815–1847", *JMBRAS*, vol. LVII, pt. 2 (1984), pp. 61–104, pp. 73 *et seq.*

295 A case of Raffles indulging in wishful thinking.

296 William Pitt (1773–1857), 2nd Baron Amherst and 1st Earl Amherst, former British Ambassador to China, and Governor-General of India between 1823 and 1828. Raffles had met him in August or September 1817 at Frogmore, at the command of Queen Charlotte, shortly after Amherst's return from China. As Governor-General, he wrote a personal letter to Raffles on 5 February 1824 in which he expressed his regret at Raffles's imminent departure from Bengkulu, as it "would have afforded me pleasure to have found myself in correspondence with you, and to have received advantage from those services which have already been so beneficially exerted in this part of our Empire". In a second letter dated 21 April 1824, he wrote of his "deep concern" at Raffles's losses in the ship *Fame*: "To the scientific world, and indeed I fear to all who take delight in the promotion of useful learning and in the improvement of their fellow creatures, the loss of your labours is irreparable. As for yourself, I trust that notwithstanding the present impaired state of your health, many years of an honorable and useful life may yet be spared to you, and that the means may be found of repairing the misfortune which no human foresight could have averted" (BL: MSS.Eur.D.742.3).

Sources

PRIMARY SOURCES

The Bute Collection at Mount Stuart, Isle of Bute, Scotland

Letter of Sir Stamford Raffles to the Marquess of Hastings,
    Bencoolen, 16 April 1818, HA/II/1/3, Leaves: 2 (245 × 203 mm)
Letter of the Marquess of Hastings to Sir Stamford Raffles,
    on the Gogra, 6 July 1818 (Draft), HA/II/5/2, Leaves: 2 (320 × 196 mm)
Letter of Sir Stamford Raffles to the Marquess of Hastings,
    Penang, 8 January 1819, HA/II/1/4, Leaves: 6 (252 × 202 mm)
Letter of Sir Stamford Raffles to Colonel James Young,
    Penang, 12 January 1819, HA/II/1/5, Leaves: 2 (252 × 203 mm)
Letter of Sir Stamford Raffles to the Hon. Colonel John Bannerman,
    Prince of Wales Island, 18 January 1819, HA/II/1/6, Leaves: 2 (252 × 202 mm)
Letter of Sir Stamford Raffles to Colonel James Young,
    Straits of Malacca, 12 February, 1819 HA/II/1/7, Leaves: 4 (255 × 200 mm)
Letter of Sir Stamford Raffles to the Marquess of Hastings,
    Penang, 15 February 1819, HA/II/1/8, Leaves: 6 (251 × 202 mm)
Letter of Sir Stamford Raffles to John Adam,
    Penang, 16 February 1819, HA/II/1/9, Leaves: 2 (251 × 205 mm)
Letter of Sir Stamford Raffles to Colonel James Young,
    Penang, 16 February 1819, HA/II/1/10, Leaves: 2 (251 × 202 mm)

Letter of Sir Stamford Raffles to the Marquess of Hastings,
 Penang, 28 February 1819, HA/11/1/11, Leaves: 4 (251 × 203 mm)
Letter of Sir Stamford Raffles to George Dowdeswell,
 Penang, 5 May 1819, HA/11/1/12, Leaves: 3 (254 × 201 mm)
Letter of Sir Stamford Raffles to the Marquess of Hastings,
 Penang, 19 May 1819, HA/11/1/13, Leaves: 4 (254 × 200 mm)
Letter of Sir Stamford Raffles to the Marquess of Hastings,
 Singapore, 8 June 1819, HA/11/1/14, Leaves: 2 (254 × 200 mm)
Letter of Sir Stamford Raffles to the Marquess of Hastings,
 Singapore, 17 June 1819, HA/11/1/15, Leaves: 4 (254 × 200 mm)
Letter of Sir Stamford Raffles to the Marquess of Hastings,
 Singapore, 17 June 1819, HA/11/1/16, Leaves: 2 (253 × 200 mm)
Letter of Sir Stamford Raffles to the Marquess of Hastings,
 Singapore, 22 June 1819, HA/11/1/17, Leaves: 8 (251 × 203 mm)
Letter of Major William Farquhar to Sir Stamford Raffles,
 Singapore, 22 June 1819, HA/11/1/17, Leaves: 2 (320 × 202 mm)
Letter of Sir Stamford Raffles to the Marquess of Hastings,
 Bencoolen, 20 August 1819, HA/11/1/18, Leaves: 4 (251 × 199 mm)
Letter of Sir Stamford Raffles to the Marquess of Hastings,
 Bencoolen, 29 September 1819, HA/11/1/19, Leaves: 4 (250 × 197 mm)
Letter of Sir Stamford Raffles to the Marquess of Hastings,
 Bencoolen, 5 October 1819, HA/11/1/20, Leaves: 2 (249 × 199 mm)
Letter of Sir Stamford Raffles to the Marquess of Hastings,
 Calcutta, 25 November 1819, HA/11/1/21, Leaves: 4 (247 × 198 mm)
Letter of Sir Stamford Raffles to the Marquess of Hastings,
 Bencoolen, 25 March 1820, HA/11/1/22, Leaves: 2 (250 × 198 mm)
Letter of Sir Stamford Raffles to the Marquess of Hastings,
 Bencoolen, 12 August 1820, HA/11/1/23, Leaves: 4 (274 × 212 mm)
Letter of Sir Stamford Raffles to the Marquess of Hastings,
 Bencoolen, 23 October 1820, HA/11/1/24, Leaves: 2 (254 × 203 mm)
Letter of Sir Stamford Raffles to the Marquess of Hastings,
 Bencoolen, 15 May 1821, HA/11/1/25, Leaves: 2 (228 × 184 mm)
Letter of Sir Stamford Raffles to the Marquess of Hastings,
 Cheltenham, 9 October 1824, HA/11/1/26, Leaves: 2 (248 × 200 mm)

Additional references to Hastings Papers:
 HA/11/5/1, HA/11/5/2, HA/11/9/2, HA/11/9/3,
 HA/11/9/7d, HA/11/9/22, HA/11/9/23, HA/11/9/25,
 HA/11/9/51, HA/11/9/65, HA/11/9/76a, HA/11/9/76b,
 HA/11/9/80, HA/11/9/84a, HA/11/9/84c

Cambridge University Library

9 Raffles letters to Thomas McQuoid, Add Ms 7386

National Library Scotland

John Murray Archives

British Library

Asia, Pacific & Africa Collections

East India Company Records:
    Bengal Secret Consultations, vols. 305, 307, 308, 309
    Bengal Secret Letters, vol. 18
    Bengal Political Letters Received, vol. 12
    Despatches to Bengal, vols. 69, 72, 74, 79, 84, 93
    Bengal Letters Received, vol. 80
    Letters from the Board to the Court, vol. 5
    Letters from the Court to the Board, vol. 6
    Java Factory Records, vols. 63, 47, 71
    Sumatra Factory Records, vols. 41, 47, 48, 49, 50

Raffles Family Papers:
    MSS.Eur.D.742.3; MSS.Eur.D.742.7; MSS.Eur.D.742.10;
    MSS.Eur.D.742.15; MSS.Eur.D.742.17; MSS.Eur.D.742.20;
    MSS.Eur.D.742.24; MSS.Eur.D.742.27

National Archives Singapore

Singapore: Letters to Bencoolen, 1819–20, L2, L4, L5, L10

National Library Singapore

Holograph letters of Raffles to John Tayler, RRARE 959.5703 RAF
Holograph letters of Raffles to Lord Lansdowne, RRARE 959.5703 RAF
and RRARE 959.8022 RAF

PRINTED SOURCES

Ali Haji ibn Ahmad, Raja. *The Precious Gift (Tuhfat al-Nafis)*, (transl.) Virginia
     Matheson and Barbara Watson Andaya (Kuala Lumpur, 1982).
Allibone, T.E. *The Royal Society and its Dining Clubs* (Oxford, 1976).
Anderson, John. *Mission to the East Coast of Sumatra in M.DCCC.XXIII* (London, 1826).
Annual Register, The, or a View of the History, Politics, and Literature, For the Year 1819
     (London, 1820).
Anon. "Address from Singapore. *To the Most Noble Francis, Marquess of Hastings,*
     K.G., G.C.B. &c. &c. &c.", *The Asiatic Journal and Monthly Register for British*
     India and its Dependencies, vol. XVI, no. 91 (July 1823), p. 72.
Anon. "Sketch of the History and Administration of the Marquess of Hastings", *The*
     Asiatic Journal and Monthly Register for British India and its Dependencies, vol. XVI,
     no. 95 (November 1823), pp. 421–30; vol. XVI, no. 96 (December 1823), pp. 525–38;
     vol. XVII, no. 97 (January 1824), pp. 1–16; vol. XVII, no. 98 (February 1824),
     pp. 117–35.
Anon. "The Honourable John Adam", *The Asiatic Journal and Monthly Register for*
     British India and its Dependencies, vol. XX, no. 119 (1825), pp. 485–504.
Anon. [J.S. Buckingham?]. "The 'Honourable' John Adam, and the Asiatic Journal",
     The Oriental Herald, and Journal of General Literature, vol. VIII (January to March
     1826), pp. 30–41.
Anon. *The East India Military Calendar; containing the Services of General and Field*
     Officers of the Indian Army (London, 1823–6), 3 vols.
Anon. "The Late Mr. Thomas Manning", *The Asiatic Journal and Monthly Register for*
     British India and its Dependencies, vol. XXXIII n.s. (November 1840), pp. 182–3.
Anon. *The Record of the Royal Society of London for the Promotion of Natural Knowledge*
     (London, Edinburgh, 1940).
Archer, Mildred. *British Drawings in the India Office Library* (London, 1969), 2 vols.
Banner, H. *These Men Were Masons: A Series of Biographies of Masonic Significance*
     (London, 1934).
Barr, Flinders. "Diary of Captain J. G. F. Crawford", *Straits Times*, 4, 11, 18, 25 October
     and 1 November 1937.
Bastin, John. "Sir Stamford Raffles's and John Crawfurd's Ideas of Colonizing the
     Malay Archipelago", *JMBRAS*, vol. XXVI, pt. 1 (1953), pp. 81–5.
Bastin, John. "Palembang in 1811 and 1812", *BKI*, vol. 109 (1953), pp. 300–20; vol. 110
     (1954), pp. 64–88 (reprinted in *Essays on Indonesian and Malayan History*
     (Singapore, 1961), pp. 53–91.
Bastin, John. "Raffles and British Policy in the Indian Archipelago, 1811–1816",
     JMBRAS, vol. XXVII, pt. 1 (1954), pp. 84–119.

Bastin, John. *The Native Policies of Sir Stamford Raffles in Java and Sumatra: An Economic Interpretation* (Oxford, 1957).

Bastin, John. *Essays on Indonesian and Malayan History* (Singapore, 1961).

Bastin, John. *The British in West Sumatra (1685–1825)* (Kuala Lumpur, 1965).

Bastin, John. "Dr Joseph Arnold and the Discovery of *Rafflesia Arnoldi* in West Sumatra in 1818", *J. Soc. Biblphy Nat. Hist.*, vol. 6, pt. 5 (1973), pp. 305–72.

Bastin, John (ed.). "The Letters of Sir Stamford Raffles to Nathaniel Wallich 1819–1824", *JMBRAS*, vol. 54, pt. 2 (1981), pp. 1–73.

Bastin, John. "Sir Stamford Raffles and the Study of Natural History in Penang, Singapore and Indonesia", *JMBRAS*, vol. LXIII, pt. 2 (1990), pp. 1–25.

Bastin, John. *The First Printing of Sir Stamford Raffles's* Minute on the Establishment of a Malay College at Singapore (Eastbourne, 1999).

Bastin, John. *The Natural History Researches of Dr Thomas Horsfield (1773–1859), First American Naturalist of Indonesia* (Singapore, 1990; reprinted Eastbourne, 2005).

Bastin, John. *John Leyden and Thomas Stamford Raffles* (Eastbourne, 2003).

Bastin, John. *Sir Stamford Raffles's* The History of Java: *A Bibliographical Essay* (Eastbourne, 2004).

Bastin, John. *William Farquhar: First Resident and Commandant of Singapore* (Eastbourne, 2005).

Bastin, John. *Letters and Books of Sir Stamford Raffles and Lady Raffles: The Tang Holdings Collection of Autograph Letters and Books of Sir Stamford Raffles and Lady Raffles* (Singapore, 2009).

Bastin, John & Christopher Bastin. "Some Old Penang Tombstones", *JMBRAS*, vol. XXXVII, pt. 1 (1964), pp. 126–65.

Boulger, D.C. *The Life of Sir Stamford Raffles* (London, 1897), reprinted in facsimile by The Pepin Press, Amsterdam, 1999, with a Preface by John Bastin.

Braddell, T. "Notices of Singapore", *Journal of the Indian Archipelago*, vol. VII (1853), pp. 325–57.

Braddell, T. "Notices of Singapore", *Journal of the Indian Archipelago*, vol. IX (1855), pp. 442–82.

Buckley, C.B. *An Anecdotal History of Old Times in Singapore* (Singapore, 1902), 2 vols.

Burkill, I.H. (ed.). "William Jack's Letters to Nathaniel Wallich, 1819–1821", *JSBRAS*, no. 73 (1916), pp. 147–268.

Bute, The Marchioness of (ed.) *The Private Journal of the Marquess of Hastings, K.G. Governor-General and Commander-in-Chief in India* (London, 1858), second edition, 2 vols.

Byrd, C.K. *Early Printing in the Straits Settlements 1806–1858: A preliminary Inquiry* (Singapore, 1970).

Calcutta Journal, The (Calcutta, 1819).

Cameron, H.C. *Sir Joseph Banks* (Sydney, 1966).

Campbell, D.M. *Java: Past & Present: A Description of the Most Beautiful Country in the World, its Ancient History, People, Antiquities, and Products* (London, 1915), 2 vols.

Carter, H.B. *Sir Joseph Banks 1743–1820* (London, 1991).

Chambers, N. (ed.). *The Letters of Sir Joseph Banks: A Selection, 1768–1820* (London, 2000).

Chatterton, Eyre. *A History of the Church of England in India Since the Early Days of the East India Company* (London, 1924).

Cholmondeley, R.H. (ed.). *The Heber Letters 1783–1832* (London, 1950).

Conner, Patrick. *George Chinnery 1774–1852: Artist of India and the China Coast* (Woodbridge, 1993).

Cowan, C.D. "Early Penang & the Rise of Singapore 1805–1832", *JMBRAS*, vol. XXIII, pt.2 (1950), pp. 1–210.

Crawfurd, J. *Journal of an Embassy from the Governor-General of India to the Courts of Siam and Cochin China; Exhibiting a View of the Actual State of Those Kingdoms* (London, 1828).

Cundall, F. (ed.). *Lady Nugent's Journal Jamaica One Hundred and Thirty-Eight Years Ago Reprinted from a Journal Kept by Maria, Lady Nugent, from 1801 to 1815, issued for Private Circulation in 1839* (London, 1939).

Curzon, George Nathaniel. *British Government in India: The Story of the Viceroys and Government Houses* (London, 1925), 2 vols.

Dawson, L.S. *Memoirs of Hydrography including Brief Biographies of the Principal Officers who have Served in H.M. Naval Surveying Service between the Years 1750 and 1885* (Eastbourne, *c.*1885), Part I. 1750 to 1830 (all published).

Dawson, W.R. (ed.). *The Banks Letters: A Calendar of the manuscript correspondence of Sir Joseph Banks preserved in the British Museum, the British Museum (Natural History) and other collections in Great Britain* (London, 1958).

Deventer, M.L. van. *Het Nederlandsch Gezag over Java en Onderhoorigheden sedert 1811* (The Hague, 1891), vol. I.

Dowden, W.S. (ed.) *The Journal of Thomas Moore* (London, Toronto, 1984), vol. II.

Elliot, George. *Memoir of Admiral the Hon[ble] Sir George Elliot Written for his Children* (London, 1863, reprinted 1891).

Embree, A.T. *Charles Grant and British Rule in India* (London, 1962).

Fortescue, J.W. *History of the British Army* (London, second edition, 1910–30), vol. 6.

Fortescue, J.W. *A Gallant Company or Deeds of Duty & Discipline from the Story of the British Army* (London, 1927).

Frankfurter, O. "The Unofficial Mission of John Morgan, merchant, to Siam in 1821", *Journal of the Siam Society*, vol. XI, pt. 1 (1914), pp. 1–7.

Gascoigne, J. *Joseph Banks and the English Enlightenment: Useful Knowledge and Polite Culture* (Cambridge, 1994).

Geike, Archibald. *Annals of the Royal Society Club The Record of a London Dining-Club in the Eighteenth & Nineteenth Centuries* (London, 1917).

Gibson-Hill, C.A. "The Singapore Chronicle (1824–37)", *JMBRAS*, vol. XXVI, pt. 1 (1953), pp. 175–99.

Gibson-Hill, C.A. "The Master Attendants at Singapore, 1819–67", *JMBRAS*, vol. XXXIII, pt. 1 (1960), pp. 1–64.

Gould, R.F. *The History of Freemasonry: Its Antiquities, Symbols, Constitutions, Customs, Etc.* (London, 1910), 6 vols.

Haan, F. de. "Personalia der Periode van het Engelsch Bestuur over Java 1811–1816", *BKI*, vol. 92 (1935), pp. 477–681.

Harfield, A. *Christian Cemeteries of Penang & Perak* (London, 1987).

Harfield, A. *Bencoolen: A History of the Honourable East India Company's Garrison on the West Coast of Sumatra (1685–1825)* (Barton-on-Sea, 1995).

Harrison, Brian. "Holding the Fort: Melaka under Two Flags 1795–1845", *MBRAS* Monograph no. 14 (1985), pp. xiv, 148.

H[aughton], H.T. "Landing of Raffles in Singapore. By An Eye-Witness", *JSBRAS*, no. 10 (1882), pp. 285–6.

Hill, A. H. "The Hikayat Abdullah: An annotated translation", *JMBRAS*, vol. XXVIII, pt. 3 (1955), pp. 345, [9].

Hooker, W.J. "Description of Malayan Plants. By William Jack. With a brief Memoir of the Author, and Extracts from his Correspondence", *Companion to the Botanical Magazine*, vol. I (1835), pp. 121–47.

Hutcheon, R. *Chinnery: The Man and the Legend* (Hong Kong, 1975).

Irwin, G. "Nineteenth-Century Borneo A Study in Diplomatic Rivalry", *VKI*, vol. XV (1955), pp. xi, 251.

[Jack, William (ed.)] *Malayan Miscellanies* (Baptist Mission Press, Bencoolen, 1820–2).

[Jack, William (ed.)]. *Proceedings of the Agricultural Society, Established in Sumatra, 1820* (Baptist Mission Press, Bencoolen, 1821), vol. I (all printed).

Jack, William. "Substance of a Report on the Condition of Society among the Native Population of Bencoolen and its immediate subordinates on the West Coast of Sumatra, October 1819", *Proceedings of the Agricultural Society, Established in Sumatra, 1820* (Baptist Mission Press, Bencoolen, 1821), vol. I, no. II, pp. 1–52.

Java Government Gazette (Batavia [Jakarta], 1812–16).

Johnson, D. *Indian Field Sports: with Observations on the Animals …* (London, 1827).

Kemp, P.H. van der. "De Sluiting van het Londensche Tractaat van 13 Augustus 1814", *BKI*, vol. 47 (1897), pp. 239–339.

Kemp, P.H. van der. "Sumatra's Westkust naar aanleiding van het Londensche Tractaat van 13 Augustus 1814", *BKI*, vol. 49 (1898), pp. 205–306.

Kemp, P.H. van der. "De Singapoorsche Papieroorlog", *BKI*, vol. 49 (1898), pp. 389–547.

Kemp, P.H. van der. "Raffles' Bezetting van de Lampongs in 1818", *BKI*, vol. 50 (1898), pp. 1–58.

Kemp, P.H. van der. "De Commissiën van den Schout-bij-Nacht C.J. Wolterbeek naar Malakka en Riouw in Juli-December 1818 en Februari-April 1820", *BKI*, vol. 51 (1900), pp. 1–100.

Kemp, P.H. van der. "Raffles' Atjeh-Overeenkomst van 1819", *BKI*, vol. 51 (1900), pp. 159–240.

Kemp, P.H. van der. "Palembang en Banka in 1816–1820", *BKI*, vol. 51 (1900), pp. xii, 331–764.

Kemp, P.H. van der. "Raffles' betrekking met Nias in 1820–21", *BKI*, vol. 52 (1901), pp. 584–603.

Kemp, P.H. van der. "De Stichting van Singapore, de Afstand ervan met Malakka door Nederland, en de Britische Aanspraken op den Linga-Riouw-Archipel", *BKI*, vol. 54 (1902), pp. 313–476.

Kemp, P.H. van der. "Benkoelen krachtens het Londensch Tractaat van 17 Maart 1824", *BKI*, vol. 55 (1903), pp. 283–320.

Kemp, P.H. van der. "De Geschiedenis van het Londensch Tractaat van 17 Maart 1824", *BKI*, vol. 56 (1904), pp. 1–244.

Kemp, P.H. van der. *Sumatra in 1818 naar Oorspronkelijke Stukken* (The Hague, 1920).

Kinnaird, D. *Remarks on the Volume of Hydrabad Papers, printed for the use of the East India Proprietors* (London, 1825).

Kraal, D. "The Circumstances surrounding the Untimely Death of Jan S. Timmerman Thijssen, Governor of Malacca 1818–1823", *JMBRAS*, vol. 83, pt. 1 (2010), pp. 9–28.

Krusenstern, Adam Johann von. *Voyage Round the World, in the Years 1803, 1804, 1805 & 1806…* (London, 1813), 2 vols.

Kwa Chong Guan. "Why did Tengku Hussein Sign the 1819 Treaty with Stamford Raffles?", *Malays/Muslims in Singapore: Selected Readings in History 1819–1965*, (ed.) Khoo Kay Kim *et al.* (Singapore 2006), pp. 1–35.

Langdon, M. and Kwa Chong Guan. "Notes on 'Sketch of the Land round Singapore Harbour, 7 February 1819'", *JMBRAS*, vol. 83, pt. 1 (2010), pp. 1–7.

Lee Kam Hing. *The Sultanate of Aceh: Relations with the British 1760–1824* (Kuala Lumpur, 1995).

Leyden, J. *The Malay Annals: Translated from the Malay Language, by The Late Dr. John Leyden, with An Introduction, by Sir Thomas Stamford Raffles, F.R.S. &c. &c.* (London, 1817).

Lisiansky, Urey. *A Voyage Round the World in the Years 1803, 4, 5 & 6* (London, 1814).

Low, C.R. *History of the Indian Navy (1613–1863)* (London, 1877), 2 vols.

Macgregor, I.A. "Johore Lama in the Sixteenth Century", *JMBRAS*, vol. XXVIII, pt. 2 (1955), pp. 48–125.

Mackenzie-Grieve, Averil. *Time and Chance: An Autobiography* (London, 1970).

McQuoid, T. "Notes of Dutch History in the Archipelago, Extracted from the Records at Batavia under the Administration of Sir Stamford Raffles", *Journal of the Indian Archipelago*, vol. I, no. 2, n.s. (1856), pp. 141–93.

Marks, Harry J. "The First Contest for Singapore 1819–1824", *VKI*, vol. XXVII (1959), pp. [vi], 262 [263].

Marshman, J.C. *The Life and Times of Carey, Marshman, and Ward: Embracing the History of the Serampore Mission* (London, 1859), 2 vols.

Maxwell. W.E. (ed.). *Notes and Queries*, Straits Branch Royal Asiatic Society (Singapore, 1887).

Maxwell, W.G. and W.S. Gibson. *Treaties and Engagements affecting the Malay States and Borneo* (London, 1924).

Mersey, Charles Clive Bigham. "Earl of Moira, Marquess of Hastings 1814–1823", *The Viceroys and Governors-General of India 1757–1947* (London, 1949), pp. 41–5.

Miller, George. "Robert Farquhar in the Malay World", *JMBRAS*, vol. LI, pt. 2 (1978), pp. 123–38.

Nelson, P.D. *Francis Rawdon-Hastings, Marquess of Hastings: Soldier, Peer of the Realm, Governor-General of India* (Madison, Teaneck, 2005).

Netscher, E. "De Nederlanders in Djohor en Siak. 1602 to 1865. Historische Beschrijving", *VBG*, vol. XXXV (1870), pp. 1–329, Bijl. pp. I–LXLIII.

O'Sullivan, L. "The London Missionary Society: A Written Record of Missionaries and Printing Presses in the Straits Settlements, 1815–1847", *JMBRAS*, vol. LVII, pt. 2 (1984), pp. 61–104.

Pearson, H.F. *People of Early Singapore* (London, 1955).

Petrie, W. *A Statement of Facts delivered to the right Honourable Lord Minto ... on his Late Arrival at Madras* (London, 1810).

Phillips, C.H. *The East India Company 1784–1834* (Manchester, 1968).

Prince of Wales Island Gazette (Pinang, 1805–1820).

Prinsep, H.T. *History of the Political and Military Transactions in India during the Administration of the Marquess of Hastings 1813–1823* (London, 1825), 2 vols.

Raffles, T.S. *Substance of a Minute Recorded by The Honourable Thomas Stamford Raffles... on the 11th February 1814; on the Introduction of an Improved System of Internal Management and the Establishment of a Land Rental on the Island of Java: ...* (London, 1814).

Raffles, T.S. "The Charges of Major General Gillespie, against The Honourable T.S. Raffles, Leutenant [*sic*] Governor of the Island of Java, with various papers and documents in refutation of them, relating to the administration of The British Government in that Island and its Dependencies" (Batavia, 1814).

[Raffles, T.S.]. *Extract Public Letter from the Honourable Court of Directors to the Supreme Government in Bengal. Dated the 13th February 1817* (privately printed, London, 1817).

Raffles, T.S. *The History of Java* (London, 1817), 2 vols.

Raffles, T.S. *On the Advantages of Affording the Means of Education to the Inhabitants of the Further East* (Baptist Mission Press, Serampur, 1819). For facsimile reprint, see John Bastin.

Raffles, T.S. [William Jack]. "Descriptive Catalogue of a Zoological Collection, made on account of the Honourable East India Company, in the Island of Sumatra and its Vicinity, under the Direction of Sir Thomas Stamford Raffles, Lieutenant-Governor of Fort Marlborough; with additional Notices illustrative of the Natural History of those Countries", *Transactions of the Linnean Society of London*, vol. XIII (1821–3), pp. 239–74, 277–340.

Raffles, T.S. "Address by the President, The Hon. Sir T. Stamford Raffles, on the Institution of the [Agricultural] Society. 1820", *Proceedings of the Agricultural Society, Established in Sumatra, 1820* (Baptist Mission Press, Bencoolen, 1821), vol. I, pp. i–xii.

[Raffles, T.S.]. "Address from Singapore. *To the Most Noble Francis, Marquess of Hastings, K.G., G.C.B. &c. &c.&c.*", *The Asiatic Journal and Monthly Register for British India and its Dependencies*, vol. XVI, no. 91 (July 1823), p. 72.

[Raffles, T.S.] *Address of the Merchants of Singapore, on the occasion of the departure of the Honorable Sir T.S. Raffles in 1823* (Sumatran Mission Press, 1823).

Raffles, T.S. *Singapore: Local Laws and Institutions, 1823* (London, 1824), reprinted in Lady Raffles, *Memoir* (London, 1830), Appendix pp. 39–73.

Raffles, T.S. *Statement of the Services of Sir Stamford Raffles* (London, 1824), reprinted with an Introduction by John Bastin (Kuala Lumpur, 1978).

Raffles, T.S. *On the Administration of the Eastern Islands* (London, 1824), reprinted in Lady Raffles, *Memoir* (London, 1830), Appendix, pp. 3–38.

Raffles, Sophia. *Memoir of the Life and Public Services of Sir Thomas Stamford Raffles, F.R.S. &c. Particularly in the Government of Java, 1811–1816, and of Bencoolen with its Dependencies, 1817–1824; with Details of the Commerce and Resources of the Eastern Archipelago, and Selections from his Correspondence* (London, 1830), reprinted with an Introduction by John Bastin (Singapore, 1991).

Ramsden, Guendolen (ed.). *Correspondence of Two Brothers: Edward Adolphus, Eleventh Duke of Somerset, and his Brother, Lord Webb Seymour, 1800 to 1819 and after* (London, 1906).

Report [Relative to the Trade with the East Indies and China,] from The Select Committee of the House of Lords, appointed to inquire into the means of extending and securing the Foreign Trade of the Country, and to report to the House; together with the Minutes of Evidence taken in Sessions 1820 and 1821, before the said Committee:- 11 April 1821. Ordered, by The House of Commons, to be Printed 7 May 1821. Brought from The Lords 7 May 1821, pp. 420.

Ridley, H.N. "The Botanists of Penang", *JSBRAS*, no. 25 (1894), pp. 163–7.

Ross-of-Bladensburg, John Foster George. *The Marquess of Hastings, K.G.,* Rulers of India series (Oxford, 1893).

Rowlandson, Thomas. *The Grand Master or Adventures of Qui Hi? in Hindostan: A Hudibrastic Poem in Eight Cantos by Quiz* [William Combe] (London, 1816).

Salmond, Francis. "Diary of a Journey across the Island of Sumatra from Fort Marlborough to Palembang, in 1818", *Malayan Miscellanies* (Baptist Mission Press, Bencoolen, 1822), vol. II, no. 3, pp. 12.

Scott, Walter. *The Journal of Sir Walter Scott 1825–32, from the Original Manuscript at Abbotsford* (Edinburgh, 1891).

Smith, E. *The Life of Sir Joseph Banks President of the Royal Society with some Notices of his Friends and Contemporaries* (London, 1911).

Smith, E.A. *George IV* (New Haven and London, 1999).

Tarling, Nicholas, *Anglo-Dutch Rivalry in the Malay World 1780–1824* (Cambridge, 1962).

Tarling, Nicholas, "The Prince of Merchants and the Lion City", *JMBRAS*, vol. XXXVII, pt. 1 (1964), pp. 20–40.

Thompson, N. *Earl Bathurst and the British Empire* (Barnsley, 1999).

Timmerman Thijssen, D. Meyer. *Twee gouverneurs en een equipagemeester: In en om Malakka 1778–1823* (Bilthoven, 1991).

Travers, T.O. *The Journal of Thomas Otho Travers (1813–1820),* (ed.) John Bastin, *Memoirs of the Raffles Museum,* no.4 (1957) (Singapore, 1960).

Visser, H. "Iets over het Landschap de Pasemah Oeloe Manna en zijne tijdelijke onderwerping door Sir Thomas Stamford Raffles", *TBG,* vol. XXVIII (1893), pp. 314–36.

Wake, C.H. "Raffles and the Rajas: The Founding of Singapore in Malayan and British Colonial History", *JMBRAS,* vol. XLVIII, pt. 1, pp. 47–73.

Wakeham, E. *The Bravest Soldier, Sir Rollo Gillespie 1766–1814: A Historical Military Sketch* (London, Edinburgh, 1937).

[Watson, T.C.] "A Journal of a Tour in the Island of Java", *The Asiatic Journal and Monthly Register for British India and its Dependencies,* vol. I (1816), pp. 124–9, 233–5.

Wright, A. *Twentieth Century Impressions of British Malaya: Its History, People, Commerce, Industries, and Resources* (London, 1908).

Wurtzburg, C.E. *Raffles of the Eastern Isles* (London, 1954).

Index

RAFFLES AND HASTINGS

Private

Singapore 22ª June 1819

My Lord,

My Official despatches will convey to your Lordship every information on the progress and present State of this Establishment, but as Major Farquhar is not yet prepared with the detailed Plan of the defences, I do myself the honor to forward under a private cover a rough Sketch shewing the position and division of the Town &c and the disposition of the principal works proposed for its defence – This Sketch does not include a considerable native

The Most Noble
The Marquess of Hastings KG. KG. &c
&c &c &c

Raffles and Hastings

Private Exchanges behind the
Founding of Singapore

JOHN BASTIN

National Library Board
Singapore

Marshall Cavendish
Editions

Published by

Marshall Cavendish Editions
An imprint of Marshall Cavendish International
1 New Industrial Road, Singapore 536196
Tel: +65 6213 9300 | Email: genref@sg.marshallcavendish.com

and

National Library Board, Singapore
100 Victoria Street, #14-01, National Library Building, Singapore 188064
Tel: +65 6332 3255 | Email: ref@library.nlb.gov.sg | www.nlb.gov.sg

First published in 2012 as *The Founding of Singapore 1819* by National Library Board, Singapore.

National Library Board, Singapore Cataloguing-in-Publication Data:

Bastin, John Sturgus, 1927–
Raffles and Hastings : Private exchanges behind the founding of Singapore / John Bastin.
– Singapore : National Library Board Singapore [and] Marshall Cavendish Editions, 2014
pages cm
ISBN : 978-981-4561-440 (paperback)
1. Raffles, Thomas Stamford, Sir, 1781–1826 – Correspondence.
2. Hastings, Francis Rawdon-Hastings, Marquess of, 1754–1826 – Correspondence.
3. Singapore – History – 1819–1867 – Sources.   I. Title.
DS598.S75
959.5703 – dc23   OCN 884843481

Printed in Singapore by Craft Print International Ltd

Frontispiece: First page of letter written by Stamford Raffles to the Marquess of Hastings,
22 June 1819 (6 leaves, 240 × 200 mm, reproduced at 80%; see full transcription on page 93).
Courtesy of the Bute Collection at Mount Stuart, Isle of Bute, Scotland.

Contents

Illustrations

Letters Printed in Full

NOTE ON THE LETTERS

The 34 letters published in this book have been transcribed from the originals as closely as possible. Editorial insertions and clarifications are enclosed in square brackets, while longer explanatory notes are indicated by superscript numbers. Variations in spelling that occur in the manuscript letters, such as place names (Singapore/Sincapore), are preserved faithfully in the transcriptions, as are all punctuation marks (including Raffles's liberal use of dashes), raised letters and capitalisation.

Most abbreviations, such as Gov^t (Government) and Servt (Servant), are clear from context; three that are rarely encountered today may be worth pointing out here: *ultimo/ulto* (last month); *instant* (this month); and *&c* (et cetera, often to shorten the formal valedictions preceding the signature).

The layout of the letters is also preserved as far as possible. In formal correspondence of Raffles and Hastings's day, the recipient's name and title were typically included at the bottom of the letter or at the foot of the first page (as seen, for example, in the facsimile facing the title page). In the transcriptions here they are always printed at the end of the letter.

Preface

This account of the founding of Singapore is based largely on Raffles's unpublished private letters to the Governor-General and Commander-in-Chief in India, Francis, 1st Marquess of Hastings, preserved in the Bute Collection at Mount Stuart, Isle of Bute, Scotland. The letters are to be distinguished from Raffles's official despatches to the Supreme Government in Bengal, his private letters to Charlotte Seymour, Duchess of Somerset, and other documents in the British Library, as well as letters to his agent, John Tayler, and Henry Petty-Fitzmaurice, 3rd Marquess of Lansdowne, in the National Library Singapore.

The part played by Hastings in the founding of Singapore and his relationship with Raffles are essential themes of the book. The text follows the chronological sequence of Raffles's letters to him, but in order to provide an explanation of their contents there is a brief introductory account of Raffles's attempts to extend British political influence in Sumatra since it was the rejection of these plans by Lord Hastings, and the adoption of an alternative policy of securing British power in the Straits of Melaka, which led to the founding of Singapore.

The book contains a good deal of original documentation, but it does not pretend to offer a comprehensive account of the founding of Singapore since it omits all reference to the correspondence between Lord Hastings and the Governor-General of the Netherlands India, Baron G.A.G.P. van der Capellen, as well as details of the protracted negotiations between the British and Netherlands governments which led to the Treaty of London in 1824 and the recognition of Singapore as a British possession. These subjects have been examined by the Dutch scholar P.H. van der Kemp in his numerous publications, and by Harry J. Marks in his monograph, *The First Contest for Singapore 1819–1824* (The Hague, 1959).

I wish to thank John, Marquess of Bute, for granting me permission to publish Raffles's private letters to the Marquess of Hastings in the Bute Collection at Mount Stuart, and Mr. Andrew McLean, former Head of Collections at Mount Stuart, and Miss Lynsey Nairn, Collections Assistant, for their help. I also wish to express my gratitude to the British Library for permission to quote from Raffles's letters to Charlotte Seymour, Duchess of Somerset, and the National Library Singapore for permission to publish Raffles's letters to Lord Lansdowne and John Tayler.

John Bastin

I trust the time is not far distant when the real value and object of the Settlement at Singapore will be fully and justly appreciated, by all parties, and that in the completion of these legitimate objects your Lordship will derive satisfaction from the contemplation of the important benefits conferred on the Commerce of Great Britain at a period when it stood so much in need of effectual aid and support –

Sir Stamford Raffles, in Bengkulu (Bencoolen),
to the Marquess of Hastings, 12 August 1820

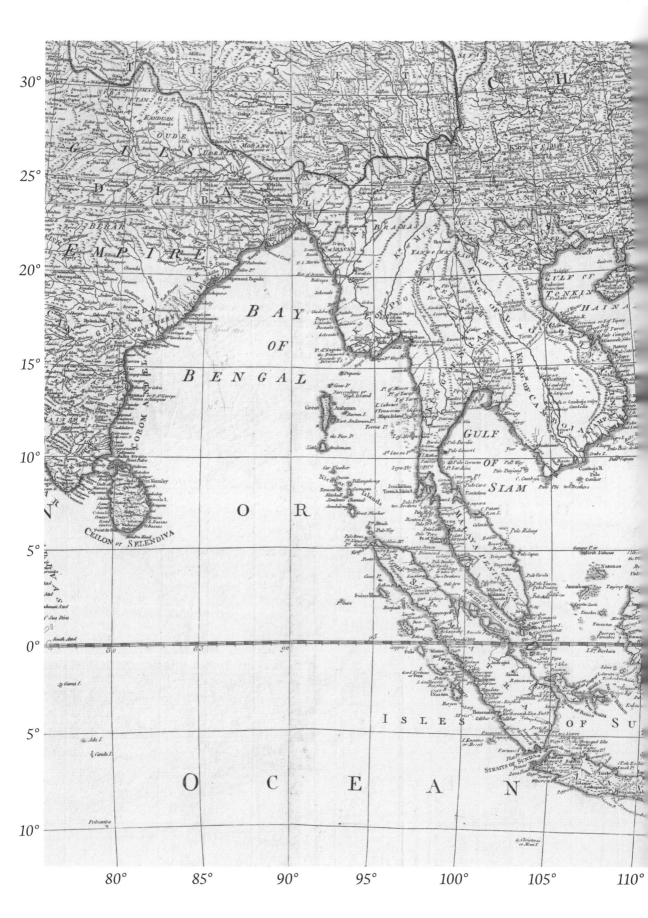

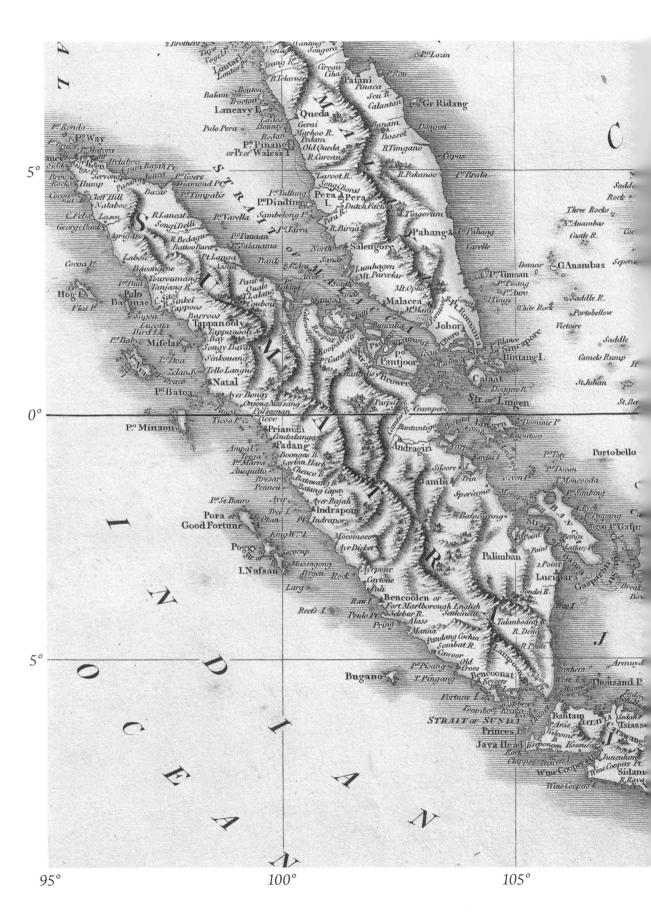

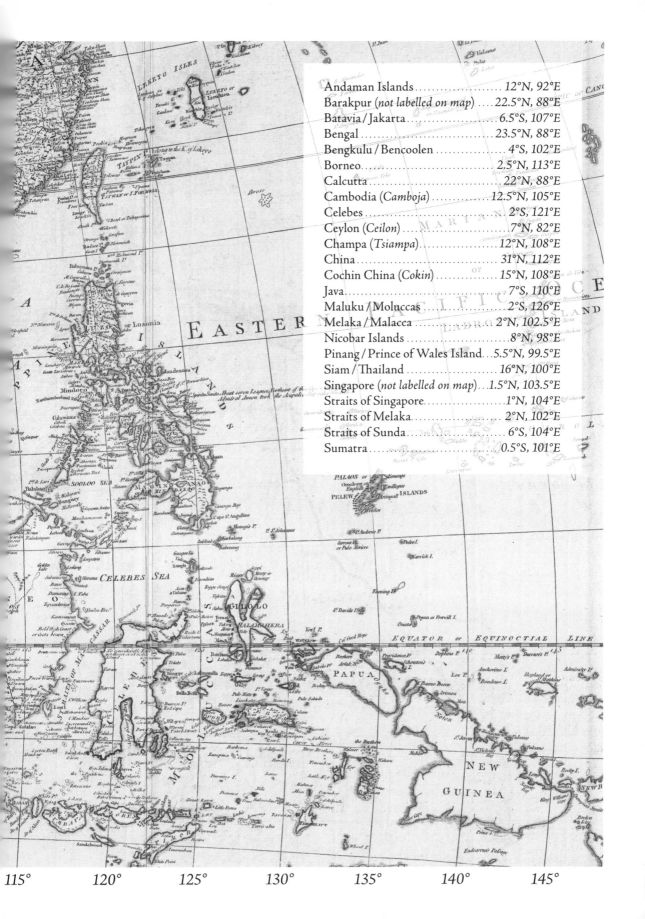

Andaman Islands............................12°N, 92°E
Barakpur (*not labelled on map*) ....22.5°N, 88°E
Batavia / Jakarta............................6.5°S, 107°E
Bengal..23.5°N, 88°E
Bengkulu / Bencoolen ....4°S, 102°E
Borneo..2.5°N, 113°E
Calcutta..22°N, 88°E
Cambodia (*Camboja*)...................12.5°N, 105°E
Celebes..2°S, 121°E
Ceylon (*Ceilon*)............................7°N, 82°E
Champa (*Tsiampa*)........................12°N, 108°E
China..31°N, 112°E
Cochin China (*Cokin*)..................15°N, 108°E
Java..7°S, 110°E
Maluku / Moluccas........................2°S, 126°E
Melaka / Malacca..........................2°N, 102.5°E
Nicobar Islands..............................8°N, 98°E
Pinang / Prince of Wales Island...5.5°N, 99.5°E
Siam / Thailand ....16°N, 100°E
Singapore (*not labelled on map*)...1.5°N, 103.5°E
Straits of Singapore........................1°N, 104°E
Straits of Melaka............................2°N, 102°E
Straits of Sunda..............................6°S, 104°E
Sumatra..0.5°S, 101°E

115°   120°   125°   130°   135°   140°   145°